LOOK AT THIS

LOOK AT THIS

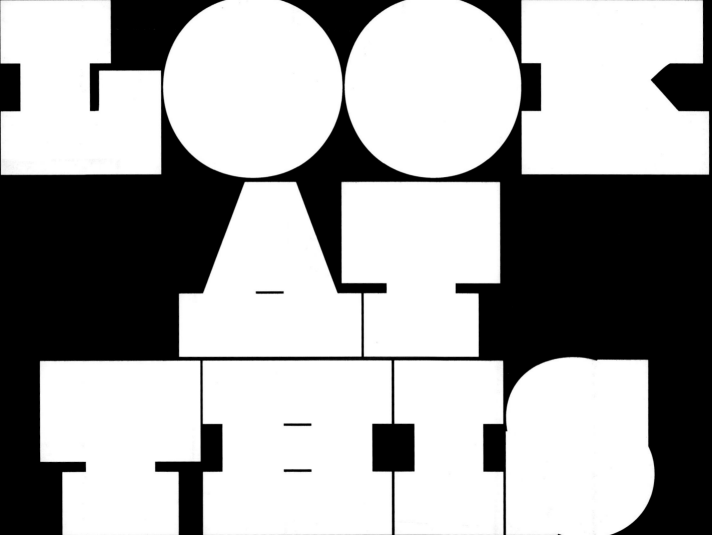

Contemporary
Brochures,
Catalogues &
Documents

Published in 2006 by
Laurence King Publishing Ltd

e-mail:
enquiries@laurenceking.co.uk
www.laurenceking.co.uk

A catalogue record for this book is available from the British Library

ISBN-13 978 185669 469 8
ISBN-10 1 85669 469 0

Designed by Non-Format

Printed in Hong Kong

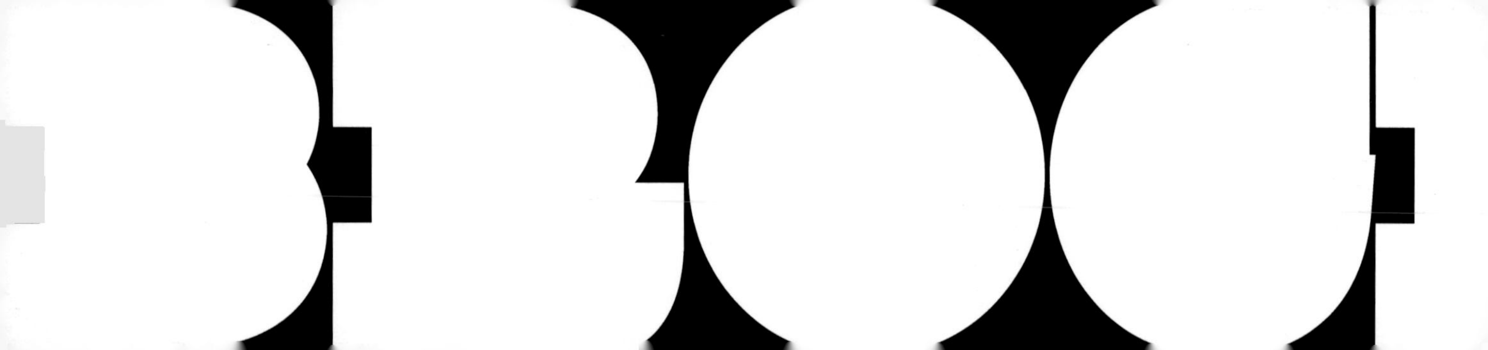

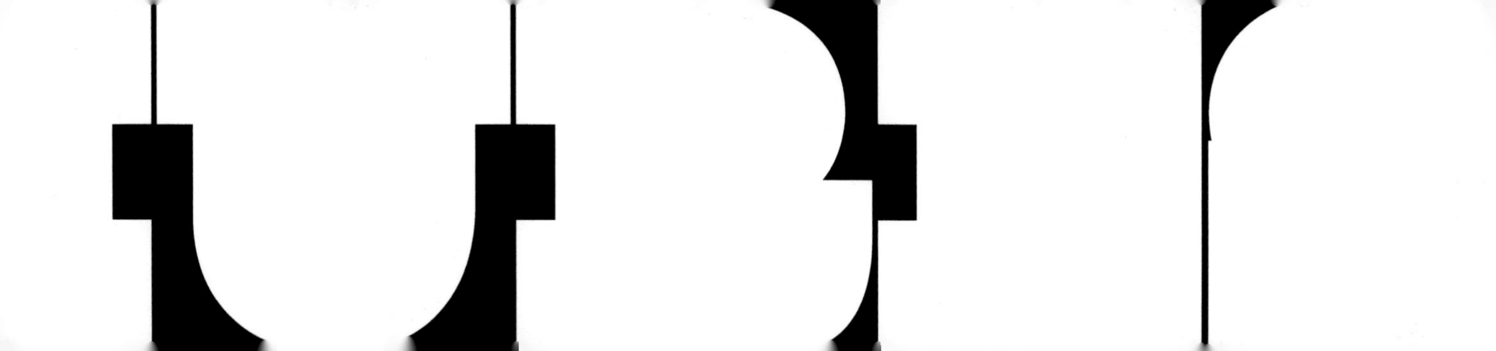

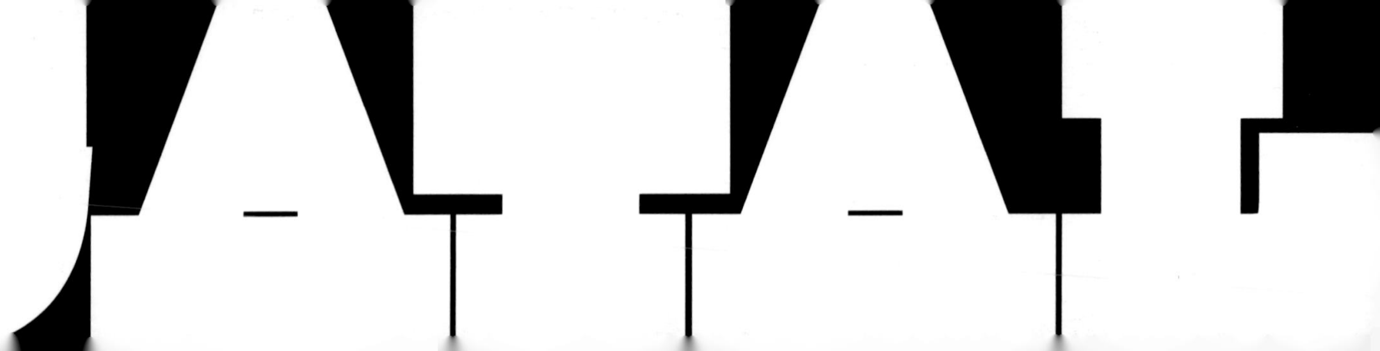

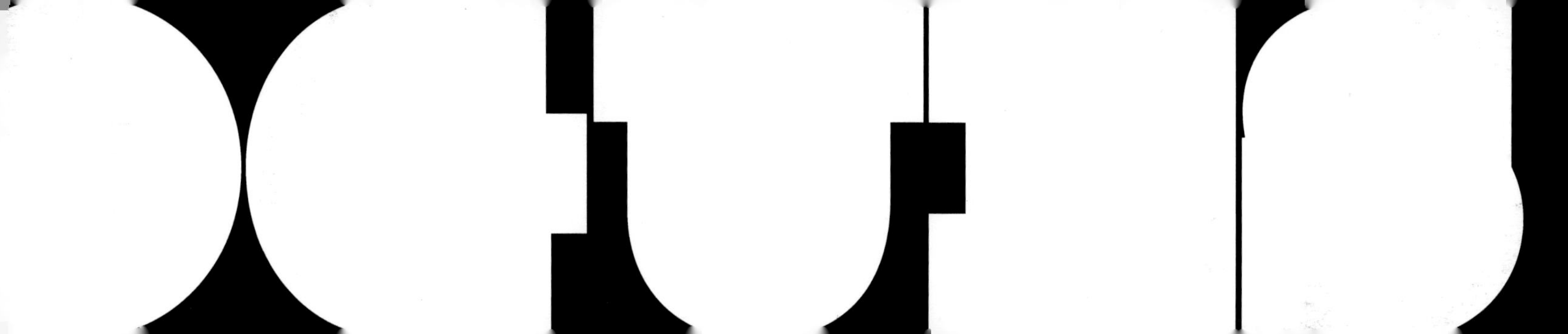

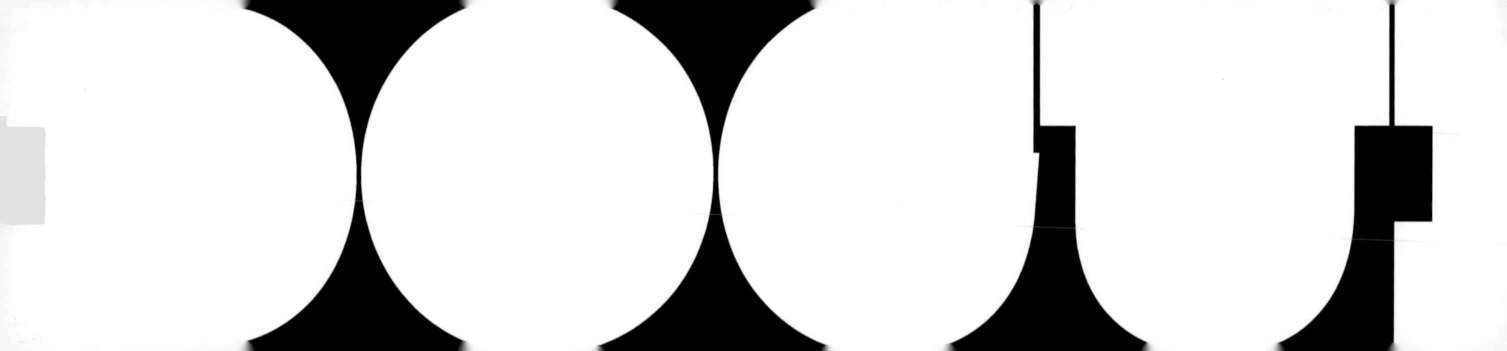

(1896)
–
–
–
–
–
–

age in the 1990s. It was no longer the stepchild of mass media or cousin of art, and we as designers became sought-after, highly trained professionals, respected by business, acknowledged by culture, needed by society. We basked in our history, criticism, and public relations.'

–

For most of the 1980s world of seamless communication was opening up, in which text would be endlessly malleable and fully interactive, and where the screen would become the main platform for written communication. Perhaps we'd have to learn complex coding languages at the same time as unlearning the old disciplines of junk mail tumbling through our letterboxes. Today electronic communication sits comfortably alongside the world of ink on paper, and the denizens of Marshall McLuhan's global electronic village move unthinkingly between the two spheres. In truth, even talking about 'two spheres' seems old-fashioned: it's (underlining, tagging, highlighting) and the functionality (menus, thumbnail images, icons) of website design have invaded print design, a phenomenon that is particularly noticeable in magazine design (Nick Bell's autumn 2001 redesign of *Eye* magazine, for example, where the indexing, signposting and navigation of the magazine bear a close resemblance, both stylistically and functionally, to website design).[1]

–

–

–

None of this, of course, alters the fact that brochures, catalogues and printed documents still form the bedrock of many graphic designers' daily practice. There's something elemental in the heft and tactile immediacy of a well-designed, well-printed, multi-page document, and for many designing multi-page documents remains a fundamental of graphic design – perhaps only the poster occupies a position of comparable importance in the designer's repertoire. The creative act of arranging typography and images on sequential pages satisfies a deep-rooted instinct found within most graphic designers. It's why many of them became designers in the first place. The dignified catalogue designs of Happy F&B for Arctic Paper (pp. 038–039 and 076–077) strike me as splendid examples of designers doing what they do best.

–

Brochures offer the designer an almost unparalleled opportunity to deploy the full range of graphic design skills. The cover of a brochure, with its frequent requirement to be eye-catching and alluring, tests the designer's ability to be seductive or impactful, informative or declamatory. (Stefan Sagmeister provides a master class in traffic-stopping cover design with his injection-moulded cover for the Zumtobel AG annual report, pp. 018–021.) Designing a cover also offers a welcome opportunity to commission (and art-direct) photography and illustration, while the 'spreads' – the inside – provide the designer with a platform for typography, layout and the integration of imagery. And what is graphic design, if not this?

–

Brochures and printed literature also provide the designer with the prospect of using a variety of materials. Paper, board and synthetics, not to mention fabric, wood and metal, all have a part to play in the creation of dynamic printed literature. Even the handmade can play a part in contemporary brochure design – as can be seen in Götz Gramlich's rough-edged but emotive experiment in the graphic depiction of music (pp. 044–045).

–

Yet most printed literature is disposable: today's hot-off-the-press document is tomorrow's landfill. It is rare to pick up a promotional brochure that has any originality of design or visual flair. Think of the stuff that falls out of magazines and Sunday newspapers. Think of the stuff that we pick up in showrooms. It is invariably dire, vapid and utterly throwaway. Think of the annual reports of large shareholder-owned corporations. These lavishly funded documents used to be dynamic platforms for big businesses to express their personality (not to mention a platform for bravura graphic design); today they are mostly limp publications, denuded of spirit by accessibility guidelines and the rules of financial compliance. Think of the countless numbers of potentially interesting brochures polluted by crass advertising and intrusive displays of sponsors' logos.[2]

–

This may sound like graphic designer carping (it is!), but there's a serious point here. When I came to compile this book, I approached numerous designers – some famous, some anonymous – to request examples of daring and mould-breaking brochure design. I was astonished by the number of times I was told the same thing: 'Sorry, haven't done a brochure for years.' This happened not once or twice but repeatedly. With ominous frequency I was told that there were few opportunities to do richly designed brochures and that the only good work was to be found in the arts and culture sectors.

–

Why is this? Clearly the Internet plays a part in the apparent scarcity of well-designed printed brochures; clients have migrated to the instantaneousness of the Internet, preferring the fact that a single website can reach millions of people a fraction of the cost of printing and distributing millions of brochures. Above all, they are attracted to the fact that a website can be amended and updated, whereas you can't change a 1 million print run.

–

But it's not only the Internet that is leading to a decrease in the numbers of gorgeously designed brochures: there is also the factor of branding. Branding is now a sophisticated science, its precepts accepted by anyone with a product or service to promote. Few would argue that good branding is essential in the modern business arena – but such is the strength of the cult of branding among clients (and many designers) that it has crushed such seemingly outmoded concepts as visual flair, expressiveness and experimentation. In branding terms these are dirty words; they have been replaced by 'consistency', 'uniformity' and 'penetration', and the result of all this 'brand engineering' is a grim homogeneity where everything looks the same – and, as a small side-effect, there is a dearth of interestingly designed brochures.

–

My response to the discovery that the heroically designed brochure was an endangered species was to push the definition of brochures, catalogues and documents to breaking-point. If it was more than one page, it was in. If it was a single sheet, but folded into a multi-faceted document, it was in. Book or brochure? Catalogue or flyer? By saying that this categorization hardly matters, I hope to show that the design of multi-page documents is not dead – it's just hiding under mossy stones.

–

–

–

Yet perhaps the biggest threat facing the printed brochure is not aesthetic; I'm thinking here of issues relating to the care of the environment and sustainability. The arguments in favour of the environmentally responsible use of paper are well known to designers and don't need restating here. But the fact is that as designers we are deeply implicated in the profligate use of paper and all the scary consequences that go with that. When we commission lavish printed documents, the environmental footprint we create is substantial, and we can't shirk our responsibility by saying it's what the client wanted. We're all quick to bemoan fossil fuel abuse, and while that gloss-laminated 144-page document you've just designed may do less damage than driving an SUV, it is not without its own substantial environmental impact. I am painfully aware that this book you are holding also comes with its own environmental price-tag.

–

So what can we do? Well, there are recycled materials we can use. These have been with us for some time and have been greatly improved in recent years; but there are commentators who say that the environmental cost of recycling is as great as the cost of creating new paper, so can we be sure they are any less harmful than virgin-fibre paper? However, there is also the option of using paper that has been made with environmentally friendly manufacturing processes. The useful website Environmental Sustainability in Print and Publishing (www.sustainprint.com) recently carried an interesting story about *Ms.* magazine's switch to environmentally friendly paper:

–

'*PrintMedia* magazine covered *Ms.* magazine's switch to eco-papers – papers with high post-consumer recycled content (PCR), cleaner manufacturing processes (including less chlorine bleaching) and without using fibre from endangered forests. But what many of you want to know is how they did it. After all, when the Feminist Majority Foundation (FMF) assumed control as publisher of *Ms.*, it inherited a $2 million-dollar debt and with it a ready-made excuse for not switching to eco-papers, as it potentially costs more to do so. But *Ms.* managed to switch to papers significantly better for the environment and human health than traditional 100 per cent virgin-fibre paper, while staying within budget.'

–

Beyond acting responsibly in our use of paper (most clients are happy to comply with a request to use environmentally friendly paper stock, so it's always worth raising the matter), there are some interesting developments in the areas of print on demand (POD). Clearly this method of production won't suit every project, but there are many areas where it is desirable, especially in the case of small-run print jobs. Yet again Götz Gramlich's bravura document illustrates the value of one-off digital printing; and while with its recondite subject-matter it is unlikely to find a publisher, by using digital technology Gramlich can give life to his extraordinary vision.

–

The one-off cost of producing a document digitally will probably be higher than that of producing it as part of a traditional print run. But there are other benefits: clients don't have to hold large quantities of stock, and there is no waste as a result of over-producing. However, digital printing is not yet as good as traditional printing, although this is likely to change, and in some areas such as art prints and photography, digital is at least the equal of traditional methods of reproduction and in many cases is the preferred choice.

–

It is inevitable that notions of sustainability will alter the future shape of printed documents. It is inconceivable that society will be able to go on consuming paper at the level we have all become accustomed to. And equally inevitably, it is designers who, once again, will have to adjust to new constraints imposed by environmental concerns.

–

–

–

Yet, as this book shows, there's still a healthy abundance of good work around. I've been astonished and delighted by the ways in which smart designers have striven to create expressive and memorable work without the advantage of big budgets. Stefan Sagmeister in the USA revels in the ingenuity of creating a newspaper for the cost of a postcard (for Anni Kuan, pp. 084–089); Spin in London demonstrate that the apparent budgetary restriction of working for an independent art gallery need not be a barrier to creating compelling work (Haunch of Venison, pp. 142–143), as do Experimental Jetset in Amsterdam, with their work for a theatre group (De Theatercompagnie, pp. 124–125); while in Tokyo, Hideki Nakajima (Ryuichi Sakamoto, pp. 054–055) demonstrates that the concert tour brochure need not be a high-gloss moment of graphic excess.

–

These and dozens of other inventive designers featured in this book, often working below the radar of commercial acceptance, manage to produce evocative and inspirational documents that inform and entertain but also communicate. With their use of unusual materials, and their bravura use of typography and imagery, designers are creating printed communications that compete with media-rich platforms such as the Internet, television, personal computers and, increasingly, even the mobile phones and hand-held devices we carry around in our pockets.

–

Surveying the work in this book, we can make some interesting observations. Chosen mainly from Europe and the USA, there is no discernible dominant aesthetic flavour; eclecticism is king, and anything goes. (See the work of French graphic designer Toffe, pp. 068–069.) Functionality seems to be a recurring theme; as printed documents become more restrained, designers seem to be moving towards more functional solutions. Chris Ashworth and his team's *Sketchbook* for Getty Images invites you to 'contribute' to the publication (pp. 050–053); you can write in it and paste your own images into it, but it is also a catalogue for an ambitious commercial organization.

–

Another interesting development is the fashion for revealing the binding of documents. Showing trim marks, printer's colour bars and other technical insignia of the designer's trade has been a well-known postmodern design trope for a number of years. But an appetite for revealing the inner construction of printed documents is a relatively new trend. There are numerous examples in this book, but perhaps the most striking is French designer's Labomatic's *Urgent Painting* catalogue (pp. 106–107); here the spine is covered in clear vinyl, a technique that simultaneously reveals and protects the exposed spine.

–

The best brochures, catalogues and documents – the really good stuff – have a permanence and organic completeness that have become increasingly important in the ephemeral world of instant communications. It is no accident that brochures from graphic design's past have become collector's items, fetching high prices and valued for their part in the history of visual culture and design history. As we look at the material featured in this book, we can't help but speculate about the shape of printed documents in the coming decades. My guess is that printed multi-page documents will still exist, but increasingly they will merge with electronic platforms to create a seamless front of cross-publishing platforms.

–

About ten years ago I was invited by the organizers of a design and publishing conference to take part in a competition to propose the most plausible shape of the magazine of the future. Half a dozen British graphic designers were each given a slot to present their 'vision' to an audience of publishing industry professionals. A prize was to be given to the best submission.

–

My crack-brained idea was electronic paper. I asked the audience to imagine a time when we travelled around, not with newspapers and magazines under our arms, but with a thin sheet of 'electronic' paper. When seated in a café or on a train we'd 'activate' the paper (how we'd do this I didn't explain) and, hey presto, text and images would appear. Using touch-screen technology, the reader would pull down more text or move around among the available information, just as in a conventional paper magazine.

–

My idea was politely received, but I got the impression that the audience wanted something a bit more plausible, and I wasn't surprised not to win the prize. However, early in 2006 I read this on the *New Scientist*'s website:

–

'There are many projects aiming to develop "electronic paper". Such a display could, for example, be used to create a fully updatable newspaper which could be rolled up to fit into a coat pocket. Flexible displays could also be used to create new mobile phones and other easily collapsible gadgets. Philips's new display was made possible by the development of a way to print organic electronics onto a thin plastic film – previously, it was only possible to print these components on glass. However, after experimenting with various different plastics, Philips now has a technique that works on polyimide film. (www.newscientist.com/article.ns?id=dn4602)'

–

Perhaps my idle speculation wasn't so far out after all. Perhaps the magazines, newspapers and brochures of the future will be produced centrally and then distributed to various platforms – newsprint, Internet, broadcast, mobile phones and, conceivably, sheets of thin plastic film. But whatever happens, to ensure that the material is properly organized and legible, designers will need to be part of the loop. As we saw earlier, there have been attempts to bypass grumpy designers with their funny ideas about layout and typefaces and letter spacing, and doubtless there will be renewed attempts in the future. Yet it seems inconceivable that there will ever be a way of communicating complex text- and image-based information without the skilled eye and space-mapping brain of a graphic designer. But I'm sure the makers of saddles and bridles once said much the same thing – and look what happened to them.

–
–
–
–
–
–

[1] Former *Eye* art director Nick Bell explains: 'I was art-directing Tom Elsner on the design of the *Eye* website at the same time as redesigning the magazine. In the magazine the keyword menus were a component in the "dashboard" approach to the beginning of each article that held together the stand-first and byline. The website fixed this concept at a less evolved stage when it was launched – the printed magazine proving strangely more changeable than the website in this instance, as it was reinterpreted every quarter. And conversely the website was influenced by print. I designed a poster to celebrate *Eye*'s 10th anniversary. The bottom half of it was filled with an index of words – all the subjects covered by *Eye* during that time. The keyword index on the *Eye* home page is inspired by that poster.'

–
–
–
–
–
–

[2] Some friends of mine recently acquired a cache of printed materials from the 1972 Munich Olympics. Designed by Otl Aicher (1922–1991), this work is widely regarded as one of the great triumphs of graphic design. My friends proudly showed me posters, leaflets, tickets and a large number of brochures and catalogues. They were wonderful artefacts; but what struck me most forcibly about this material – especially the multi-page documents – was the almost total absence of advertising and sponsors' logos. Today it would be festooned with ads from giant corporations and the insignia of sponsors. The purity and directness of communication that Aicher and his team achieved in 1972 are impossible to replicate in the twenty-first century.

–
–
–
–
–
–

Contem
Broc
Cat
Doc

Title:
Public Buildings/
Berlin – City in Space

Origin:
Germany/Switzerland

Client:
Vice Versa Verlag

Studio:
Prill, Vieceli &
Fickentscher

Dimensions:
165mm x 120mm
6.4" x 4.7"

Contemporary
Brochures
Catalogues
Documents

Description:
The graphic designers Tania Prill and Alberto Vieceli, assisted here by Lisa Fickentscher, are a Zurich-based studio, producing highly sophisticated printed matter – books, brochures and documents.

–

Prior to setting up his own practice with Prill, Vieceli worked at Lars Müller, the celebrated Swiss publishing house. Prill is currently Visiting Professor of Graphic Design at the School for New Media at Karlsruhe in Germany. Her work with Vieceli, although sharply contemporary, is in the grand tradition of classic Swiss design.

–

As part of the 'Berlin – City in Space' project, Prill and Vieceli produced two A5 booklets. The first is lavishly illustrated with black-and-white photography and black text, while the second is a meticulously executed, typography-only document printed entirely in red. Both editions come bound in a detachable clear vinyl wallet, with embossed letterforms.

Autohaus Winter

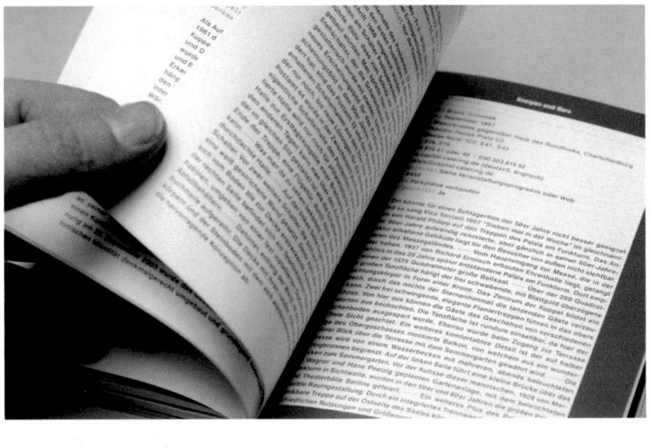

Contem
Broc
Cat
Doc

Title:
Zumtobel AG
Annual Report

Origin:
USA/Austria

Client:
Zumtobel AG

Studio:
Sagmeister Inc.

Dimensions:
272mm x 211mm
10.7" x 8.3"

–
–
–

–
–
–
–
–
–
–
–
–

Description:
Stefan Sagmeister is one of the foremost graphic designers of his generation. Irreverent, iconoclastic and invariably witty, he was born in Austria but has lived and worked in New York City since 1993. Before setting up Sagmeister Inc., he worked for the great Tibor Kalman.

–

His annual report for Austrian company Zumtobel AG is a *tour de force* of graphic inventiveness. Zumtobel make lighting systems. The plastic moulded relief cover of this document shows a vase containing five flowers – each representing a Zumtobel sub-brand. Inside the document the moulded image is used repeatedly, but photographed using radically changing lighting conditions on each occasion.

–

As the writer Peter Noever noted, Sagmeister is 'more of an inventor than a designer'. He is never afraid to challenge conventions; this is not a conventional annual report.

–
–
–
–
–
–

ZUM
TO 01 02
BEL AG

REISS INTERNATIONAL GMBH

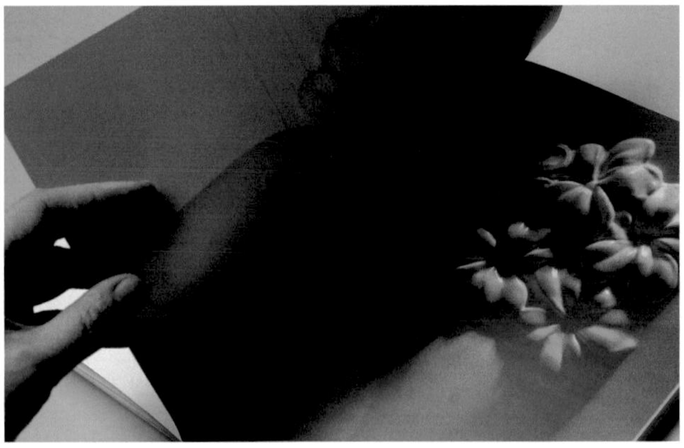

Contem
Broc
Cat
Doc

Title:
Elvis Swift
–
Origin:
USA
–
Client:
Joanie Bernstein
–
Studio:
Werner Design Werks, Inc.
–
Dimensions:
241mm x 175mm
9.5" x 6.9"

Description:
Werner Design Werks is a two-person studio based in Minneapolis, Minnesota, USA. They have clients ranging from large companies such as Moët Hennessy and Chronicle Books to smaller ones such as Mrs. Meyer's Clean Day ('small when we started working with them, but now growing fast'). WDW work primarily in print and specialize in graphic design with strong tactile qualities.
–
Artist representative Joanie Bernstein was the studio's first client when it opened for business 14 years ago. One of the artists represented by Bernstein's is Elvis Swift, an illustrator whose particular talent is for calligraphy and calligraphic illustrations.
–
'The brochure is to promote Elvis and his unique style', explains WDW designer Sarah Nelson. 'Elvis creates his art on scraps of paper, bits of this and that, and collects them all together; we wanted to capture that feeling but also reproduce it in larger quantities. To do so, we selected a variety of paper stocks, some new, some old, and some found – like the vintage wallpaper that we cut down – and the paperback romances we cut apart. Most of the art is letterpress-printed to feel as if it was individually drawn on. No two booklets are the same, just like no two portfolios Elvis sends out are ever the same.'

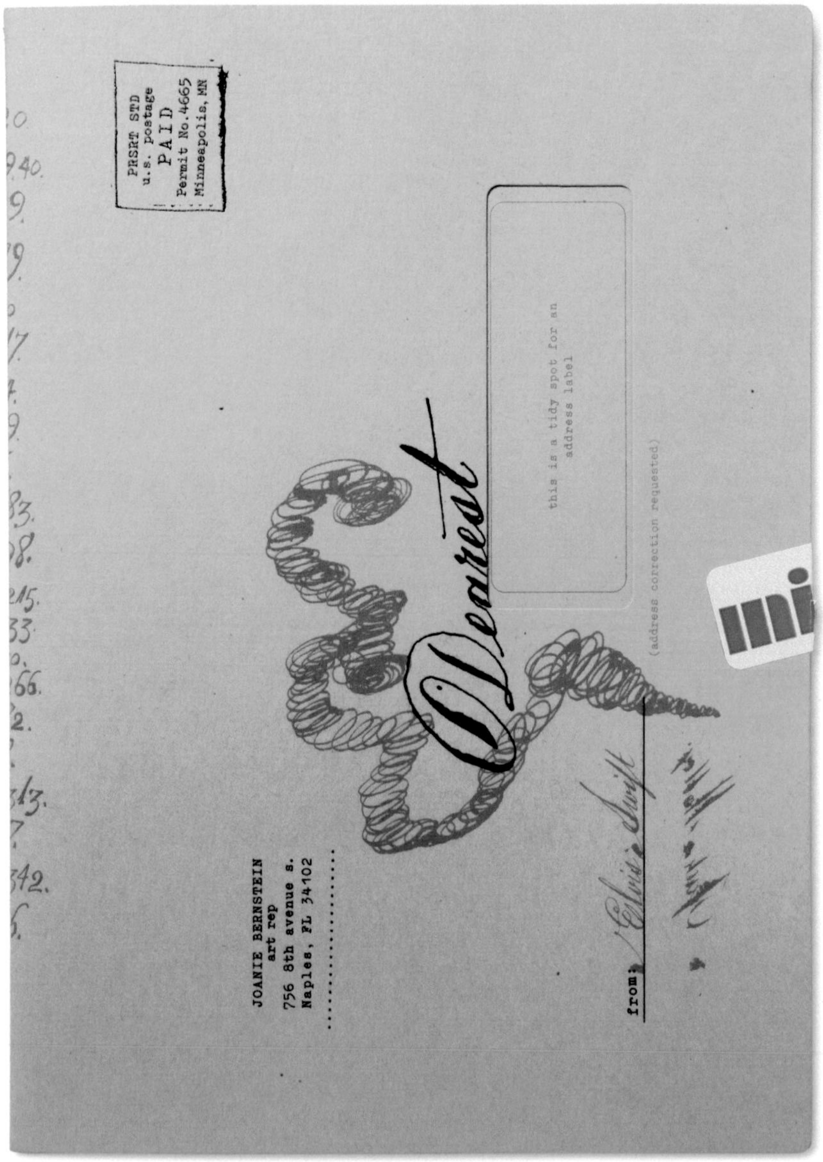
PRSRT STD
u.s. postage
PAID
Permit No.4665
Minneapolis, MN
this is a tidy spot for an
address label
(address correction requested)
Dearest
JOANIE BERNSTEIN
art rep
756 8th avenue s.
Naples, FL 34102
from:

bits and

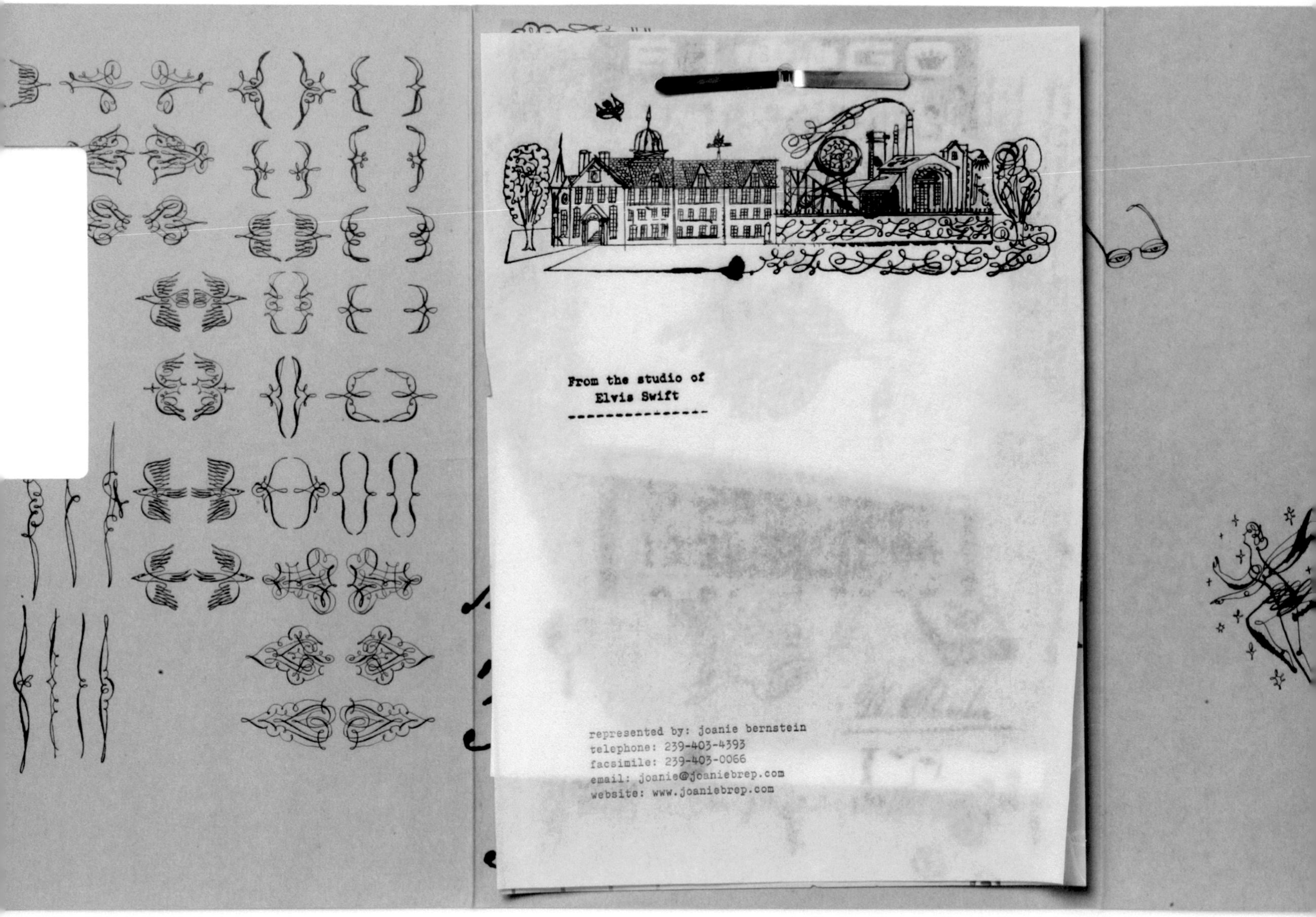
From the studio of
Elvis Swift
represented by: joanie bernstein
telephone: 239-403-4393
facsimile: 239-403-0066
email: joanie@joaniebrep.com
website: www.joaniebrep.com

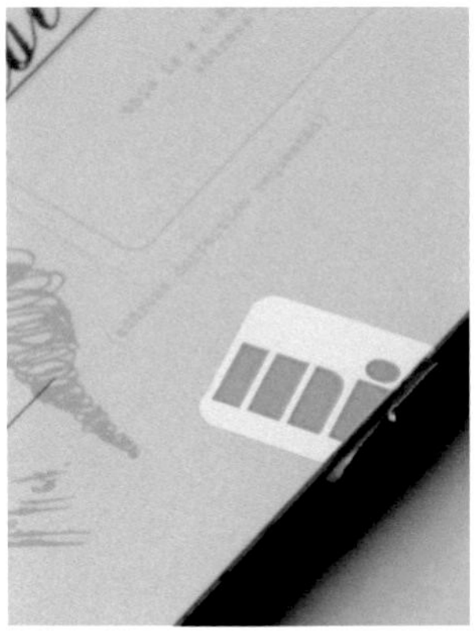

Conte
Broc
Cat
Doc

Title:
White: Jubilee Book

Origin:
Sweden

Client:
White Arkitekter AB

Studio:
Happy F&B

Dimensions:
210mm x 170mm
8.3" x 6.7"

Page 025

Contemporary
Brochures
Catalogues
Documents

Description:
A celebration of the 50th anniversary of Sweden's largest firm of architects. Rather than a retrospective yearbook, the firm elected for a manifesto, with the aim of stimulating debate.

This chunky document is a bravura display of graphic design and print production. Designed by leading Swedish design studio Happy F&B, it contains nearly every mode of graphic expression: handwriting, stencil type, formal typography, photography, 3-D rendering, maps, schematics and diagrams.

The production techniques deployed are equally wide-ranging. The 300+ page document is bound by white plastic bolts. The front and back covers have a clear vinyl sheet for protection. Inside, a vast array of stock is used. Litho is mixed with screen-printing to create a rich panoply of visual and tactile effects. The spine is hand-stamped with the legend 'Just White'.

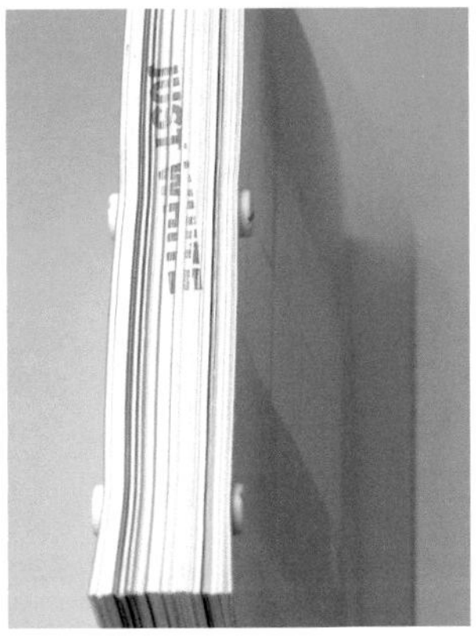

–

Contem
Broc
Cat
Doc

–

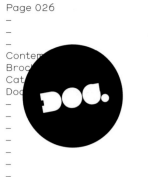

Title:
Stedelijk Museum CS
–
Origin:
The Netherlands
–
Client:
Stedelijk Museum
–
Studio:
Experimental Jetset
–
Dimensions:
210mm x 148mm
8.3" x 5.8"

–

Description:
Experimental Jetset is one of the most interesting and consistently innovative design groups at work today. The members of this Amsterdam-based trio are masters of graphic expressiveness. For the world-famous Stedelijk Museum CS they were asked to create the house style for the institution's temporary exhibition space in a former post office while the Stedelijk's home was undergoing renovation.
–
As they state on their website: 'It was an honour to be asked to undertake this assignment. After all, the Stedelijk Museum used to be the ultimate embodiment of social-democratic and modernist values, values which are important to us.'
–
One of their first tasks was to produce a series of document-like invitations consisting of several single-sided A3-sized posters, each one folded to an A5 format. The first invitation, the one for the opening of the building itself, shows the unveiling of the logotype: all four versions of the logo are used, in various grades of abstraction.

Geel Metalliek

Geel Metalliek
Metallic Yellow
Goud voor / Gold for Robert Smit

for Robert
You are invited to a reception
to celebrate the opening of
exhibition Metallic Yellow
Robert Smit at
Museum CS.

Agenda Mei 2004
Program May 2004
16.05 - 29.08
Tussenstand: een keuze
uit de collectie
Intermission: a choice
from the collection
16.05 - 29.08
Kramer vs. Rietveld
/Contrasten in
de meubelcollectie
Kramer vs. Rietveld
/Contrasts in
the furniture collection
16.05 - 03.10
20/20 Vision
Gemeente
Amsterdam
Economische Zaken
Meubelindustrie Gelderland BV
Mondriaan Stichting

Time

Time

and

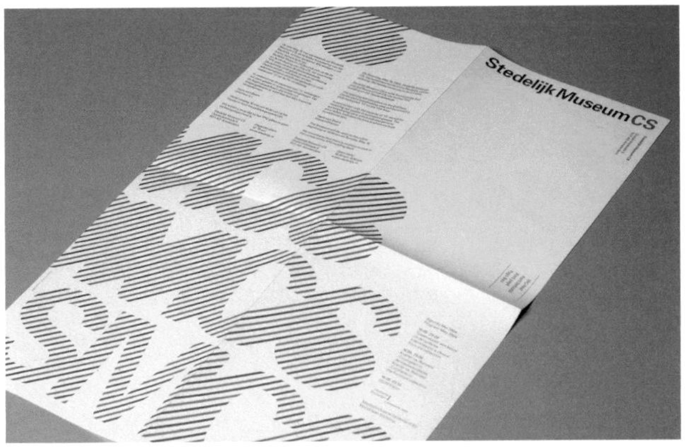
Stedelijk Museum CS

Again*

–
–
–
Conte
Broc
Cat
Doc
–
–
–
–
–
–
–
–
–
Title:
Pompei –
il romanzo della cenere
–
Origin:
UK
–
Client:
The Venice Biennale
–
Studio:
Non-Format
–
Dimensions:
240mm x 170mm
9.4" x 6.7"
–
–
–
–
–
–

la Biennale di Venezia
La Biennale di Venezia
La Biennale di Venezia
37. Festival Internazionale
del Teatro
Pompei
il romanzo della cenere
Venezia
Arsenale
15 – 25 Settembre
2005
Direttore Romeo Castellucci
ubulibri

la Biennale di Venezia
La Biennale di Venezia
37. Festival Internazionale
del Teatro
www.labiennale.org
Pompei
il romanzo della cenere
Venezia
Arsenale
15 – 25 Settembre
2005
Direttore Romeo Castellucci
ubulibri

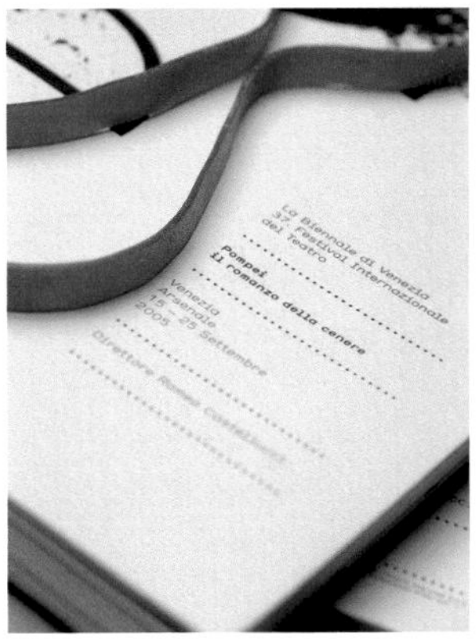

Contemporary
Brochures
Catalogues
Documents

Description:
The organizers of the 37th Venice Theatre Biennale invited Non-Format to design a catalogue for this famous event. In previous years the document had worked both as programme and catalogue, but Non-Format elected to separate the two components: 'We decided to split it into two parts,' notes designer Kjell Ekhorn, 'one 144-page catalogue and one 32-page programme, both held together with a rubber band. The idea was to keep the programme light and easy to carry around, allowing festival visitors to keep the more book-like catalogue pristine.'

As with so much of Non-Format's work, there is a conscious attempt to re-invent the ordinary. Here the clichés of cultural publishing are inverted: 'A lot of the performances were commissioned specially for the festival,' explains Ekhorn, 'so there were no performance photographs, and we did not like the idea of using portraits of the directors, theatre groups or shots from previous shows in the catalogue. Instead, the attitude of the festival was communicated by a custom-made typeface and unrelated photographs by the Italian photographer Francesco Raffaelli. All the information about the individual theatre troupes and performances was text-only.'

Ultramodern typography sits beside the designers' trademark 'illustrated' lettering; black-and-white predominates – only the red flash of the organizers' logo intrudes into this refined mono world.

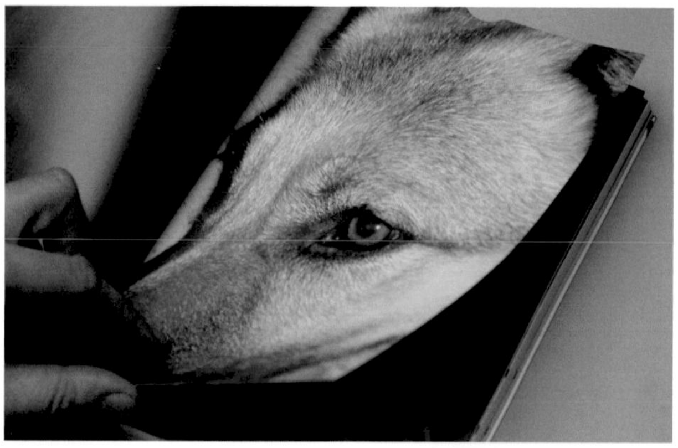

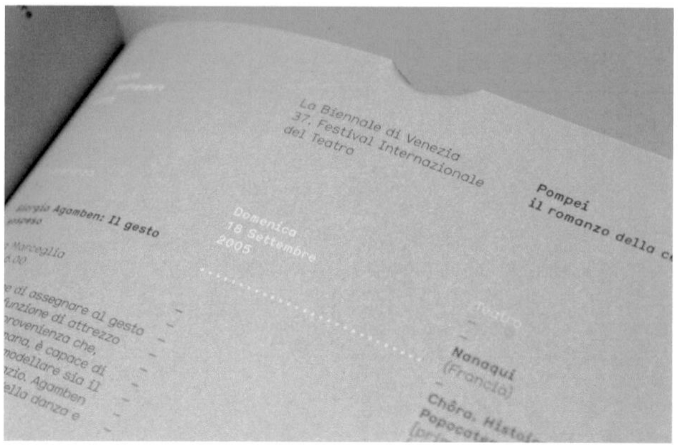
La Biennale di Venezia
37. Festival Internazionale
del Teatro
Domenica
18 Settembre
2005
Nanaqui
(Francia)

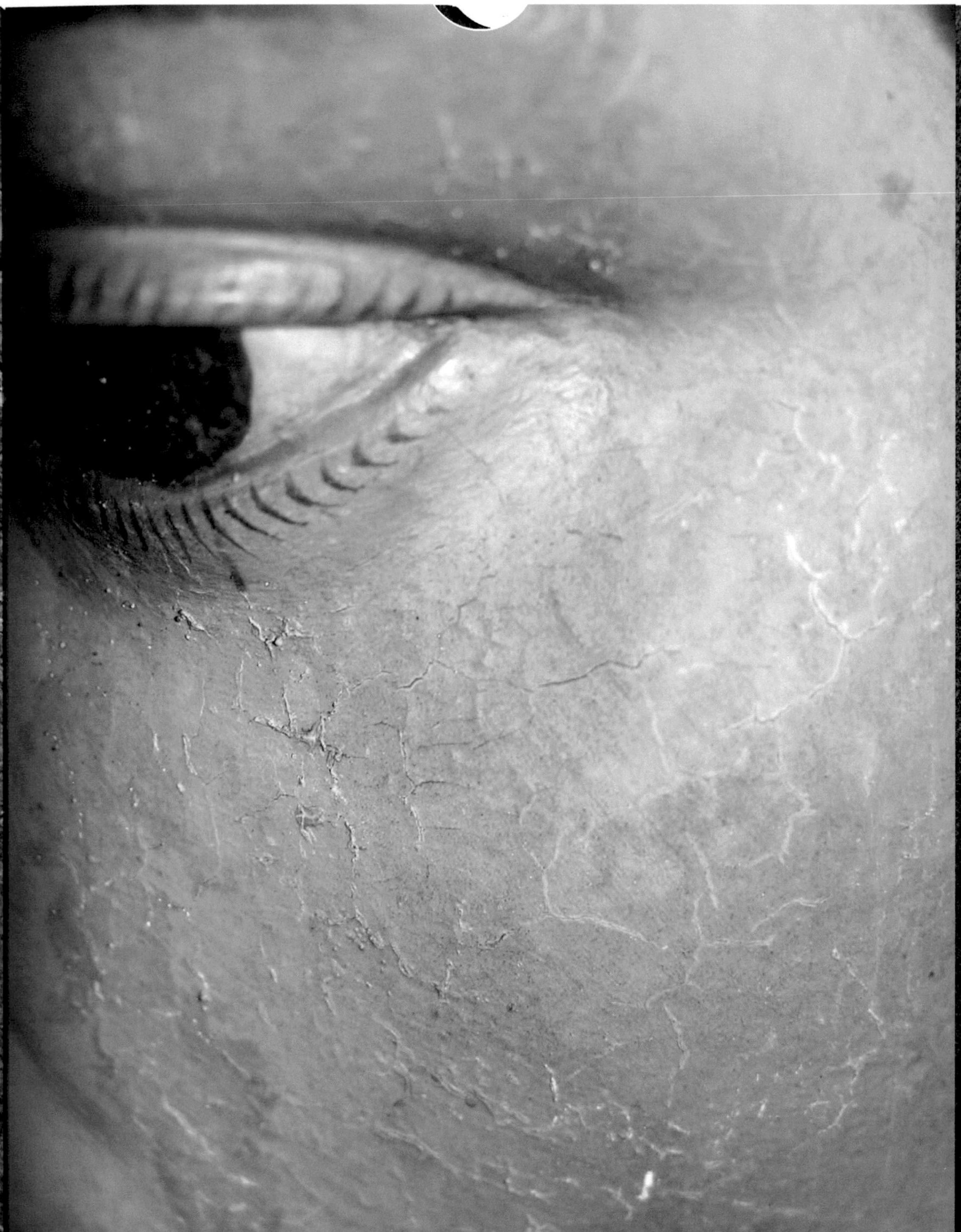

Conte…
Broc…
Cat…
Doc…

Title:
The Hugo Boss Prize 2004

Origin:
USA

Client:
Hugo Boss

Studio:
Sagmeister Inc.

Dimensions:
342mm x 270mm
13.5" x 10.5"

The
HUGO BOSS PRIZE
2004
GUGGENHEIM
ACKERMANN
de RIJKE & de ROOIJ
NEUENSCHWANDER
STARLING
TIRAVANIJA
YANG

THE HUGO BOSS PRIZE
2004
GUGGENHEIM Museum
ACKERMANN
de RIJKE & de ROOIJ
NEUENSCHWANDER
STARLING
TIRAVANIJA
YANG

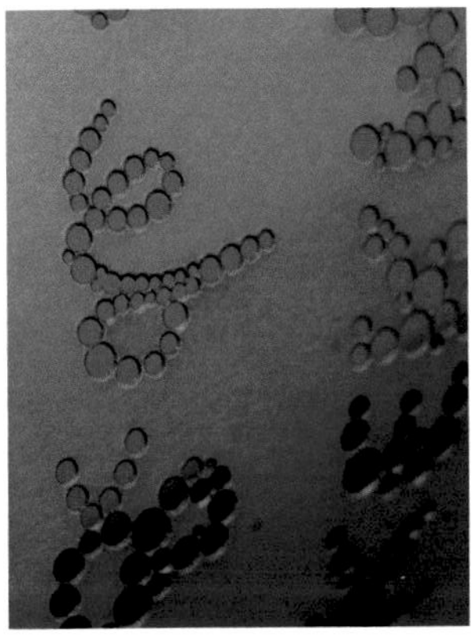

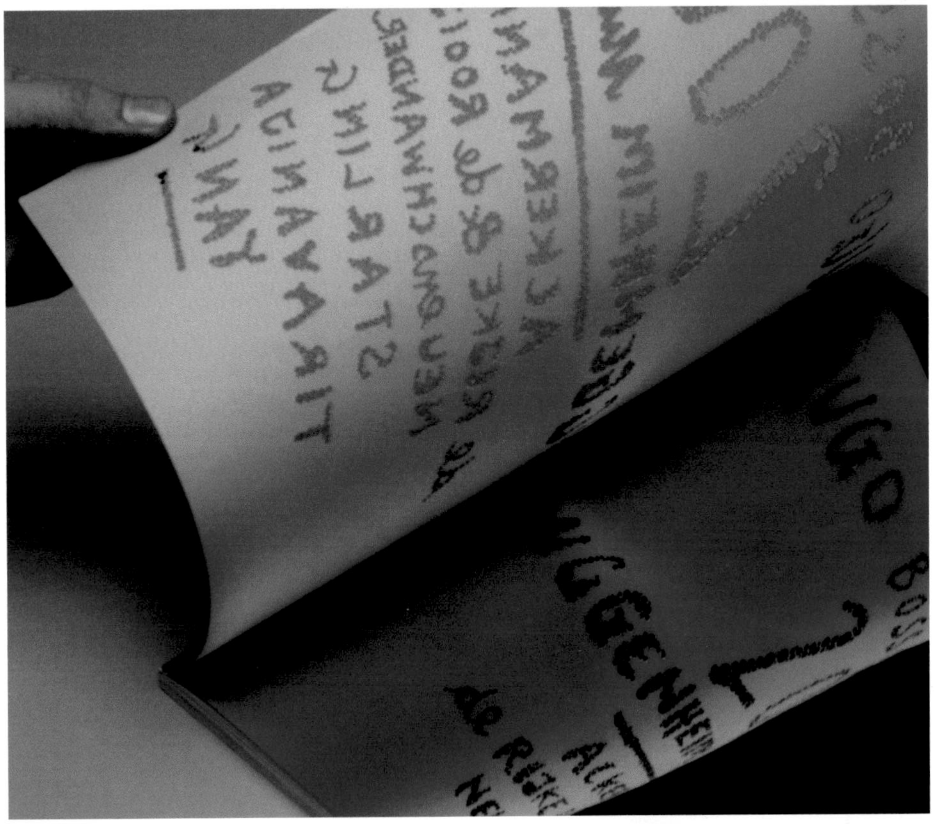

Description:
Art catalogues are easy to design. You just let the art do the work. If you've got beautiful art, how can you fail to make a beautiful catalogue?

Stefan Sagmeister, with his customary insouciance, challenges this notion. Although his handsome, large-format brochure for the Hugo Boss Prize 2004 is a surprisingly restrained statement from one of the great showmen of contemporary graphic design, there is enough Sagmeister fizz about it to lift it above the run-of-the-mill art catalogue.

Large blow-ups of the work of the various artists selected for the prize's shortlist are accompanied by unobtrusive typography and an abundance of white space. But Sagmeister manages to inject a signature gesture into the cover: he uses muted, grey, matt stock, but then die-cuts molecular lettering out of it, through which we glimpse a sheet of shimmering mirror board. The effect is to create a memorable and eye-catching document cover, without upstaging or overshadowing the artwork reproduced inside.

–
–
–
Contem
Broc
Cat
Doc
–
–
–
–
–
–
–
–
Title:
Gràfiques Ocultes ('Hidden Graphics')
–
Origin:
Spain
–
Client:
KRTU
–
Designer:
David Torrents
–
Dimensions:
235mm x 165mm
9.2" x 6.4"
–
–
–
–
–
–

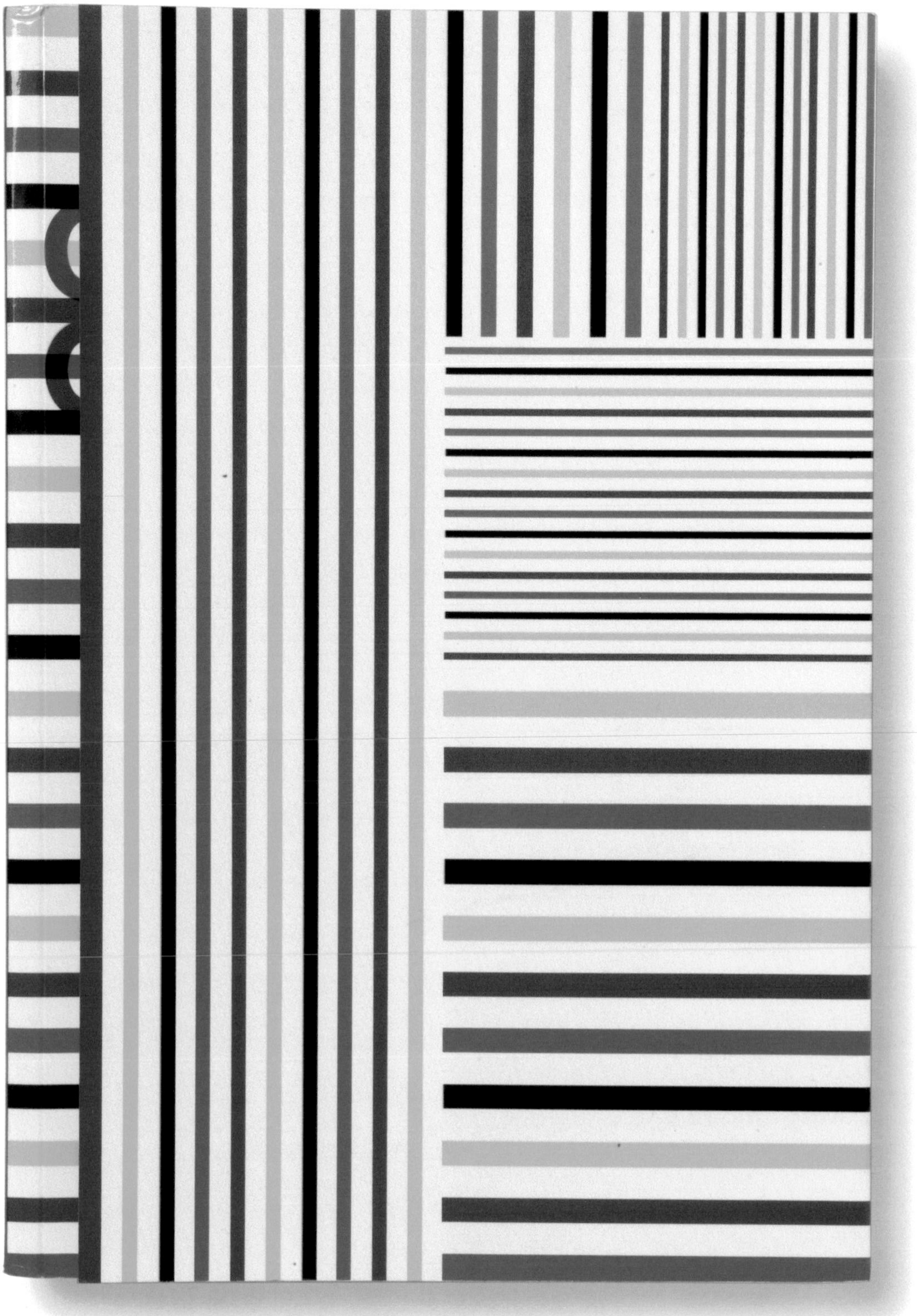

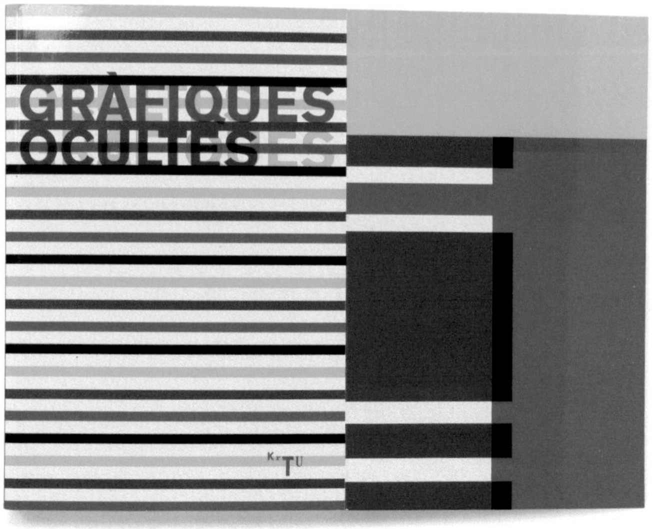
GRÀFIQUES
OCULTES

Contemporary
Brochures
Catalogues
Documents

Description:
Gràfiques Ocultes ('Hidden Graphics') was an exhibition and catalogue presenting graphic design from Catalonia in Spain. The show was so called because it featured work produced in small quantities for small audiences: party invitations, limited-edition books, flyers, comics, handmade one-offs etc. As designer David Torrents observes: 'It is "hidden" work because it is unknown.'

The sturdy 272-page catalogue comes with a striking CMYK linear design on the cover. 'It is based on offset litho cropping marks,' explains Torrents, 'which are normally hidden. I made them into a sort of Op Art effect. It was my way of not showing one particular project from the book on the cover. There were lots of designers, and nobody was more important than anyone else.'

As well as designing a handsome catalogue brimful of stimulating work, Torrents produced posters, a TV commercial and flyers for the exhibition. 'The show was a big success, and people in Barcelona still remember it', he notes.

GO-254-GO CAGA TIÓ
GO-142-GO USERDA
S. ARGENTE + S. SAURA + R. TORRENTE
caga tió
a la plaça de sant jaume. dissabte dia 22 de desembre al matí.
ajuntament de barcelona i barna centre
userda
14 NUCLEARES EN EL PLAN
FEM LA CIUTAT HABITABLE
"UNHA NAVALLADA A NOSA TERRA"
EZETZA LEMONIZEKO ZENTRALARI
Los ordenadores contra Gutemberg
TESTIMONIO DE DOS SINDICALISTAS

GRÀFIQUES OCULTES

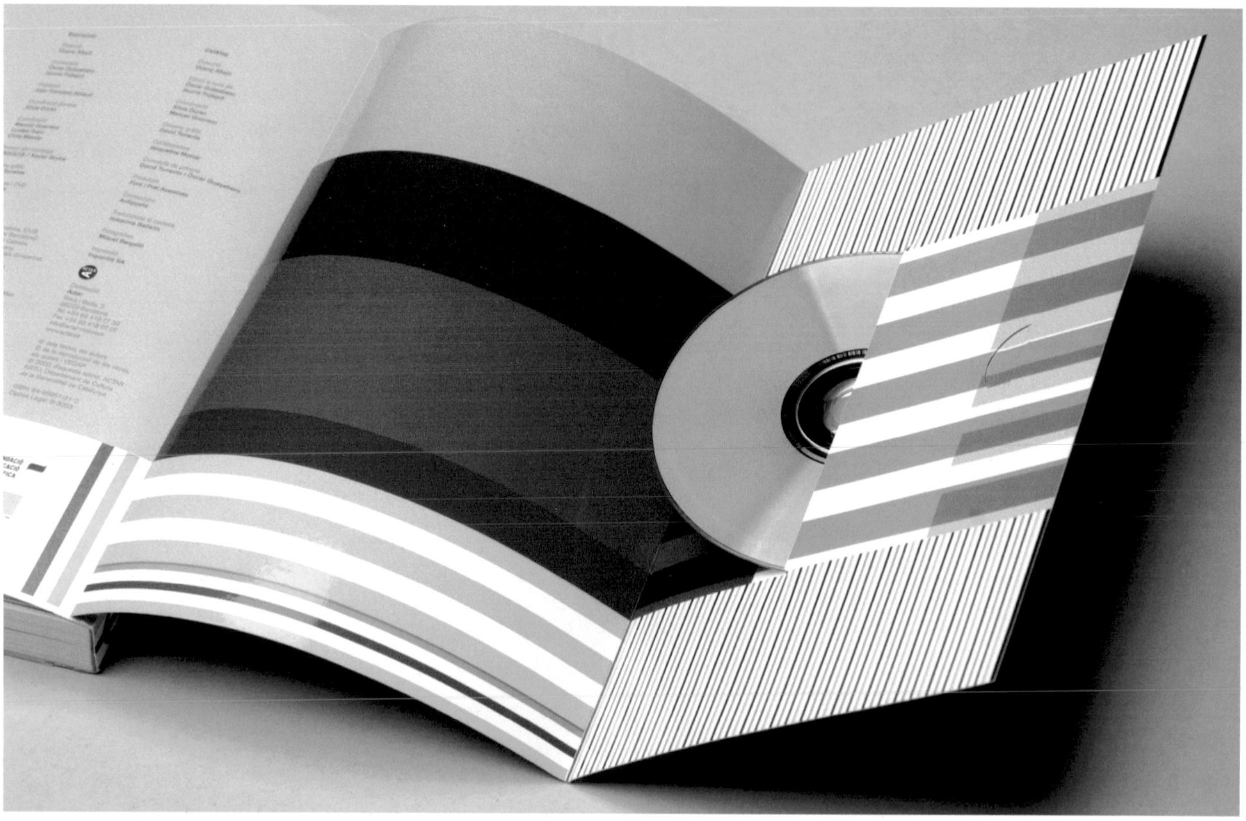

Piccolino
VO
DEL MAR
OBSESION

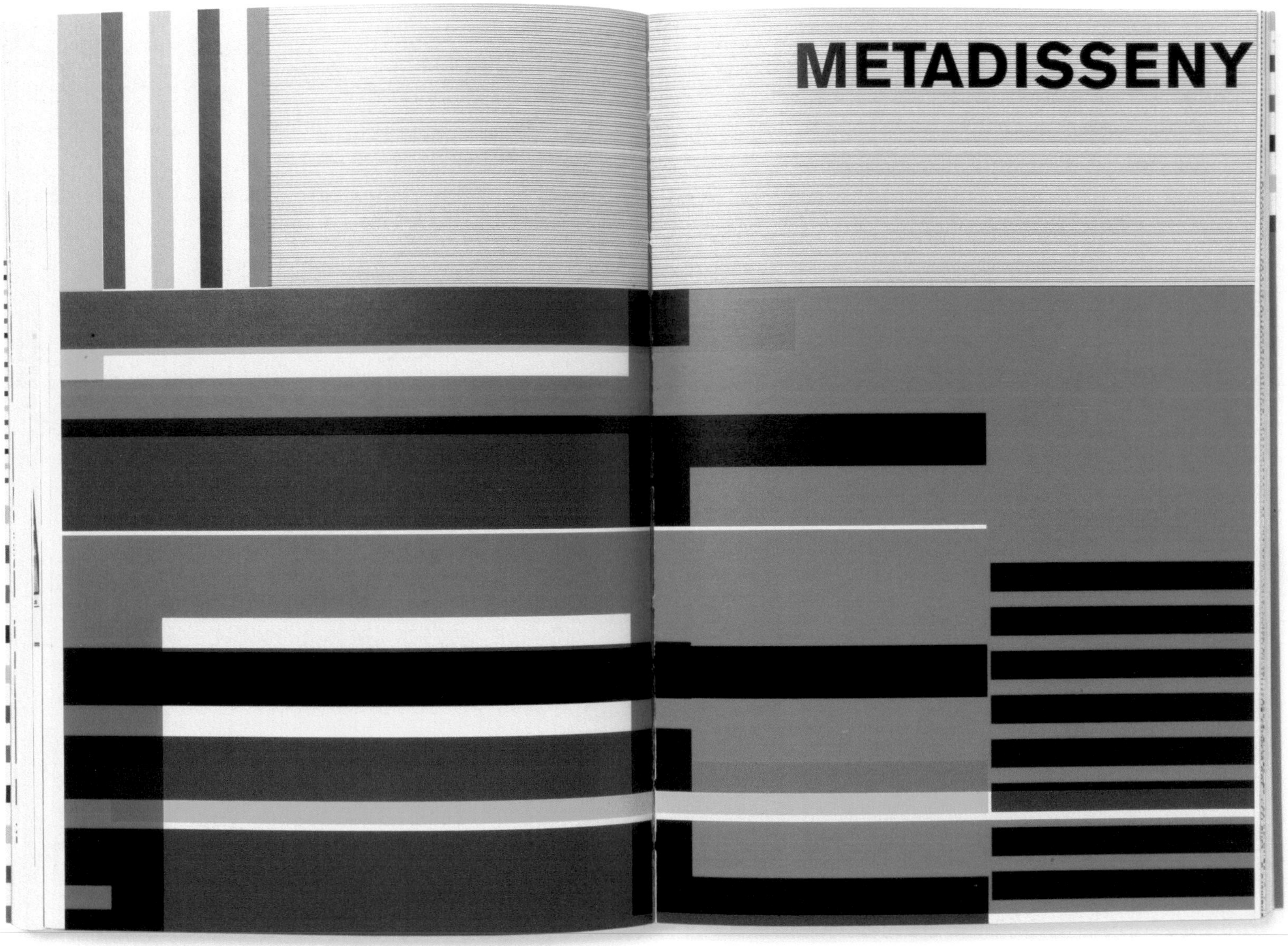
METADISSENY

Contem
Broch
Cat
Doc

Title:
Faces and Surfaces

Origin:
Sweden

Client:
Arctic Paper

Studio:
Happy F&B

Dimensions:
230mm x 180mm
9" x 7.1"

Faces
and
sur-
faces

–
–
–

Contemporary
Brochures
Catalogues
Documents

–
–
–
–
–
–
–
–
–

Description:
A confident, unfussy brochure for Arctic Paper's Munken range. One hundred people were photographed (by Jager Aren) in revealing, almost brutal, close-up. 'Paper has a lot in common with the texture of skin,' explains designer Lisa Careborg, 'from soft and smooth when we are young to rougher and frailer as we get older. In the book we started with a one-year-old baby on page 1 and ended with a 100-year-old person on page 100. The book begins with Munken's smoothest and whitest stock, followed by creamier and rougher material, finally becoming smooth and pale again towards the end of the document.'

–

The photography and the severely functional design (the front cover uses barely visible embossing for the title) impart an appealing honesty and immediacy. The models look like ordinary people, which is exactly what they were: 'It was surprisingly easy to find people', notes Careborg. 'We used friends, friends of friends and people who worked in shops around our studio. The most difficult ones to find were the last ten people. We ended up setting up a studio in an old people's home. When the book was printed, we arranged a party for all the "models", which was great fun.'

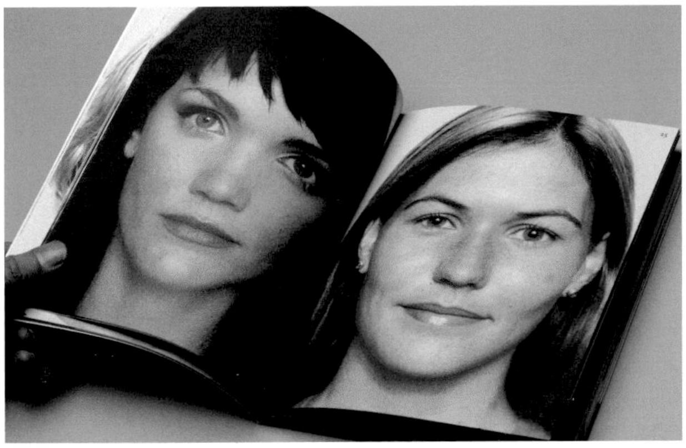

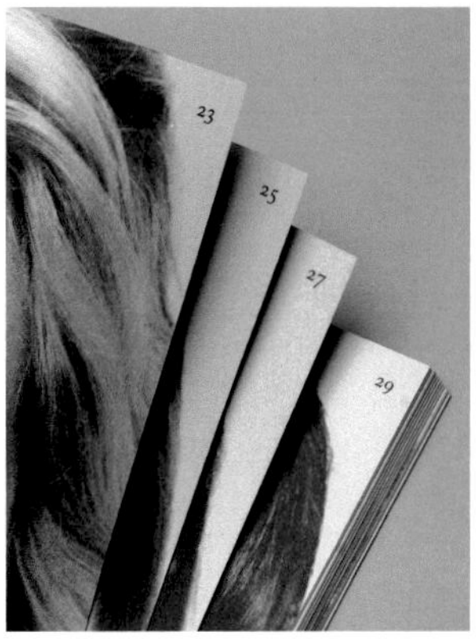
23
25
27
29

–
–
–
–
–
–
–

–
–
–
Conte
Broc
Cat
Doc
–
–
–
–
–
–
–
–
–

Title:
4
–
Origin:
UK
–
Client:
4th Floor
–
Studio:
North
–
Dimensions:
210mm x 150mm
8.3" x 5.9"
–
–
–
–
–
–

4TH_FLOOR
INTRODUCTION
4_SHAMPOOS
4_CONDITIONERS
4_STYLING_PRODUC
MOISTURIS
HAIR TYPE
HAIR THAT
RICH, NOU
ACTIVE IN
AND NOURI
SWEET ALM
THE HAIR

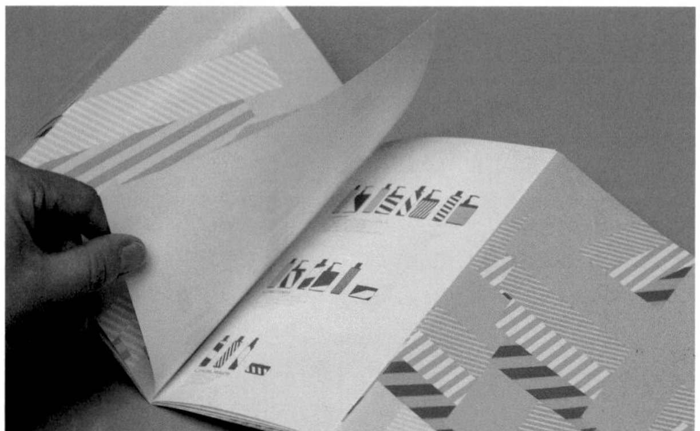

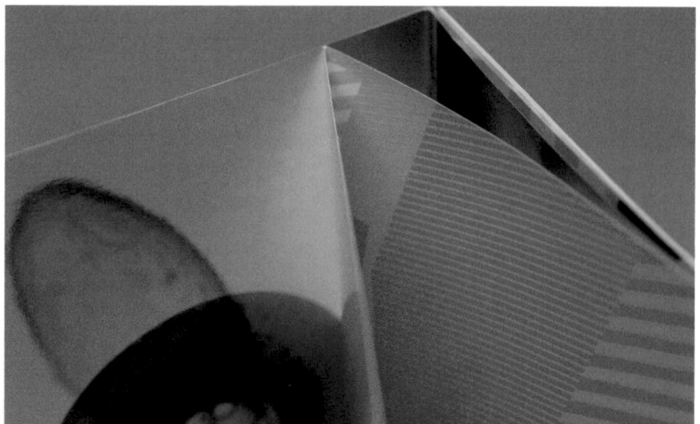

EVERYDAY
CONDITIONER

250ml/1000ml℮

DITIONER
ITABLE FOR ALL HAIR TYPES, AND LIGHT ENOUGH
DAILY BASIS, IF REQUIRED, THIS CONDITIONER
LES AND ADDS SHINE TO THE HAIR.
DIENTS THE NATURAL ANTIOXIDANT PROPERTIES
ER HELP TO RESTRUCTURE DRY AND BRITTLE
AVE IT SOFT AND PROTECTED, WHILE EXTRACT
L MOISTURISES AND CONDITIONS.

JRISING
IONER

1000ml℮

IONER
CTIVE ON DRY AND CHEMICALLY TREATED
RE-MOISTURISING, THIS IS A VERY
EATMENT CONDITIONER.
THE PROTEINS IN KUKUI MILK REPAIR
) HAIR, WHILE THE COMBINATION OF
) PANTHENOL SOFTENS AND PROTECTS
AGAINST EVERYDAY DAMAGE.

LEAVE-IN
CONDITIONER

200ml℮

LEAVE-IN_CONDITIONER
HAIR TYPE THIS CONDITIONER DOUBLES AS A LIGHT GROOMING AID AND IS PARTICULARLY EFFECTIVE WHEN USED AS A STYLING PRODUCT – TO GIVE DEFINITION AND CONTROL TO TEXTURED, CURLY OR FRIZZY HAIR.
ACTIVE INGREDIENTS COCONUT OIL BOTH NOURISHES AND PROTECTS THE HAIR.
DIRECTIONS FOR USE APPLY TO DAMP HAIR. DO NOT RINSE OUT; JUST PROCEED TO STYLE IN THE USUAL WAY.

TREATMENT

250ml℮

TREATMENT
HAIR TYPE THIS IS A DEEP AND INTENSE MOISTURISING CONDITIONER, A PARTICULARLY EFFECTIVE TREATMENT FOR DRY, CHEMICALLY TREATED OR DAMAGED HAIR.
ACTIVE INGREDIENTS THE RICH PROTEINS IN KUKUI MILK REPAIR AND NOURISH STRESSED HAIR, WHILE THE ANTIOXIDANT PROPERTIES OF SHEA BUTTER HELP TO RESTRUCTURE DRY AND BRITTLE HAIR. NATURAL LUSTRE AND ELASTICITY IS RESTORED BY SILK PROTEINS AS THE HAIR IS MOISTURISED AND SOFTENED BY SWEET ALMOND OIL AND EXTRACT OF CASTOR OIL.
DIRECTIONS FOR USE AFTER SHAMPOOING, APPLY THE TREATMENT TO WET HAIR, WORKING FROM THE ROOTS TO THE ENDS. COMB THROUGH AND LEAVE FOR FIVE MINUTES – OR LONGER IF POSSIBLE – BEFORE RINSING THOROUGHLY.

–
–
–
–
–
–
–
–
–

Description:
The design group North has a reputation for sharp-brained, disciplined graphic design. Under founder Sean Perkins the studio has been responsible for some of the most engaging and systematically executed graphic design of the past decade. North are pioneers of the neo-Modernist style. Everything they do is suffused with the spirit of the great European Modernists, yet they always manage to inject a shot of contemporary adrenalin into their work, an ingredient that neatly parries any charge of parody and which makes North's work superbly contemporary.

–

The studio is responsible for the brand identity of fashionable London hair salon Fourth Floor. The salon's innovative product catalogue, shown here, is part of an ongoing programme of brand-building by North.

–

The catalogue – which is given away in the Fourth Floor salon and at various retail outlets – is a continuous play on the number four. The brochure is made up of groups of four pages; the cover features a graphic abstract of the numeral 4; in addition to the standard four process colours, four special colours have been used. The cleverly folded document also contains four pages of mirror board – presumably to allow customers to view the efficacy of the salon's hair care products!

–
–
–
–
–
–

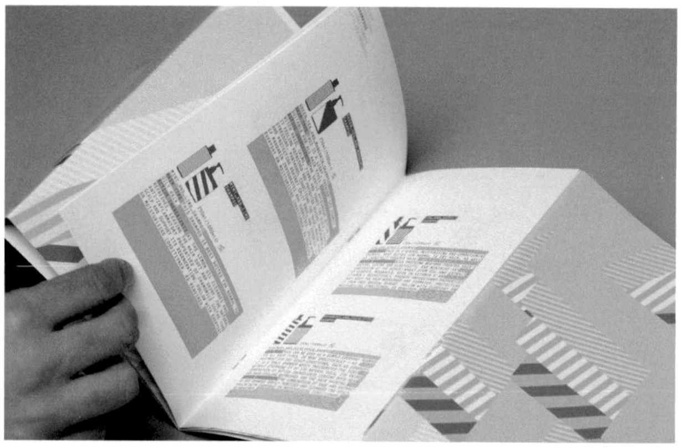

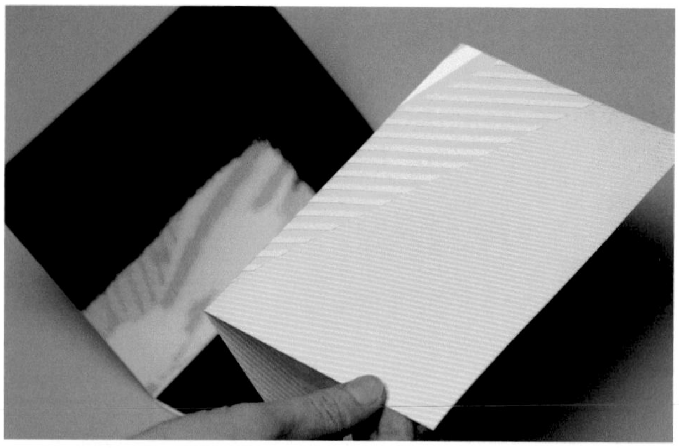

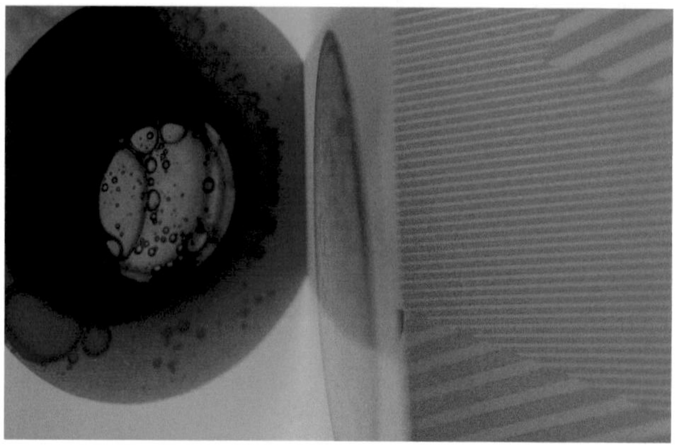

ROSEMARY_AND_EUCALYPTUS
SHAMPOO
250ml/1000ml

FOUR

Conte
Broc
Cat
Doc

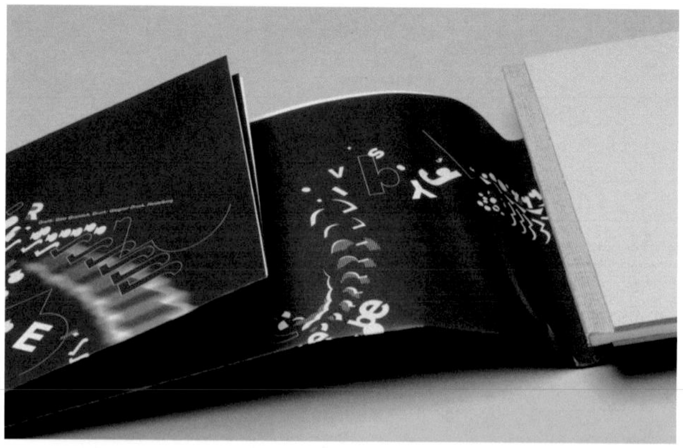

Title:
Musik Typographisch Visualisieren
–
Origin:
Germany
–
Client:
Self-initiated
–
Studio:
Götz Gramlich
–
Dimensions:
235mm x 165mm
9.2" x 6.4"

Description:
An intriguing, handmade, limited-edition, mono-coloured document by the Heidelberg-based designer Götz Gramlich, cataloguing his experiments into the graphic depiction of music. Gramlich asked himself the question 'How can I see what I can hear?' and set out to answer it.
–
'To visualize music is a highly abstract task', he notes. 'Visual artists have often attempted to make invisible emotions visible. Between the abstract and the material the artist acts as a medium, transforming subjective sensations into tangible entities – a sort of filter with a defined space and limited means of expression.'
–
Working with a computer programmer, Gramlich created generative software that turns music into optical signals, allowing him to turn printed paper into sonic space. Linear forms and basic patterns in various shades of grey convey qualities of tone and sound, and serve as a method of making the audible visible. The process is based on a strictly defined number of forms generated from Berthold Akzidenz Grotesk Bold and another cut of the same font.

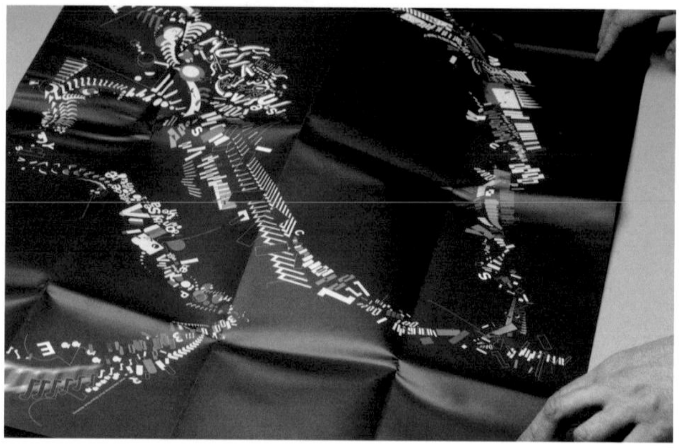

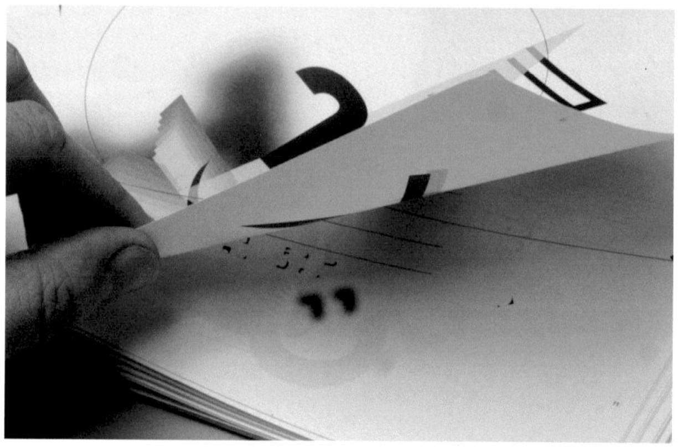

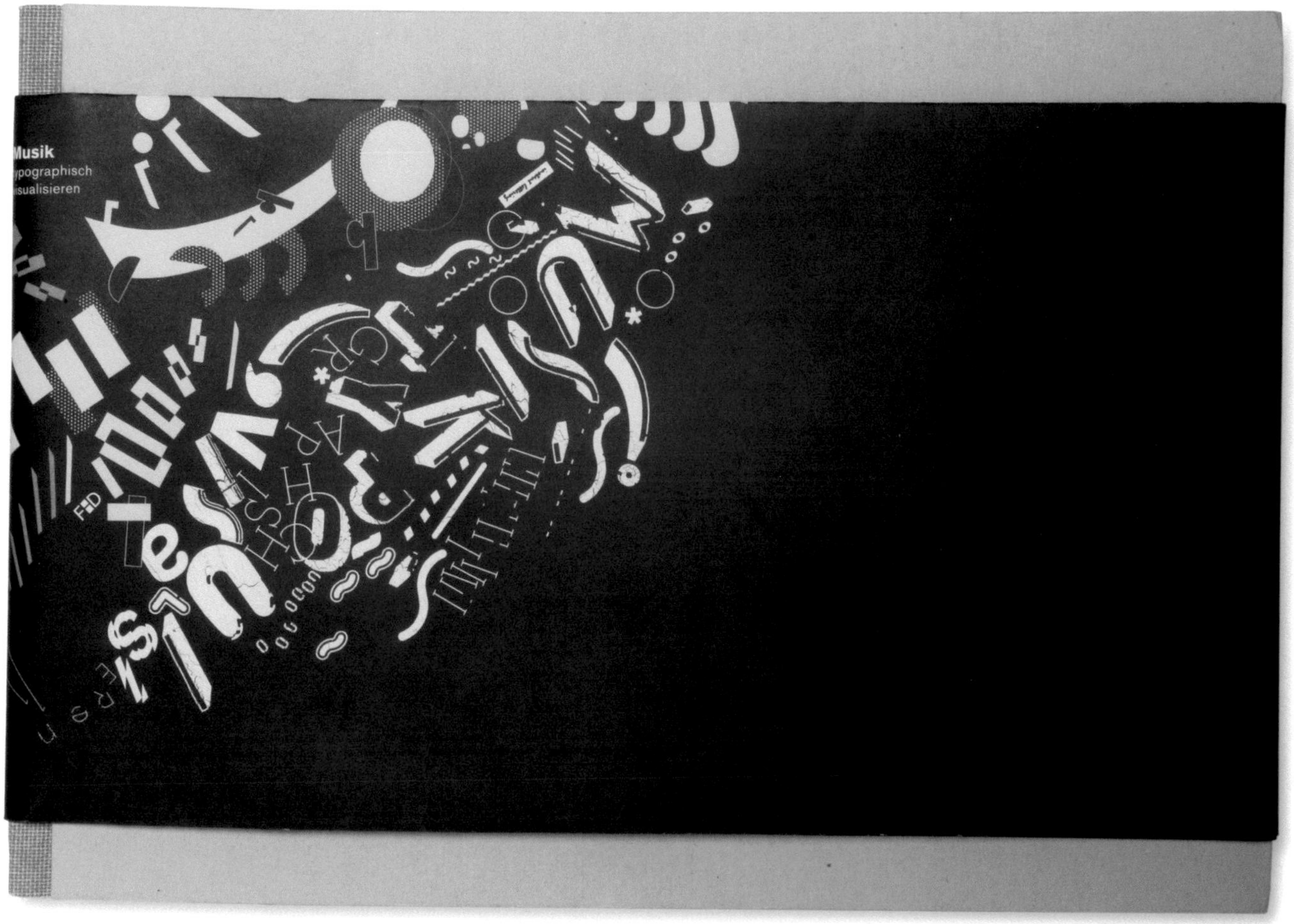
Musik
ypographisch
isualisieren

H.J. Bennink, Drums, Donnerwetter, live in Willisau
16
40
56

Title:
Below the Fold:
–
Origin:
USA
–
Client:
Winterhouse
–
Studio:
Winterhouse
–
Dimensions:
450mm x 274mm
17.7" x 10.8"

Description:
Described as an 'occasional journal from the Winterhouse Institute' (the studio and publishing venture run by US designers Jessica Helfand and William Drenttel), *Below the Fold:* is a whip-smart, tabloid-style publication exuding the authorial design ethos for which the duo is justifiably famous.
–
As Helfand and Drenttel explain on their website: 'Within the limitations of a printed publication, each issue of *Below the Fold:* will explore a single topic through visual narrative and critical inquiry, examining ideas that are technically "below the fold" in an effort to reveal alternative ways of looking at the world we live in.'
–
The publication is an invigorating example of the notion of the designer as author and editor. Helfand and Drenttel, and their fellow contributors, have created a stimulating piece of visual and textual communication that extends the growing library of designer-authored publications and demonstrates how graphic communication can aid our understanding of the world in ways that more traditional modes of editorial exposition cannot always match.
–
The document is 16 pages long, wire-stitched, and deploys two colours throughout. Paper is Carnival Ice Vellum Text, and the principal typeface is Peter Bilak's Fedra Mono.

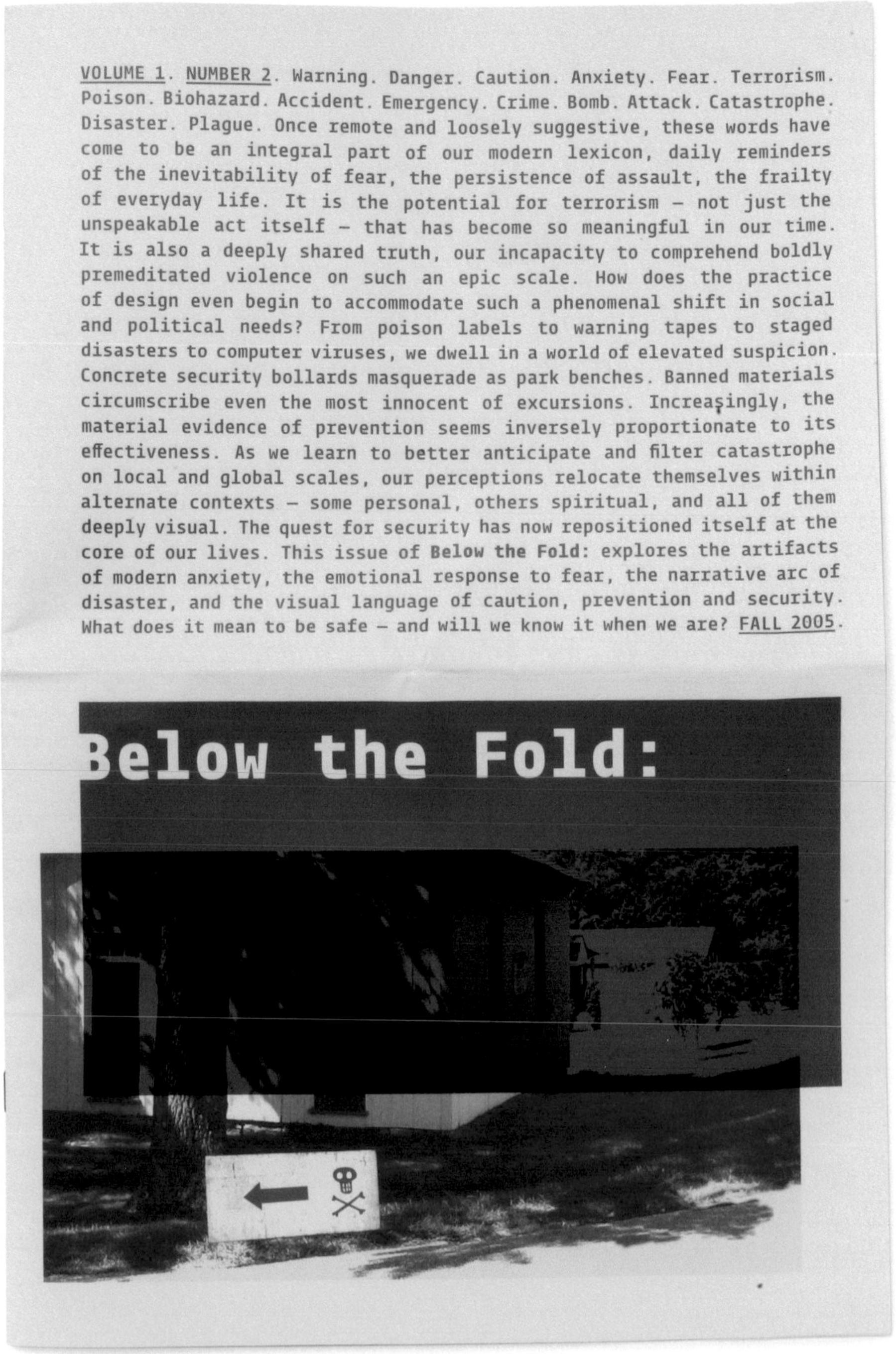
VOLUME 1. NUMBER 2. Warning. Danger. Caution. Anxiety. Fear. Terrorism. Poison. Biohazard. Accident. Emergency. Crime. Bomb. Attack. Catastrophe. Disaster. Plague. Once remote and loosely suggestive, these words have come to be an integral part of our modern lexicon, daily reminders of the inevitability of fear, the persistence of assault, the frailty of everyday life. It is the potential for terrorism – not just the unspeakable act itself – that has become so meaningful in our time. It is also a deeply shared truth, our incapacity to comprehend boldly premeditated violence on such an epic scale. How does the practice of design even begin to accommodate such a phenomenal shift in social and political needs? From poison labels to warning tapes to staged disasters to computer viruses, we dwell in a world of elevated suspicion. Concrete security bollards masquerade as park benches. Banned materials circumscribe even the most innocent of excursions. Increasingly, the material evidence of prevention seems inversely proportionate to its effectiveness. As we learn to better anticipate and filter catastrophe on local and global scales, our perceptions relocate themselves within alternate contexts – some personal, others spiritual, and all of them deeply visual. The quest for security has now repositioned itself at the core of our lives. This issue of Below the Fold: explores the artifacts of modern anxiety, the emotional response to fear, the narrative arc of disaster, and the visual language of caution, prevention and security. What does it mean to be safe – and will we know it when we are? FALL 2005.

Below the Fold:

Below the Fold:

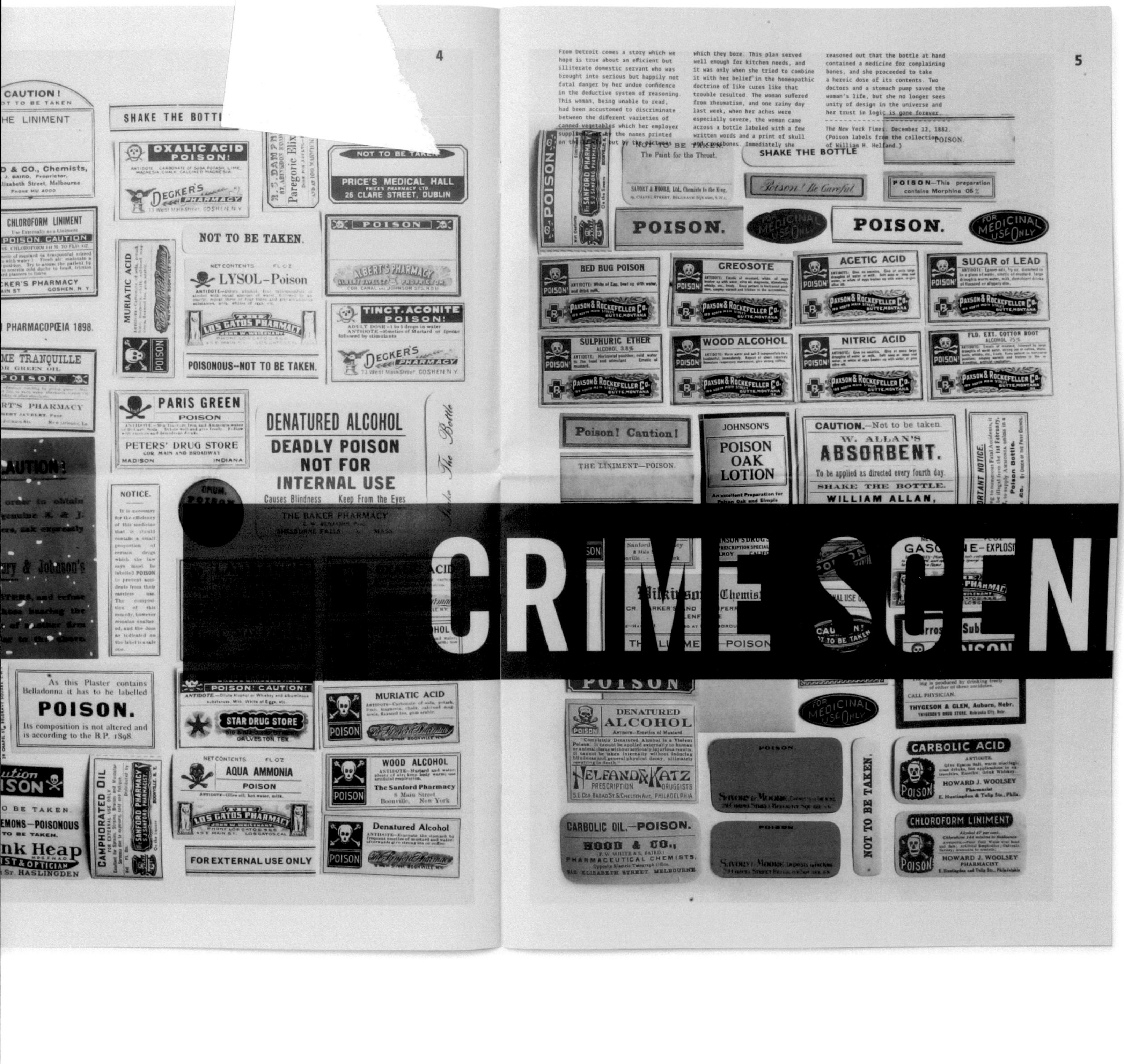
4
5
From Detroit comes a story which we hope is true about an efficient but illiterate domestic servant who was brought into serious but happily not fatal danger by her undue confidence in the deductive system of reasoning. This woman, being unable to read, had been accustomed to discriminate between the different varieties of canned vegetables which her employer supplied, not by the names printed on the labels but by the pictures which they bore. This plan served well enough for kitchen needs, and it was only when she tried to combine it with her belief in the homeopathic doctrine of like cures like that trouble resulted. The woman suffered from rheumatism, and one rainy day last week, when her aches were especially severe, the woman came across a bottle labeled with a few written words and a print of skull and crossbones. Immediately she reasoned out that the bottle at hand contained a medicine for complaining bones, and she proceeded to take a heroic dose of its contents. Two doctors and a stomach pump saved the woman's life, but she no longer sees unity of design in the universe and her trust in logic is gone forever.
The New York Times. December 12, 1882.
(Poison labels from the collection of William H. Helfand.)
CRIME SCEN

Below the Fold:

Conte
Broc
Cat
Doc

Title:
Burberry

Origin:
UK

Client:
Burberry

Studio:
Multistorey

Dimensions:
Various

THOMASBURBERRY.COM

Description:
British retailer and fashion brand Burberry handed a batch of photographs to design duo Multistorey and asked them to design a brochure with them. This was as close as Multistorey came to receiving a formal brief. The document was intended for use as an item of Burberry in-store marketing literature, and to be sent to press and media contacts.

Designer Rhonda Drakeford explains the process: 'We began by talking to photographer Barnaby Roper about what he had been trying to achieve in the shoot. The photographs had been shot on a windy day on a Cornish beach. We wanted to capture that timeless feeling of a day trip to an English coast.'

Drakeford and design partner Harry Woodrow created a brochure design where the pages were cut to different sizes to resemble loose photographs that had been found and bound together in a hurry. 'The paper stock we specified', she explains, 'had lots of visible flecks in it that, when printed, looked like bits being blown around in the wind. The style of the layout uses frames and the colour palette of old photographs. Finding a binding company that would take this job on was the hardest part, especially as it was a very large run.'

1835
Thomas Burberry
AUTUMN/WINTER 03/04

–
–
–
Contem
Broc
Cat
Doc
–
–
–
–
–
–
–
–
–

Title:
Sketchbook
–
Origin:
USA
–
Client:
Getty Images
–
Art Direction and Design:
Mark Fraser
–
Copywriting:
Mike Benson
Jason Graham
–
Illustration:
Jimmy Turrell
–
Photography:
Getty Images
–
Creative Direction:
Chris Ashworth
–
Dimensions:
245mm x 210mm
9.6" x 8.3"
–
–
–
–
–
–

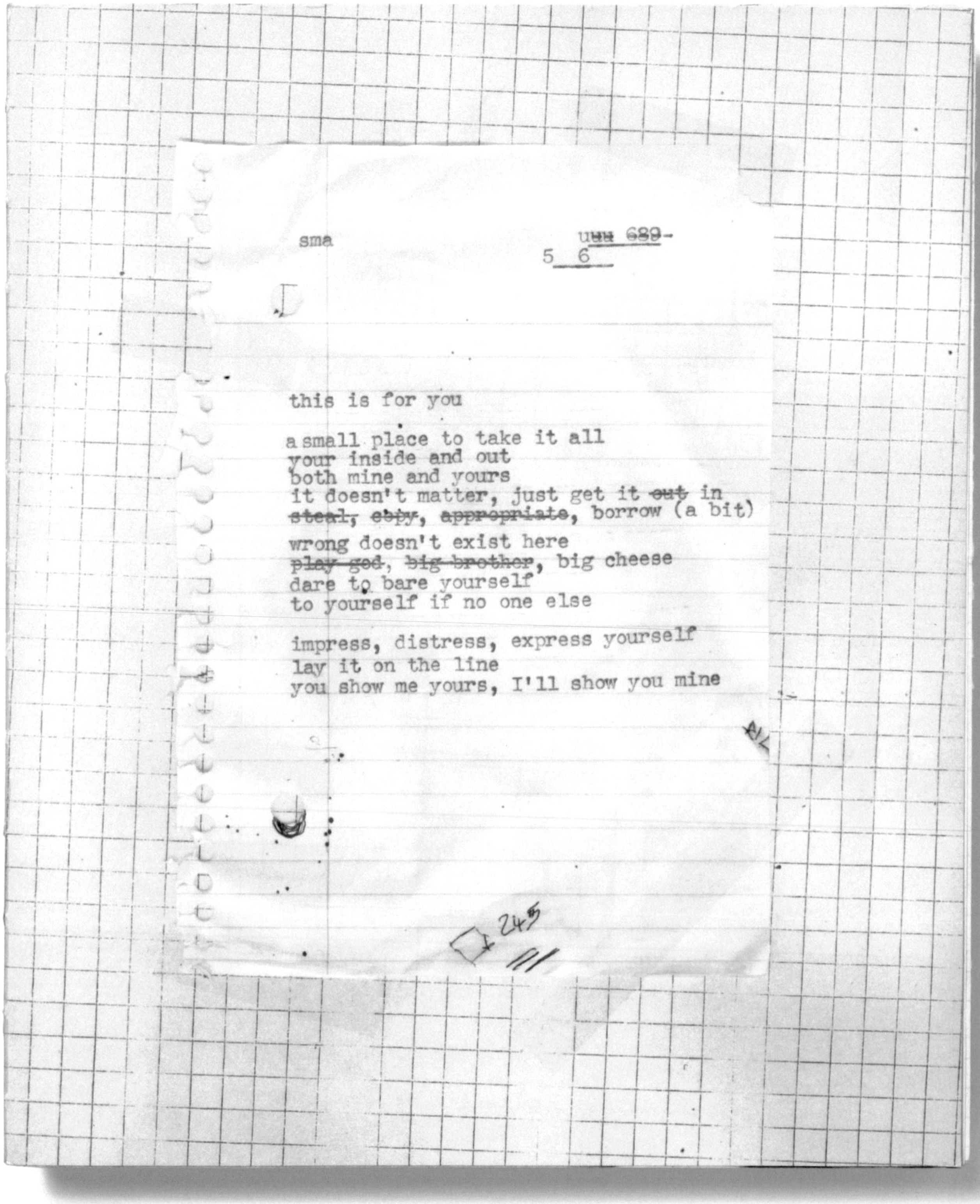
sma
5 6
this is for you
a small place to take it all
your inside and out
both mine and yours
it doesn't matter, just get it ~~out~~ in
~~steal~~, ~~copy~~, ~~appropriate~~, borrow (a bit)
wrong doesn't exist here
~~play god~~, ~~big brother~~, big cheese
dare to bare yourself
to yourself if no one else
impress, distress, express yourself
lay it on the line
you show me yours, I'll show you mine

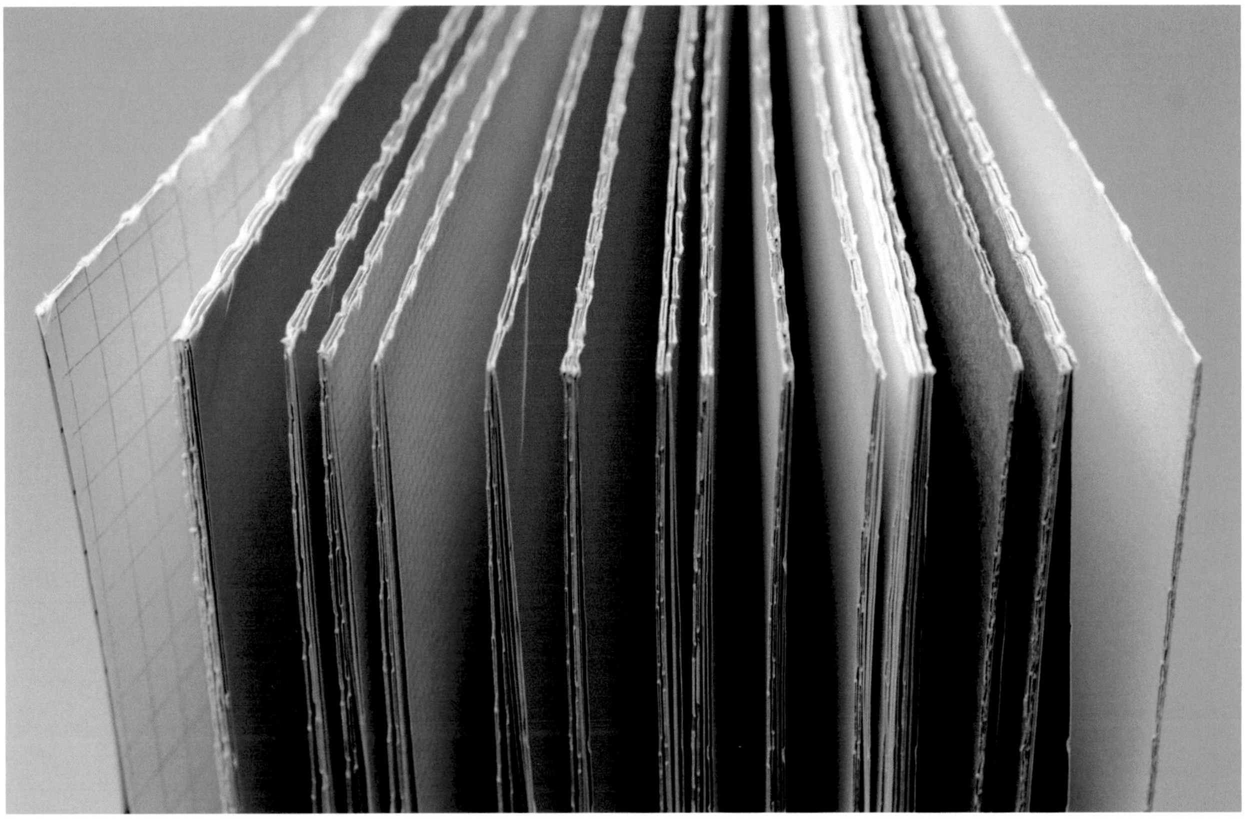

Description:
Modern photo libraries rely on the Web to display and deliver imagery. Yet the printed catalogue remains a key promotional tool. Getty Images, under Seattle-based Chris Ashworth's creative direction, consistently produces high-quality printed literature.

–

But 'Sketchbook' bears zero resemblance to a typical photo-library catalogue. It's a striking piece of graphic wizardry, using a mix of coloured stock, uncut pages and exposed binding. Most of the photographic imagery is, somewhat contrarily, printed on the reverse of the sealed pages.

–

'The thinking was to design a sketchbook where anything goes,' explains designer Mark Fraser, 'a book for all your thoughts, ideas, things that catch your eye, words etc. It's about the start of the creative process, when things are open and thrown into the pot. We made it very raw aesthetically to encourage people to gets things out, good and bad, to have to rip it and not to be too precious about it.'

–

Does Fraser see the end of the glossy photo-library catalogue? 'Things have moved on in our approach and our thinking about how we communicate with our imagery. Now we're interested in creating communications and sharing ideas with people that may help them in their everyday lives.
So, with this piece the imagery and illustrations are there to express the concept and encourage its use and hopefully ... inspire.'

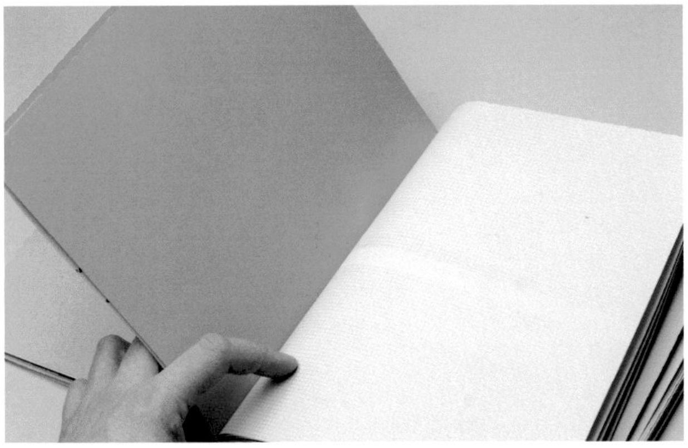

–
–
–
–
–
–

drop
5:41 pm Page 2

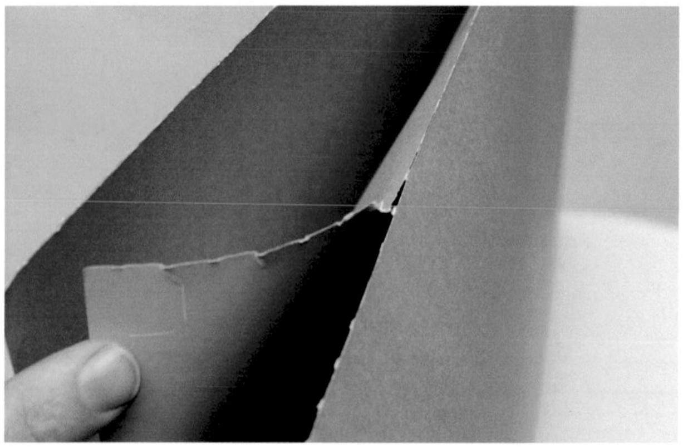

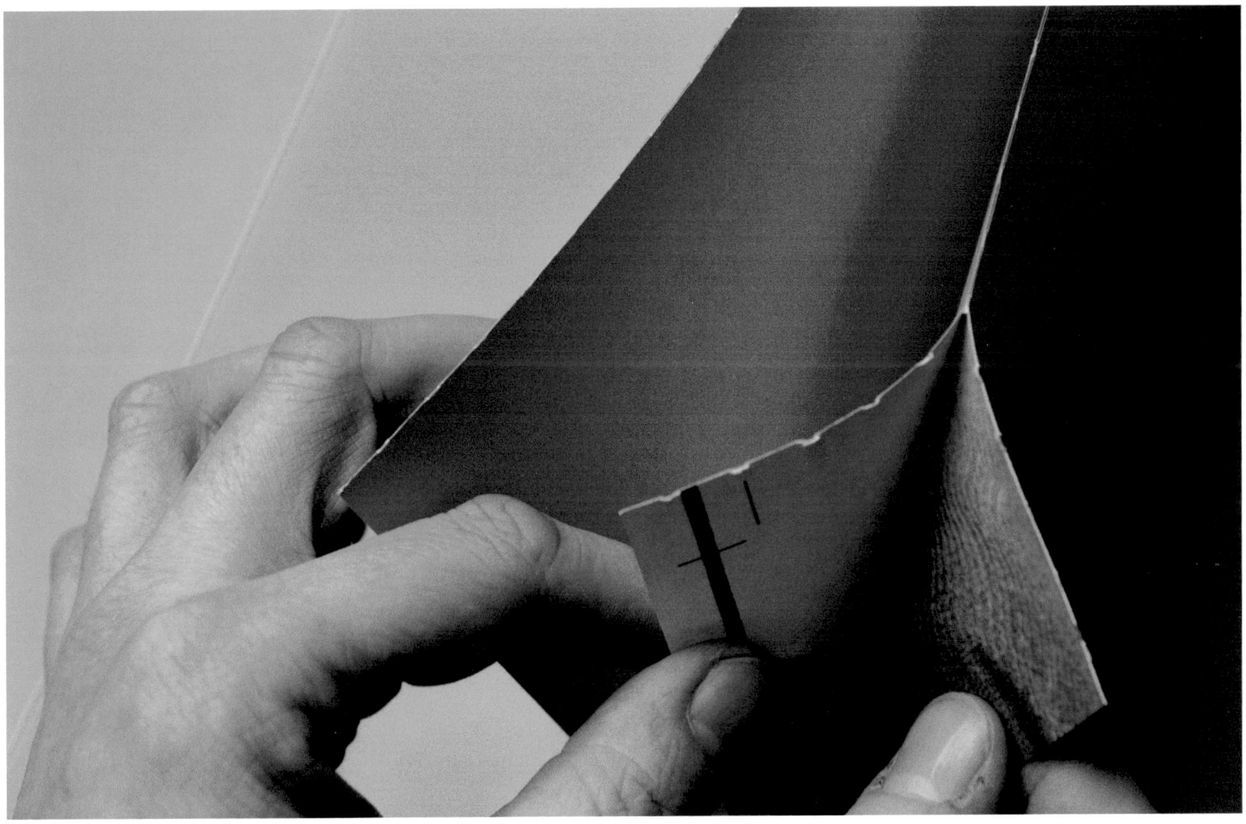

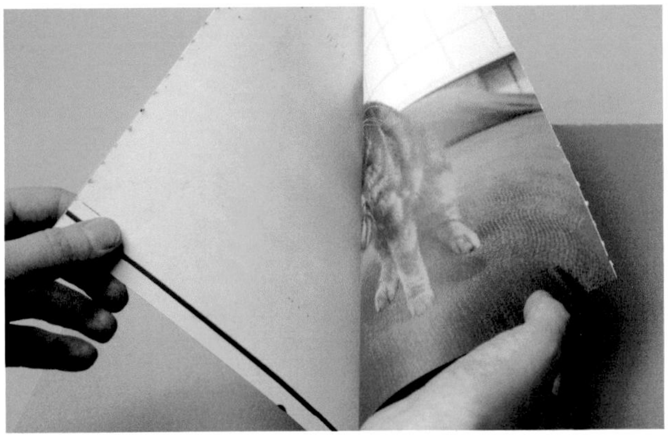

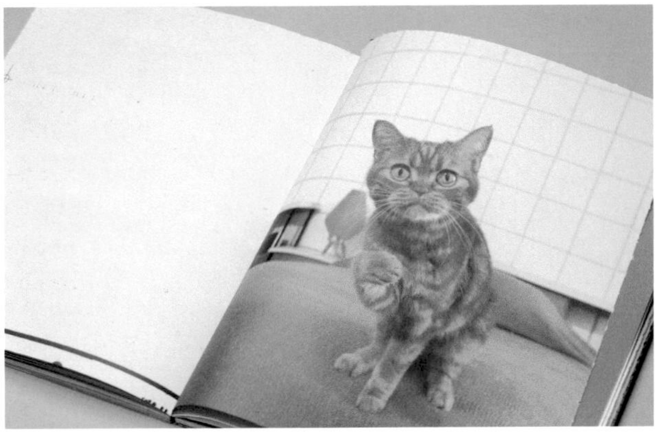

Conte
Broc
Cat
Doc

Title:
Ryuichi Sakamoto
Tour 2005 Brochure

Origin:
Japan

Client:
Ryuichi Sakamoto

Studio:
Hideki Nakajima

Dimensions:
330mm x 240mm
13" x 9.4"

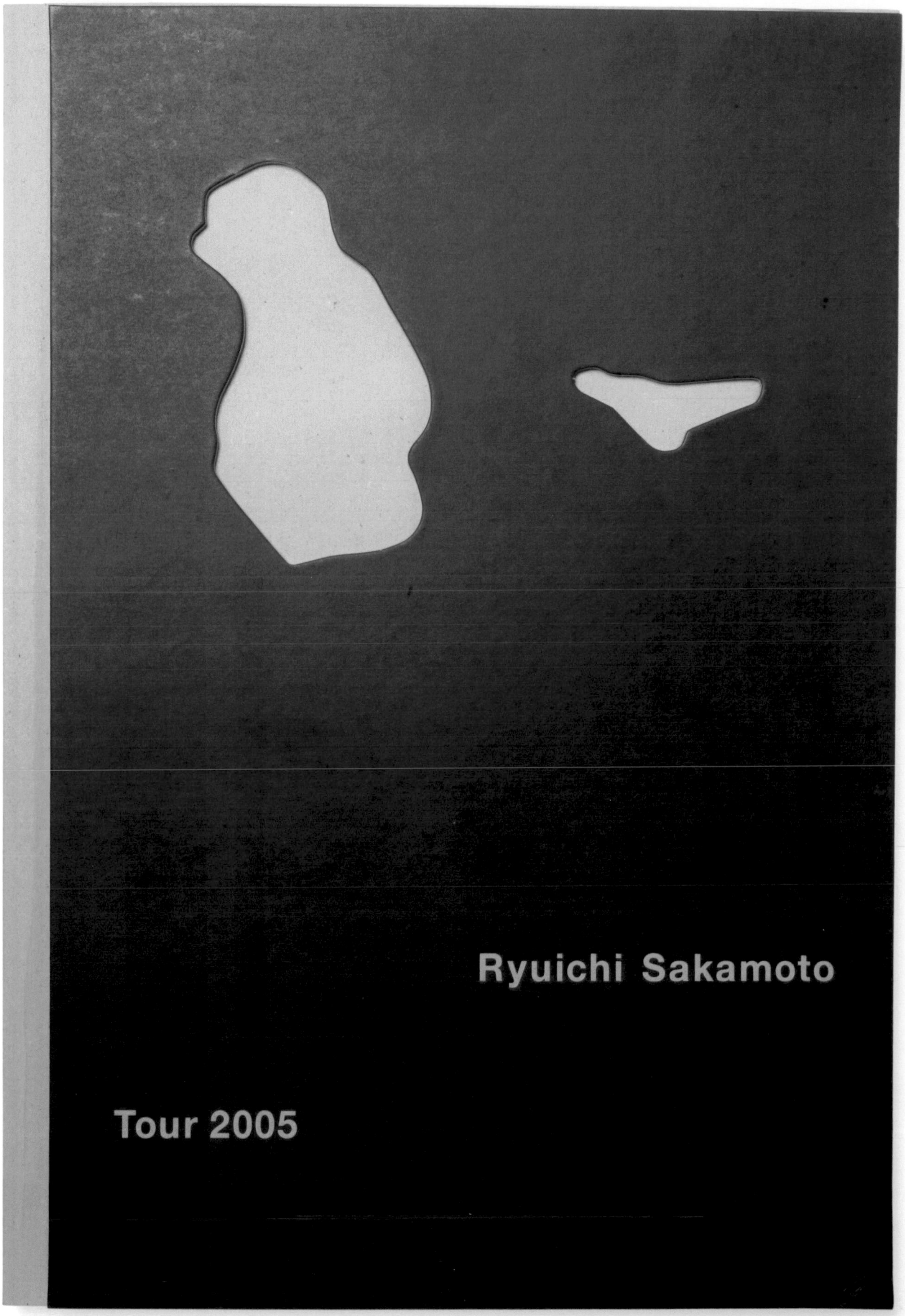
Ryuichi Sakamoto
Tour 2005

–
–
–

Contemporary
Brochures
Catalogues
Documents

–
–
–
–
–
–
–
–
–

Description:
Hideki Nakajima, the Tokyo-based graphic designer, has a worldwide reputation for his work and his constant experimentation with materials. Long associated with the cult musician Ryuichi Sakamoto, famous for his minimalist, neo-classical, electronic music, Nakajima has produced numerous iconic album covers and printed literature for Sakamoto over the past decade.

–

Tour brochures were once glorious examples of graphic enterprise. Today they are disposable 'merchandise' – usually thrown together on the eve of the tour, and with the sole aim of squeezing an extra buck or two from concert-goers. For his 2005 tour Sakamoto commissioned Nakajima to create a document that flew in the face of the customary glossy and ephemeral 'tour brochure'.

–

Tour

As in so much of his work, Nakajima makes inspired use of materials. His heavy-duty board covers, with taped spine, and die-cut abstract shapes, combine to make an arresting first impression. Inside, the judicious use of full-colour photography of natural phenomena makes for a compelling counterpoint to the more austere cover. The result is a collector's item.

–
–
–
–
–
–

ap bank
ap bankは、アーティストたちによる未来への融資だ。

–
–
–
Contem
Broc
Cat
Doc
–
–
–
–
–
–
–
–
–

Title:
Khadi – Textile of India
–
Origin:
Switzerland
–
Client:
Kontrast Verlag
–
Designers:
Tania Prill
Alberto Vieceli
–
Dimensions:
245mm x 163.5mm
9.6" x 6.4"
–
–
–
–
–
–

EXTILE OF INDIA KHADI – TEXTILE OF IND
TEXTILE OF INDIA KHADI – TEXTILE OF
ISBN 3-906729-12-5

KHADI – TEXTILE OF INDIA
KONTRAST

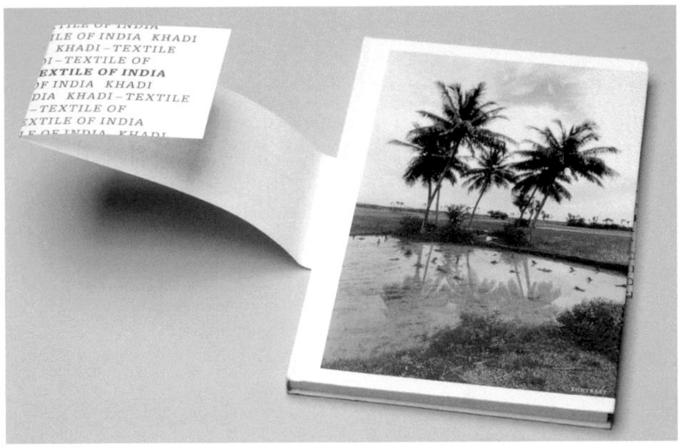

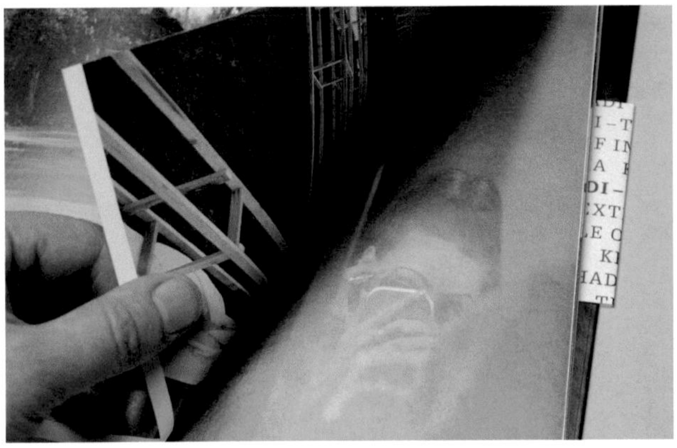

–
–
–

Contemporary
Brochures
Catalogues
Documents

–

Description:
A beautifully designed and impeccably produced documentary account of textile manufacture in rural southern India, with reportage-style photography by Manuel Bauer. Designed by Swiss duo Tania Prill and Alberto Vieceli, the book exhibits the trademark thoughtfulness and unhurried poise of their graphic design.

–

Unusually for a printed account of Indian life and culture, most of the photography is black-and-white. There are a few colour spreads, but the overall effect is of muted authenticity. The paper stock resembles superior quality newsprint, and French folding is deployed throughout to give added heft to what might otherwise be a disappointingly slim volume. The typography is robust, and a detachable, wraparound paper band carries the document's title.

–

Contem
Broc
Cat
Doc

Title:
Centrefold 1 & 2

Origin:
UK

Client:
Self-initiated

Studio:
BB/Saunders

Dimensions:
420mm x 297mm
16.5" x 11.7"

centrefold
1

centrefold
1
Noun.
Illustrated centre spread
that is extra long and has
to be folded into a

Description:
BB/Saunders is a London-based design studio. Its clients include Nike, MTV, Penguin Books and Philips. *Centrefold* is a self-initiated, self-published studio project. Originally conceived as a selling tool for a photographer, it developed into an ongoing project with other contributors. As creative director Warren Beeby explains: 'The brief was to design a magazine featuring young eclectic design, fashion and image-making talent. I always wanted the magazine to work on more than one level. I wanted to find a format that could showcase the mainly image-led content in a unique way.'

–

Centrefold is designed as a series of unbound, interleaved pages working sequentially, just like any other publication. But the unbound format allows each centrefold to be removed from the publication and to exist independently. 'The idea is intended to be playful', notes Beeby, 'and presents endless possibilities with each new issue. I've always been fascinated by images that have been removed from magazines to be displayed elsewhere, giving them another life away from the original publication. I also like the way a sheet from a newspaper, if removed from the paper, may have hard news on one side and sport or gossip on the other. Removing the sheet changes the context of both pieces, and their relationship to one another.'

–

Centrefold 1 was encased in a screen-printed poly bag. Issue 2 comes inside a paper sleeve, sewn on three sides.

–
–
–
–

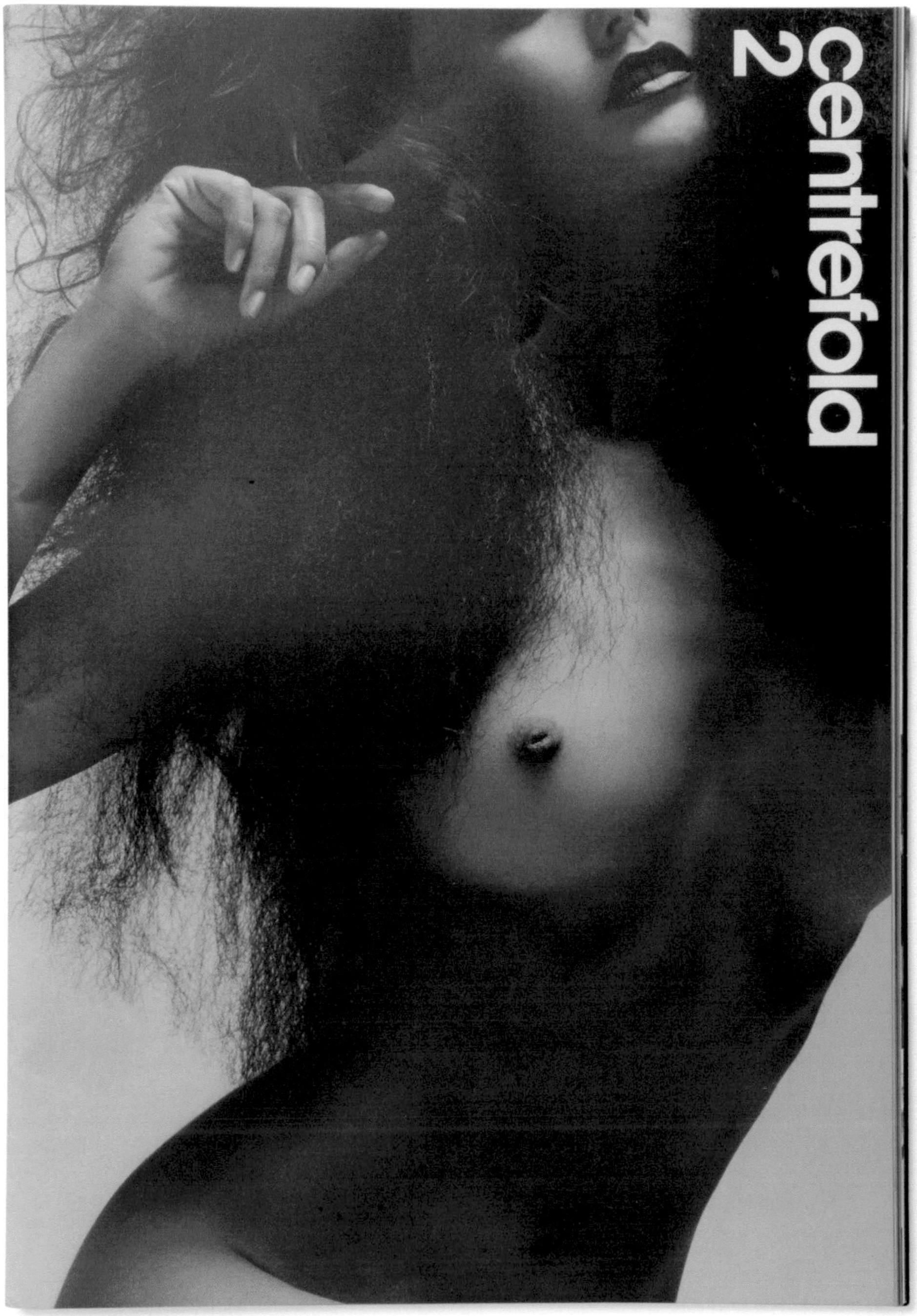
centrefold
2

9

cent

17

7
5a
5b
5c
5d
5e
3a

16

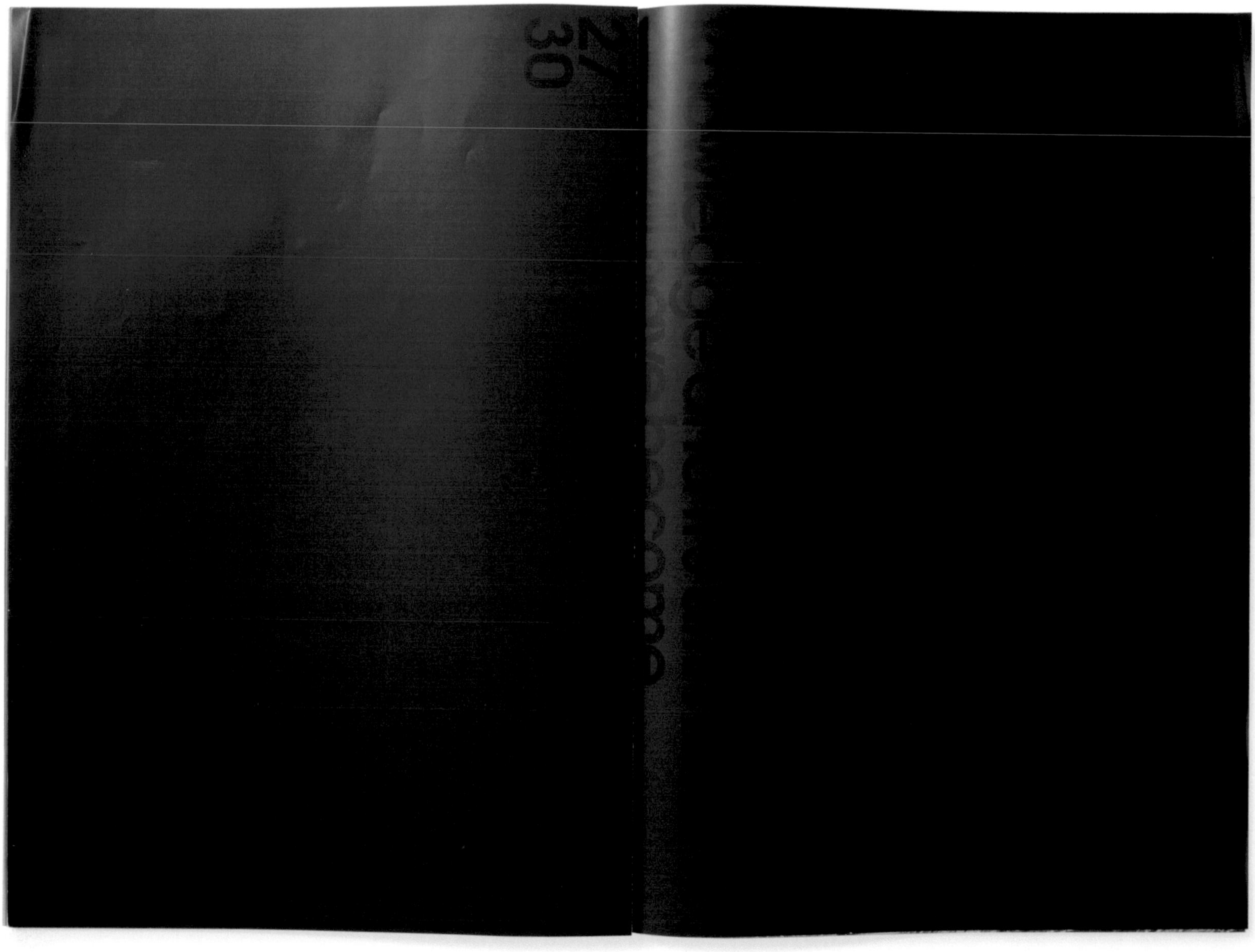

11
46
47
10

–
–
–
Contem
Broc
Cat
Doc
–
–
–
–
–
–
–
–
–
Title:
Esse
–
Origin:
USA
–
Client:
Gilbert Paper
–
Concept:
Rick Valicenti
Louise Sandhaus
at Wild LuV
–
Designers:
Rick Valicenti
Gina Vieceli
John Pobojewski
–
Studio:
Thirst
–
Dimensions:
287mm x 294mm
11.3" x 11.6"
–
–
–
–
–
–

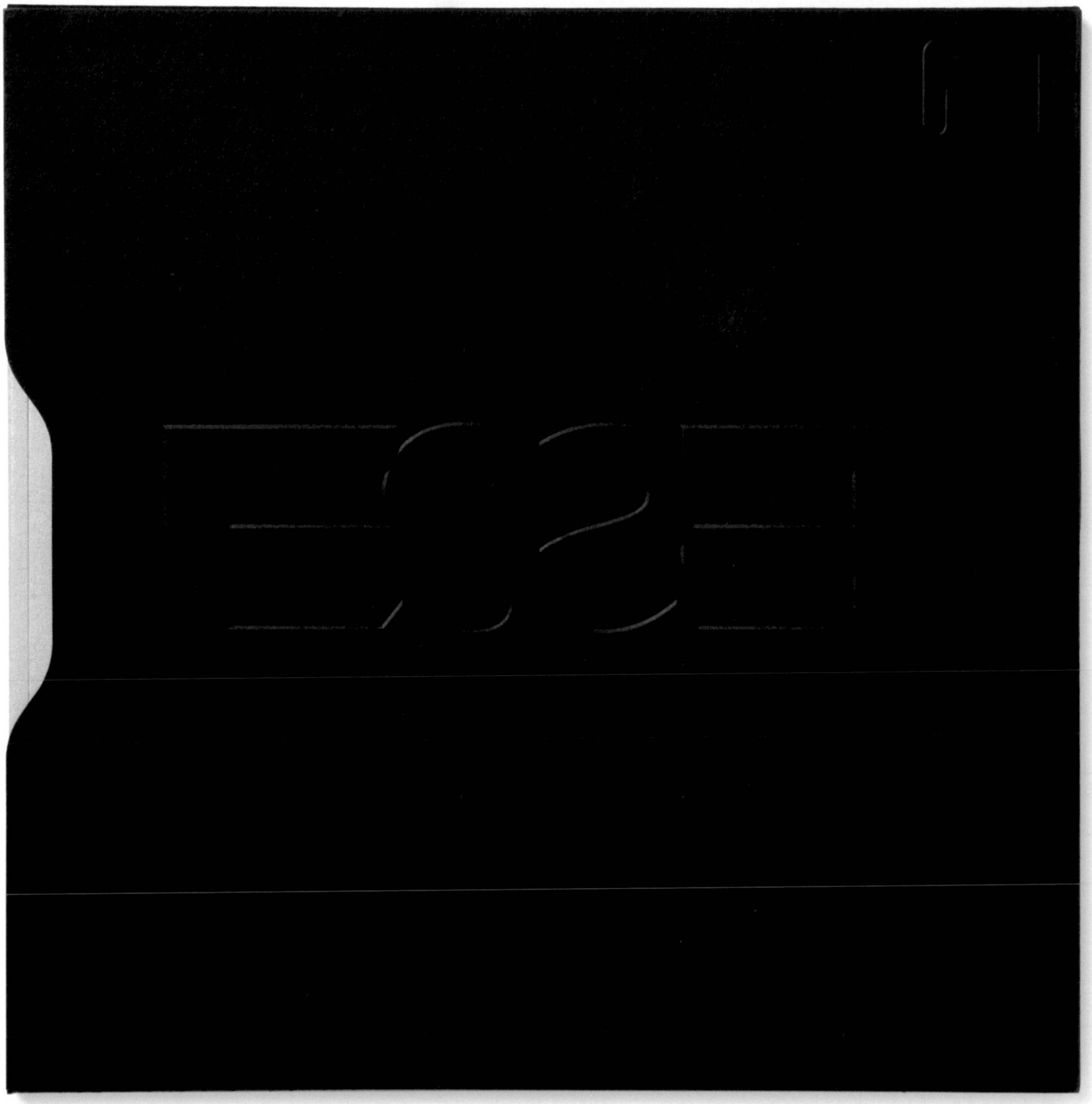

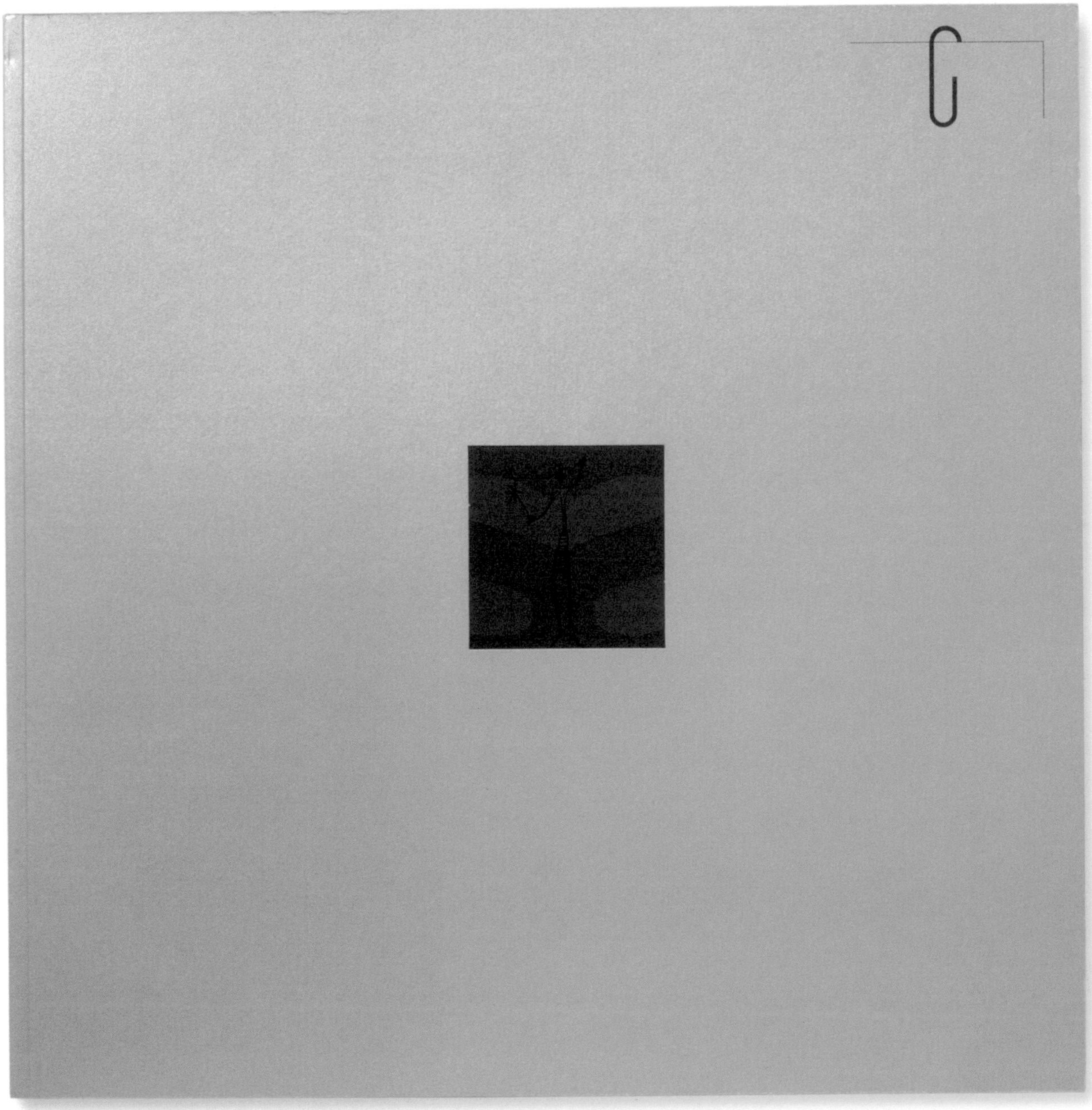

–
–
–
–
–
–
–
–
–

Description:
A bravura brochure that road-tests three types of Gilbert Paper stocks – textured, smooth and pearlized. Designer Rick Valicenti and members of his Thirst studio working with noted colourist Beatrice Santiccioli, have created a paper company catalogue that demonstrates the colour- and detail-holding capabilities of the Esse range of papers.
–
The designers use a circus of production tricks and graphic conjuring to create a nearly square document that exudes Valicenti's graphic signature. The brochure is a riot of colour and textural effects. It is a delight to look at, and a delight to hold. Extensive die-cutting throughout adds to the sense of drama created by this lavish document.
–
A sober matt-black slip-case houses the brochure. The Esse logo is blind-embossed, as is an illustrated figure on the reverse, which utters the word 'Ciao'. The slip-case is the only note of restraint in an otherwise finely judged exercise in excess.
–
–
–
–
–
–

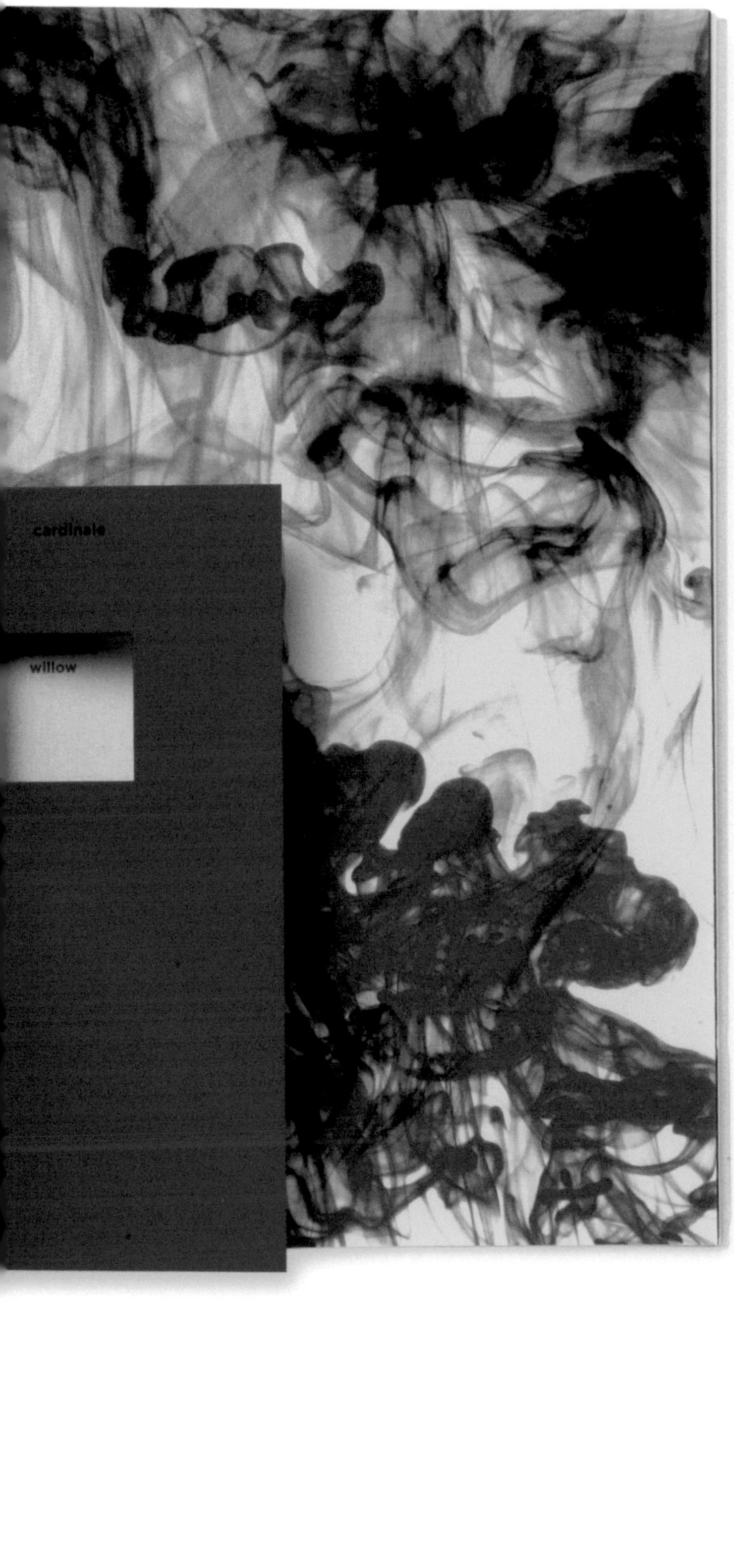
cardinale
willow

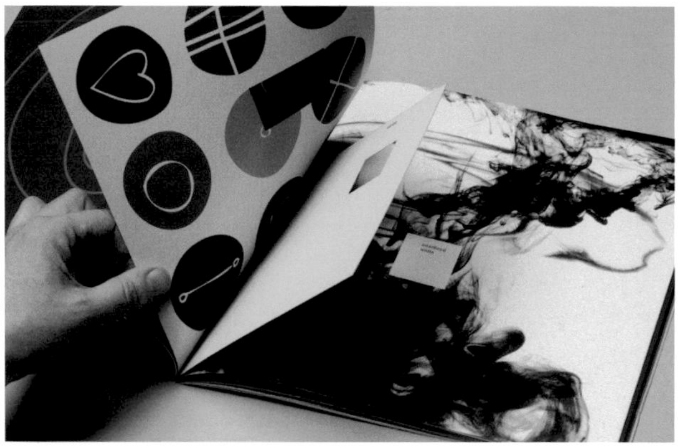

Conten
Broc
Cat
Doc

Title:
Centre Culturel Français d'Alger

Origin:
France

Client:
Centre Culturel Français d'Alger

Studio:
Christophe Jacquet (*a.k.a.* Toffe), Giancarlo Oprandi

Dimensions:
297mm x 210mm
11.7" x 8.3"

Description:
He works under the *nom de plume* Toffe, but his real name is Christophe Jacquet and he is one of France's leading graphic designers. His work is not well known outside Gallic design circles, yet he is among the most intelligent and experimental forces in modern design. An early adopter of the Apple Mac (he first used one in 1984), his work is a hybrid of digital motifs and effects ('I like work that shows its method of construction') and elegant graphic formalism.

One of Toffe's most challenging clients is the Centre Culturel Français d'Alger, a government body dedicated to 'the renewal of a dialogue between the two banks of the Mediterranean'. The CCF is committed to 'contemporary thought and creation, artistic gestures, risk-taking and discovering ideas'.

Toffe produces books, documents, journals and graphic materials of all kinds for the Centre. He uses a stylistic voice that incorporates Arabic ornamentation, computer default settings, traditional French typography and personal expression, in a lively graphic soup that is neither European nor Arabic, but rather a sophisticated and modern statement about cross-cultural communication.

2004

28.04.2005 * 18:00
POTESTAD

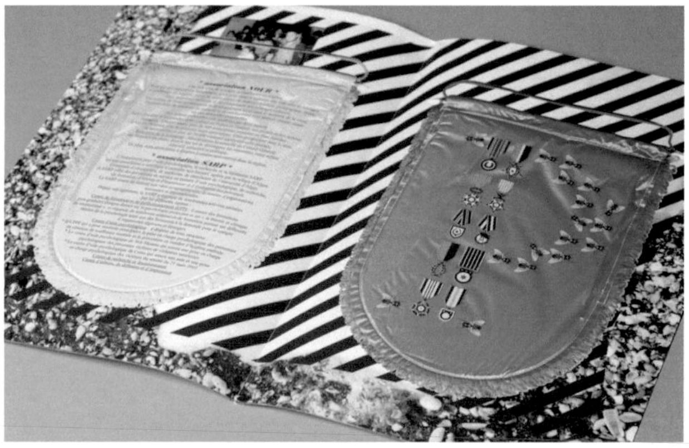

du 14 au 23 septembre 2004
pour
jean sénac

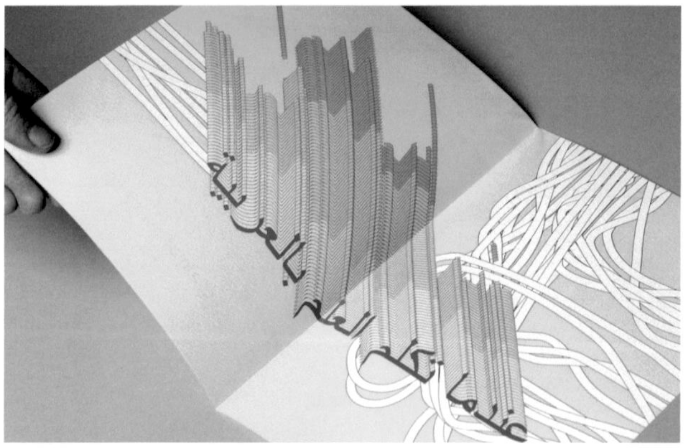

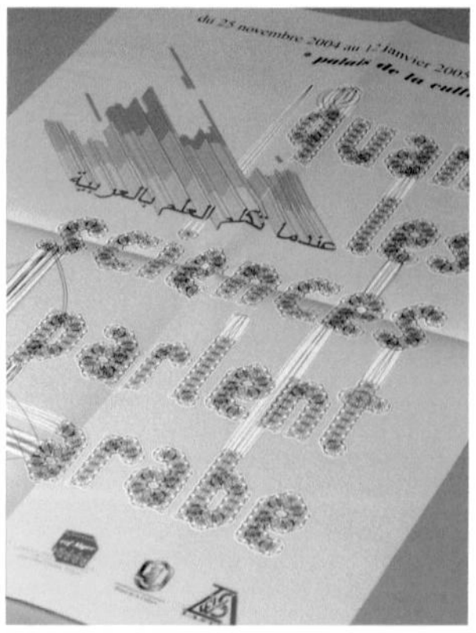

26 avril au 9 mai 2004
Louis Winsberg

ccf Alger
centre culturel français d'Alger
affiche
programme
THÉÂTRE
NATIONAL
ALGÉRIEN
* 28.04.2005 * 18:00 *
EDUARDO PAVLOVSKY
INTERPRÉTÉ PAR JEAN-LOUIS BÉRARD
POTESTAD
MISE EN SCÈNE JEAN-LOUIS TRINTIGNANT
LA MORT DE
MARGUERITE
DURAS
MISE EN SCÈNE SOPHIE PINCEMAILLE

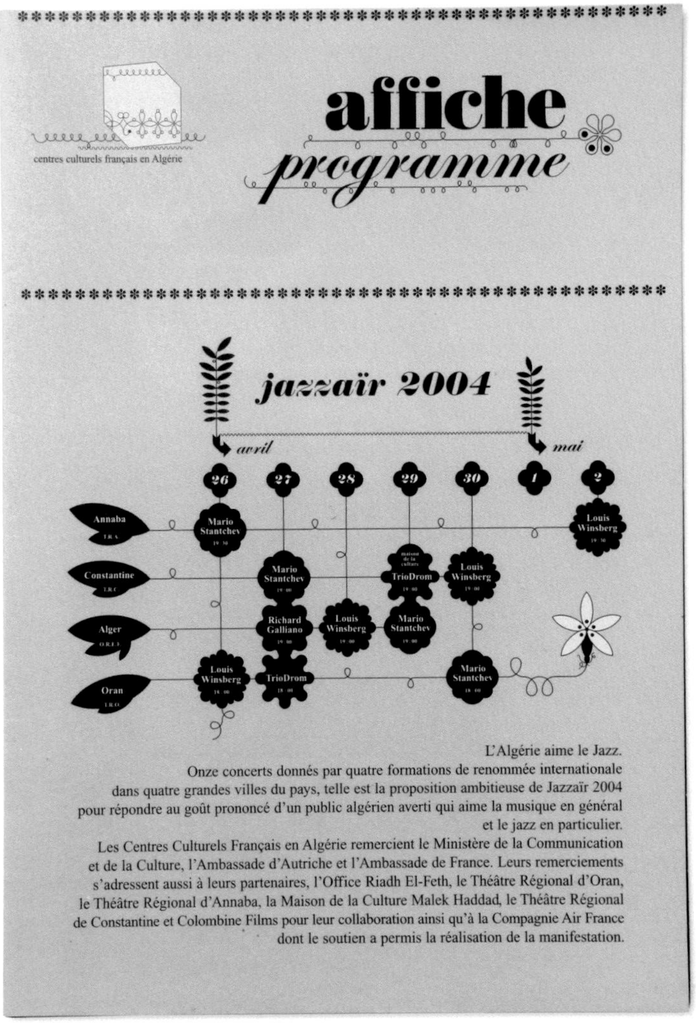
centres culturels français en Algérie
affiche
programme
jazzaïr 2004
avril
mai
26
27
28
29
30
1
2
Annaba
Constantine
Alger
Oran
Mario Stantchev
Louis Winsberg
Richard Galliano
TrioDrom
L'Algérie aime le Jazz.
Onze concerts donnés par quatre formations de renommée internationale
dans quatre grandes villes du pays, telle est la proposition ambitieuse de Jazzaïr 2004
pour répondre au goût prononcé d'un public algérien averti qui aime la musique en général
et le jazz en particulier.
Les Centres Culturels Français en Algérie remercient le Ministère de la Communication
et de la Culture, l'Ambassade d'Autriche et l'Ambassade de France. Leurs remerciements
s'adressent aussi à leurs partenaires, l'Office Riadh El-Feth, le Théâtre Régional d'Oran,
le Théâtre Régional d'Annaba, la Maison de la Culture Malek Haddad, le Théâtre Régional
de Constantine et Colombine Films pour leur collaboration ainsi qu'à la Compagnie Air France
dont le soutien a permis la réalisation de la manifestation.

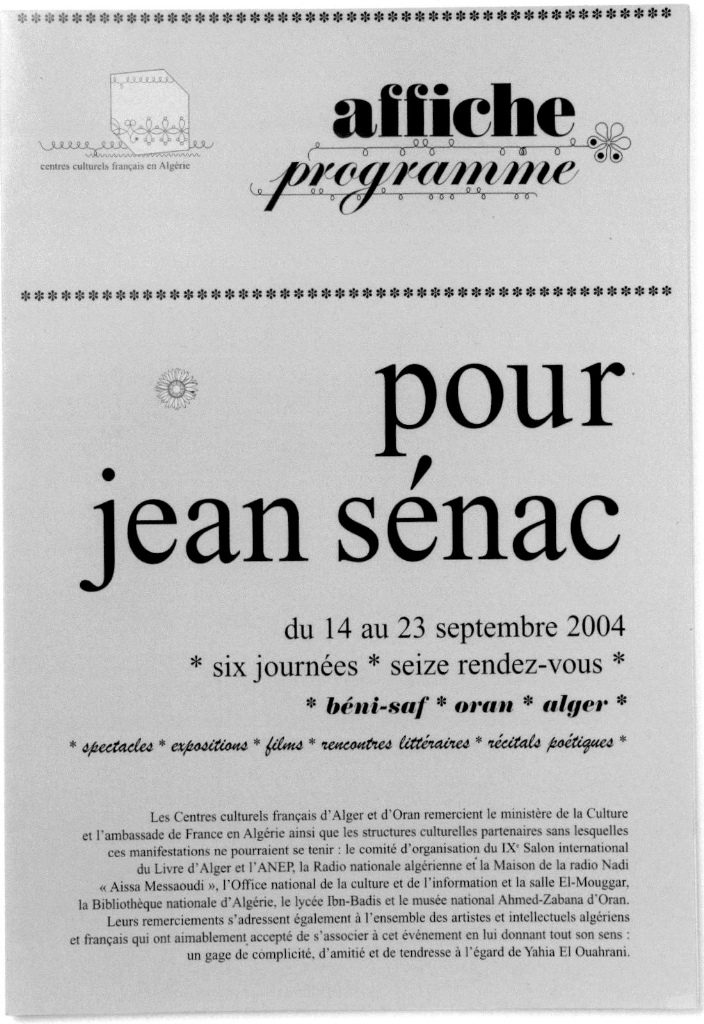
centres culturels français en Algérie
affiche
programme
pour
jean sénac
du 14 au 23 septembre 2004
* six journées * seize rendez-vous *
* béni-saf * oran * alger *
* spectacles * expositions * films * rencontres littéraires * récitals poétiques *
Les Centres culturels français d'Alger et d'Oran remercient le ministère de la Culture
et l'ambassade de France en Algérie ainsi que les structures culturelles partenaires sans lesquelles
ces manifestations ne pourraient se tenir : le comité d'organisation du IXe Salon international
du Livre d'Alger et l'ANEP, la Radio nationale algérienne et la Maison de la radio Nadi
« Aissa Messaoudi », l'Office national de la culture et de l'information et la salle El-Mouggar,
la Bibliothèque nationale d'Algérie, le lycée Ibn-Badis et le musée national Ahmed-Zabana d'Oran.
Leurs remerciements s'adressent également à l'ensemble des artistes et intellectuels algériens
et français qui ont aimablement accepté de s'associer à cet événement en lui donnant tout son sens :
un gage de complicité, d'amitié et de tendresse à l'égard de Yahia El Ouahrani.

ccf Alger
centre culturel français d'Alger
affiche
programme
quand
les
sciences
parlent
arabe
* du 25 novembre 2004 *
* au 12 janvier 2005 * 13:00 - 17:00 *
* palais de la culture * alger *
كان هناك زمن كان العلماء يجوبون فيه العالم، من بغداد إلى سمرقند، من غرناطة إلى القاهرة، من
دمشق إلى الهند. وكانت لغتهم المشتركة هي العربية.
وكان هؤلاء علماء فلك وعلماء رياضيات واطباء وفلاسفة... وقد اتخذ العلم بعداً عالمياً. وصارت
العربية لغة عدة شعوب وعدة ثقافات ومعارف.

Contem
Broc
Cat
Doc

Title:
Strategic Rail Authority Annual Report 2003–2004

Origin:
UK

Client:
Strategic Rail Authority

Studio:
Spin

Dimensions:
320mm x 230mm
12.6" x 9"

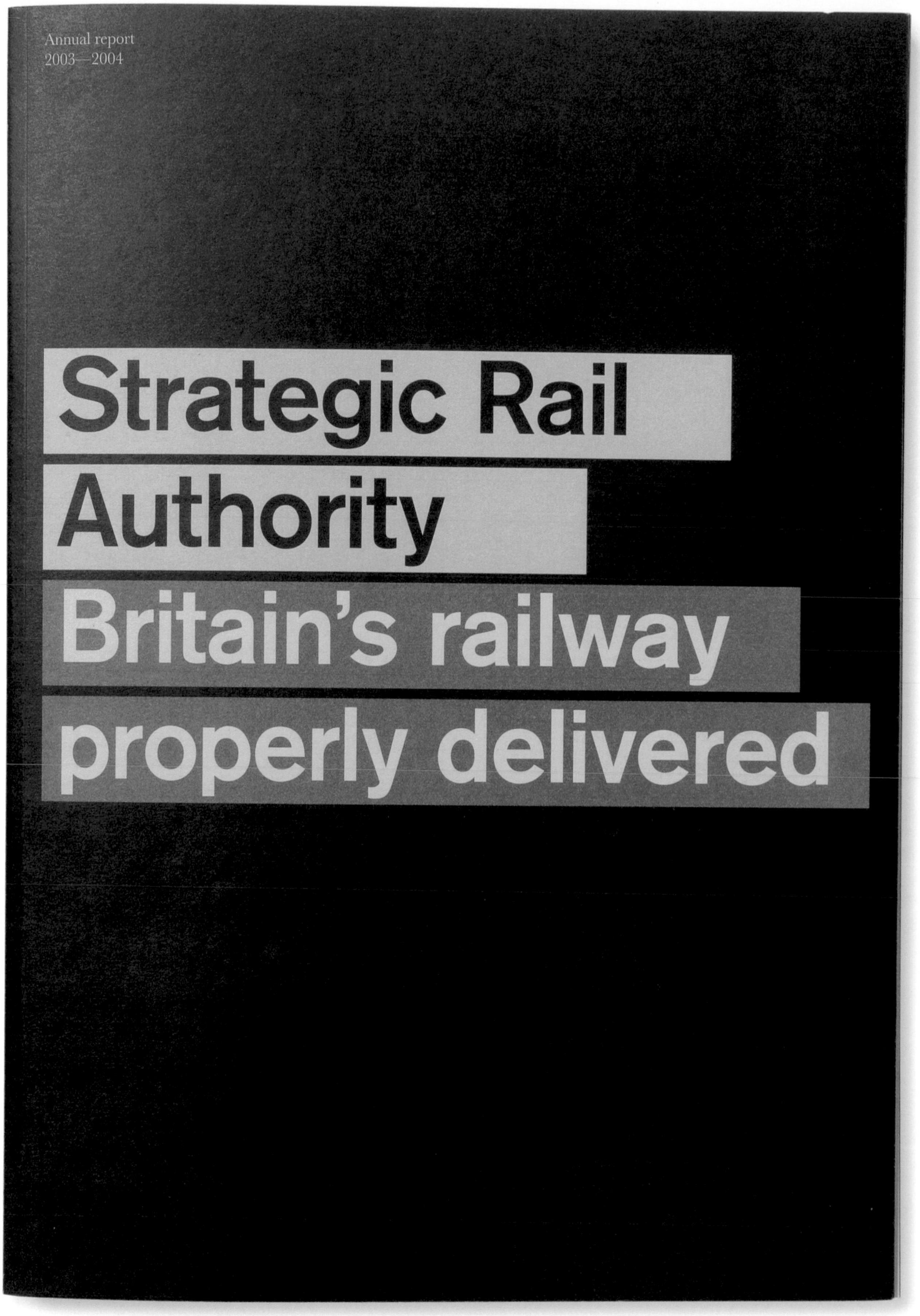
Annual report
2003—2004
Strategic Rail
Authority
Britain's railway
properly delivered

–
–
–

–
–
–
–
–
–
–
–
–

Contents

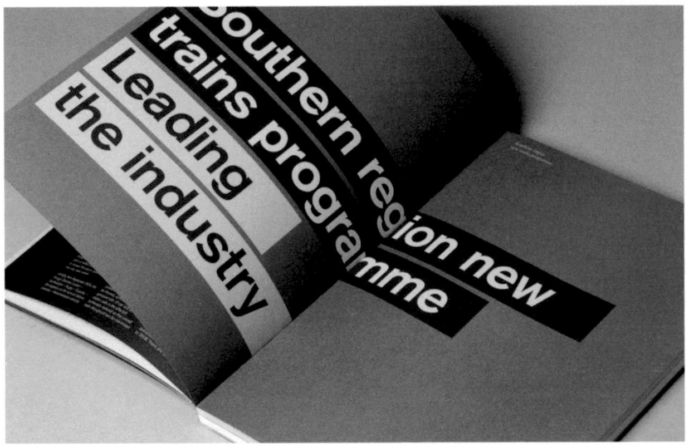
Southern region new
trains programme
Leading
the industry

Strategic Rail Authority
76—77
MAERSK

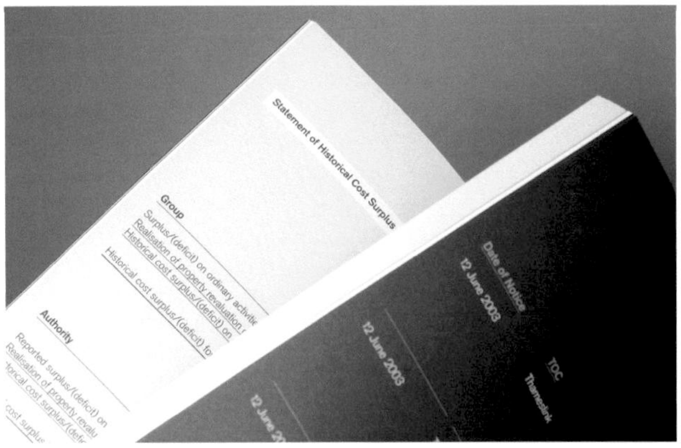
Statement of Historical Cost Surplus
Group
Authority
Date of Notice
12 June 2003
12 June 2003
TOC
Thameslink

Description:
London design group Spin is best known for its cool, measured, neo-Modernist graphic style. It works with many of the leading media and arts organizations, including Channel 4, Five, The Photographers' Gallery, D&AD and a host of other forward-thinking bodies.

–

At a time when annual reports have largely descended into super-bland functionality (they once provided a glorious opportunity for a corporation to display its personality), it is intriguing to study Spin's take on this important category of graphic design.

–

Spin's creative director, Tony Brook, describes the group's approach: 'We were briefed to give the document a serious and practical feel. It wasn't required to be glossy or flashy in any way. It was going to end up on the Prime Minister's desk and needed to be strong and impactful with a serious dose of *gravitas*. In short, it had to look like it meant business.'

–

Brook and his team applied their updated Swiss Modernism to create a document that is a model of well-crafted graphic communication. Three specials and two paper stocks were used. But did Brook find the constraints of designing an annual report to be limiting? 'Playing around with tables, charts and dense text can be taxing, engaging and enjoyable in equal measure', he notes. 'Check out the way Wolfgang Weingart handles information. Annual reports can be good design, and every client has limitations; you have to be able to turn them into inspiration.'

–
–
–

Conte
Broc
Cat
Doc

Title:
Adolf Hitler: Reden zur Kunst- und Kulturpolitik, 1933–1939

Origin:
Germany

Client:
Revolver

Studio:
Markus Weisbeck/surface

Dimensions:
175mm x 102mm
6.9" x 4"

Adolf Hitler
Reden zur Kunst- und Kulturpolitik
1933–1939
herausgegeben und kommentiert von Robert Eikmeyer
mit einer Einführung von Boris Groys

–
–
–
–
–
–
–
–
–

Adolf Hitler
Reden zur Kunst-
1933–1939

Description:
Revolver Books in Frankfurt, a small independent art book publisher, commissioned Markus Weisbeck/surface to create a design for one of the titles in a series of 'Art Propaganda Documents'. The series features original texts, speeches, programmes and manifestoes crucial to cultural politics in the context of twentieth-century totalitarian movements; these are documents that either haven't been published before or which are no longer available.
They are important sources for research into the subject of totalitarianism as a 'transgressive cultural phenomenon'.
–
Each volume in the series contains an introductory essay by an important contemporary author and is edited with a critical commentary. Weisbeck's design reinforces the notion of a recovered or reclaimed document. 'I was walking through a flea market', he explains. 'It was late at night, and I found a very damaged book lying on the ground. It gave me the idea of a book which is not finished. No cover. More like a bad photocopy from a copy shop with old equipment.'
–
–
–
–
–
–

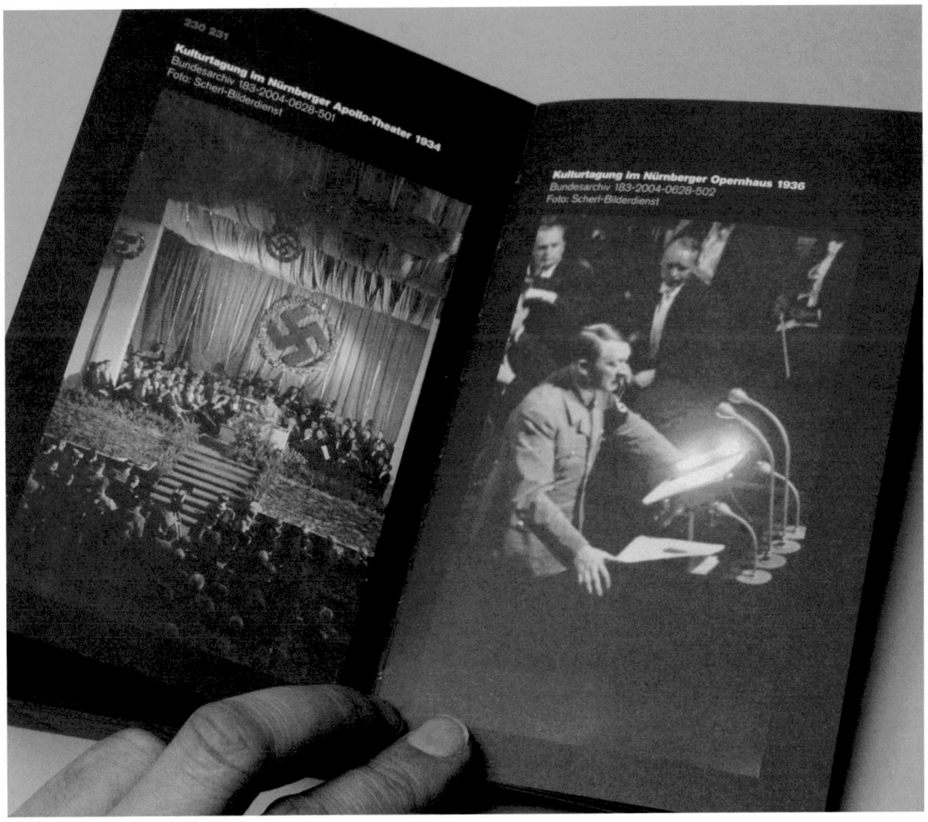
230 231
Kulturtagung im Nürnberger Apollo-Theater 1934
Bundesarchiv 183-2004-0628-501
Foto: Scherl-Bilderdienst
Kulturtagung im Nürnberger Opernhaus 1936
Bundesarchiv 183-2004-0628-502
Foto: Scherl-Bilderdienst

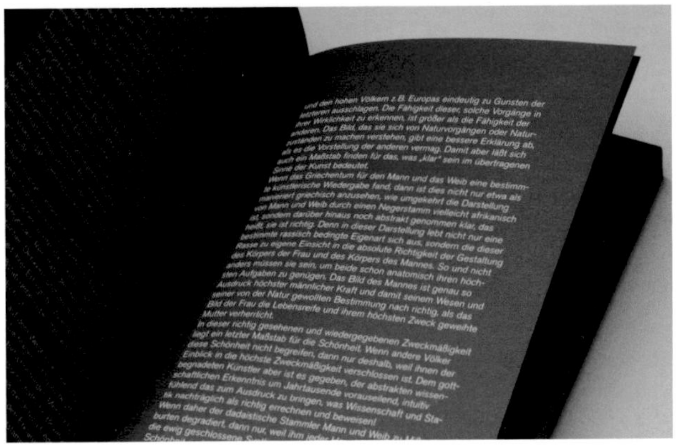

Contem
Broc
Cat
Doc

Title:
The Point
Issue no. 3, spring 2004

Origin:
Canada

Client:
Society of Graphic
Designers of Canada
British Columbia Chapter
(SGDC/BC)

Designer:
Marian Bantjes

Dimensions:
254mm x 203mm
10" x 8"

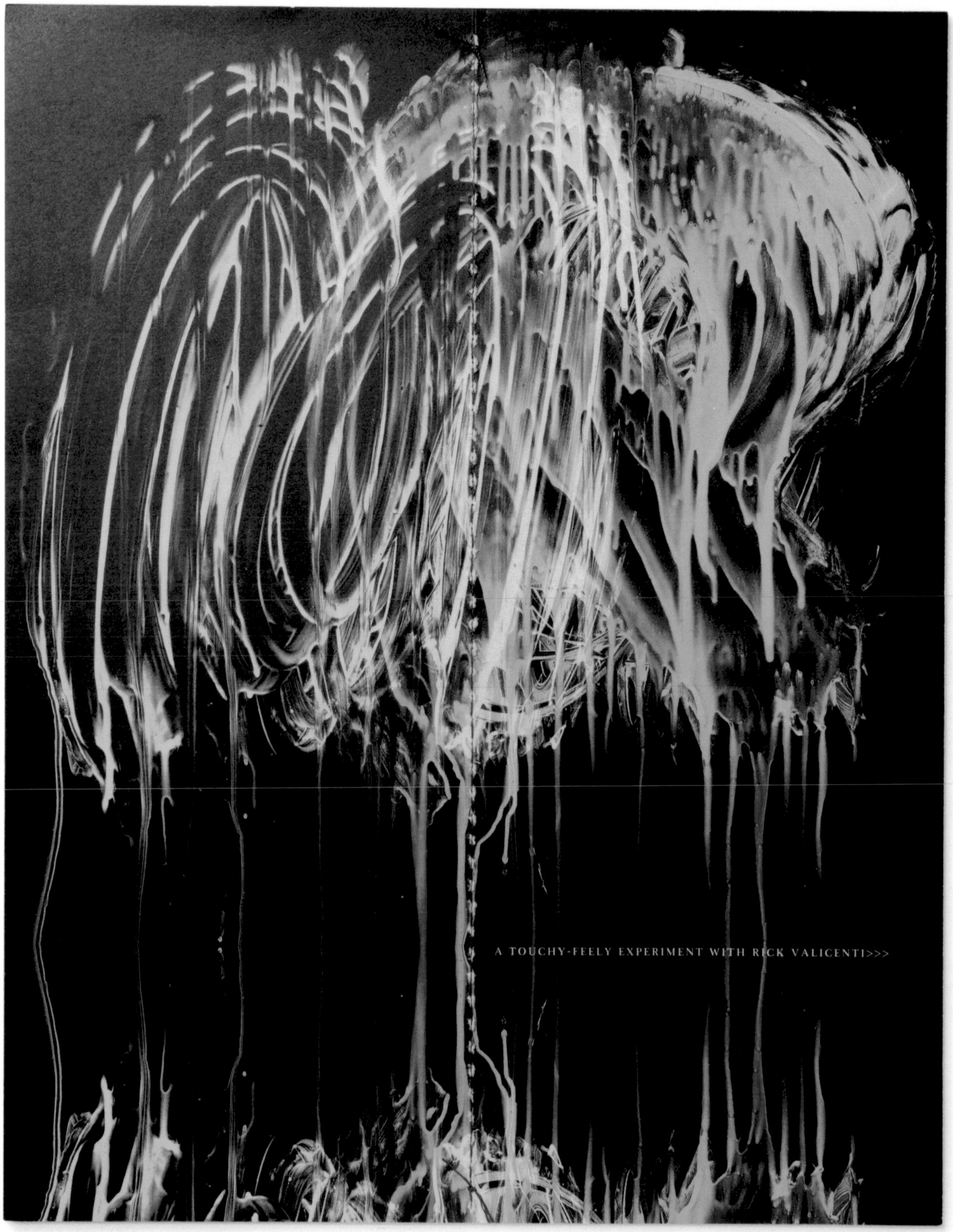
A TOUCHY-FEELY EXPERIMENT WITH RICK VALICENTI>>>

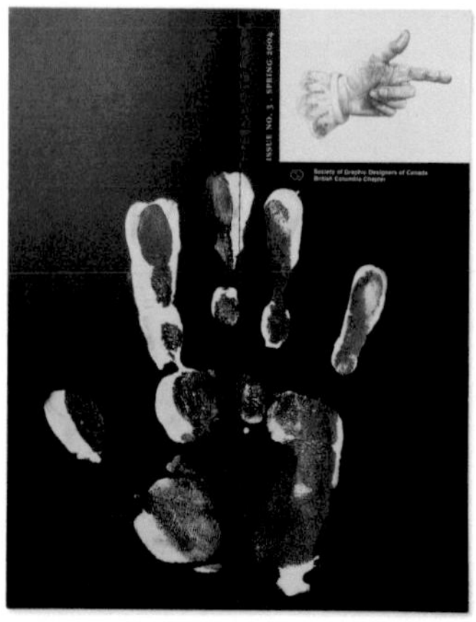

–
–
–
–
–
–
–
–
–

Description:
Marian Bantjes epitomizes the new breed of enterprising, multi-tasking graphic designer. She writes, edits and designs *The Point*, an unpaid 'labour of love' that demands a large amount of her time and energy. 'As the Communications Vice-President on the Board of the SGDC/BC, it is theoretically my responsibility to produce a newsletter', she explains. 'The society gives me *carte blanche* with a heavy dose of trust, and it was my crazy-ass decision to take a Helvetica-template newsletter and turn it into a graphic artefact, quadrupling my investment in time, care and reward.'

–

Bantjes' quirky document contains an extraordinary 'calligraphic' interview with US designer Rick Valicenti. 'The concept behind Issue 3 was "hand work"', she notes. 'I also wanted to provide a venue for some of the SGDC/BC's sponsors, so I ran an article on an illustration rep, and a feature on a company that does stitching and hand-binding. We have a large Chinese community in Vancouver, so I was able to include a Chinese calligrapher; and the final touch was getting Rick Valicenti to do a little hands-on graphic conversation.'

–

With its centrally stitched spine, Bantjes' publication hardly looks like a typical newsletter. 'Deciding to stitch down the centre was a way to stay inside my 8" x 10" [255mm x 203mm] format,' she says, 'while at the same time flexing it.'

–
–
–
–
–
–

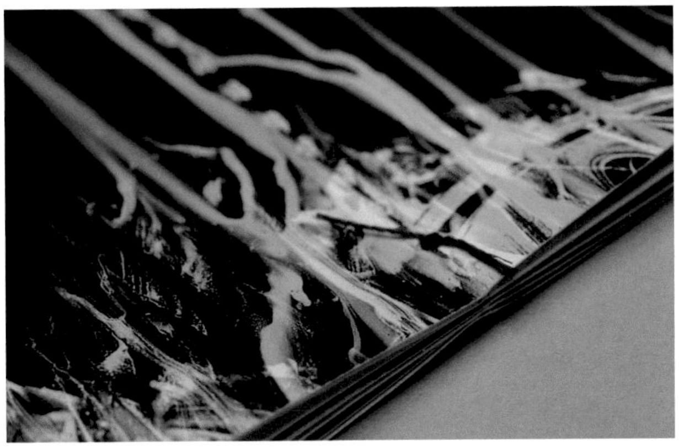

THANKS, RICK

–
–
–
Contem
Broc
Cat
Doc
–
–
–
–
–
–
–
–
–

Title:
Wood on Wood
–
Origin:
Sweden
–
Client:
Arctic Paper
–
Studio:
Happy F&B
–
Dimensions:
273mm x 226mm
10.7" x 8.9"
–
–
–
–
–
–

Description:
Graphic designers relish the challenge of designing for other designers. Here, at least, is an opportunity to be subtle, expansive, even mysterious, although we also know that we have to be at our best, as our fellow designers will look at our work with added critical scrutiny.

–

Gothenburg-based Happy F&B, through their work with Arctic Papers, have amassed an impressive portfolio of promotional paper catalogues. Their *Wood on Wood* brochure is a remarkable design statement. 'We wanted to show the connection between wood and paper,' explains designer Lisa Careborg, 'as well as the tactile properties of uncoated paper and what the surface can do for printed images. To do this we used numerous types of wood.'

–

The discreet use of pencil lettering adds a strong whiff of the carpentry workshop. Was this intentional? 'Yes. Working on the book, we visited carpentry shops and timber yards, and found that to mark out the wood they all used pencil lettering. We photographed timber workers' handwriting and imitated the style to make it look as authentic and natural as possible.'

Munken
BY ARCTIC PAPER

16

–
–
–
Conte
Broc
Cat
Doc
–
–
–
–
–
–
–
–
–
Title:
V-Series
–
Origin:
UK
–
Client:
Nike
–
Studio:
Spin
–
Dimensions:
250mm x 344mm
9.8" x 13.5"
and
280mm x 390mm
11" x 15.3"
–
–
–
–
–
–

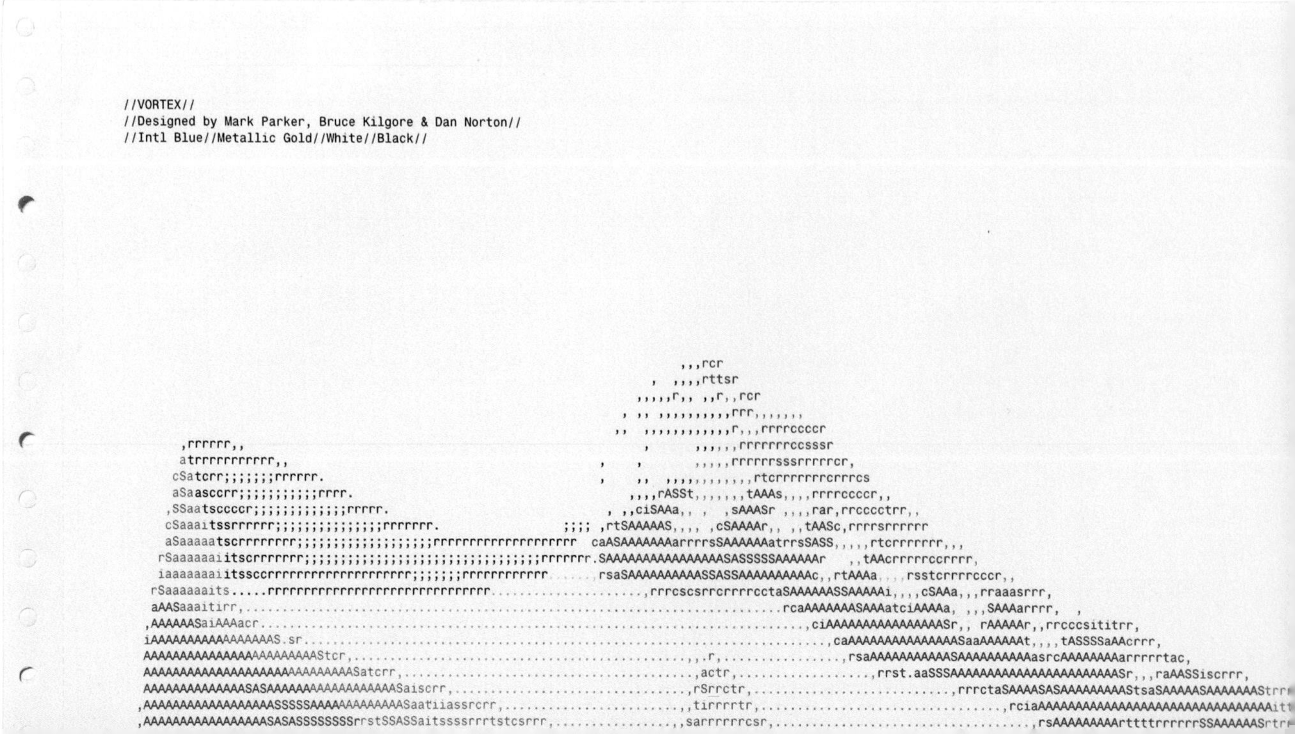
//VORTEX//
//Designed by Mark Parker, Bruce Kilgore & Dan Norton//
//Intl Blue//Metallic Gold//White//Black//

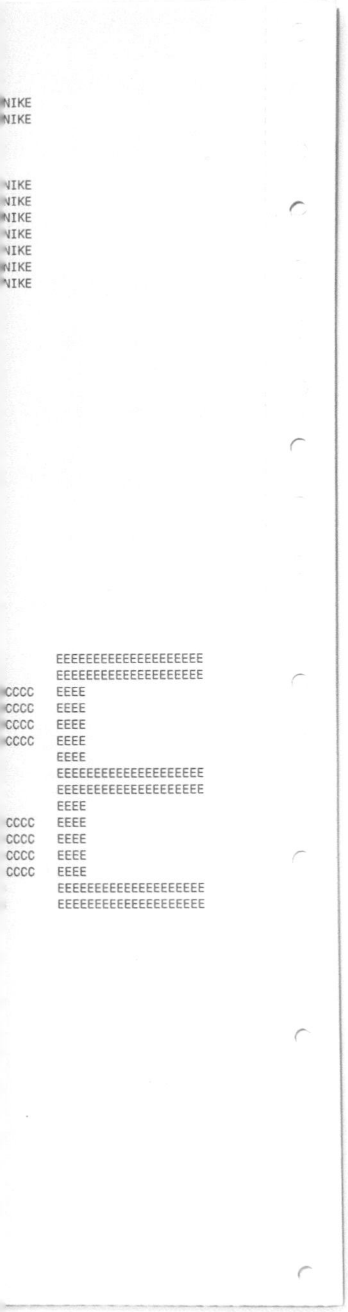
NIKE
NIKE
NIKE
NIKE
NIKE
NIKE
NIKE
NIKE
NIKE
EEEEEEEEEEEEEEEEEEEE
EEEEEEEEEEEEEEEEEEEE
CCCC EEEE
CCCC EEEE
CCCC EEEE
CCCC EEEE
EEEE
EEEEEEEEEEEEEEEEEEEE
EEEEEEEEEEEEEEEEEEEE
EEEE
CCCC EEEE
CCCC EEEE
CCCC EEEE
CCCC EEEE
EEEEEEEEEEEEEEEEEEEE
EEEEEEEEEEEEEEEEEEEE

SERIES
VECTOR
VENGEANCE
VORTEX

rrrcscsrrc
,actr,
rSrrctr,
tirrrrtr,
sarrrrrrcsr,
rsiirrrrrrrrrctr
ttccrrrrrrrrrrcrir

```
NIKE            NIKE                                 NIKENIKENIKE       NIKENIKENIKENIKENIKE   NIKENIKENIKENIKE           NIKENIKENIKE       NIKENIKEN
NIKE            NIKE                                 NIKENIKENIKE       NIKENIKENIKENIKENIKE   NIKENIKENIKENIKE           NIKENIKENIKE       NIKENIKEN
NIKE            NIKE                             NIKE            NIKE   NIKE                   NIKE            NIKE           NIKE           NIKE
NIKE            NIKE                             NIKE            NIKE   NIKE                   NIKE            NIKE           NIKE           NIKE
NIKE            NIKE                             NIKE                   NIKE                   NIKE            NIKE           NIKE           NIKE
NIKE            NIKE                             NIKE                   NIKE                   NIKE            NIKE           NIKE           NIKE
NIKE            NIKE                             NIKE                   NIKE                   NIKE            NIKE           NIKE           NIKE
NIKE            NIKE   NIKENIKENIKENIKENIKE      NIKENIKENIKENIKENIKE   NIKENIKENIKENIKENIKE   NIKENIKENIKENIKE               NIKE           NIKENIKEN
NIKE            NIKE   NIKENIKENIKENIKENIKE      NIKENIKENIKENIKENIKE   NIKENIKENIKENIKENIKE   NIKENIKENIKENIKE               NIKE           NIKENIKEN
NIKE            NIKE                                             NIKE   NIKE                   NIKE            NIKE           NIKE           NIKE
NIKE            NIKE                                             NIKE   NIKE                   NIKE            NIKE           NIKE           NIKE
NIKE            NIKE                                             NIKE   NIKE                   NIKE            NIKE           NIKE           NIKE
    NIKE    NIKE                                 NIKE            NIKE   NIKE                   NIKE            NIKE           NIKE           NIKE
    NIKE    NIKE                                 NIKE            NIKE   NIKE                   NIKE            NIKE           NIKE           NIKE
        NIKE                                         NIKENIKENIKE       NIKENIKENIKENIKENIKE   NIKE            NIKE       NIKENIKENIKE       NIKENIKEN
        NIKE                                         NIKENIKENIKE       NIKENIKENIKENIKENIKE   NIKE            NIKE       NIKENIKENIKE       NIKENIKEN
>
////////////////////////////////////////////////////////////////////////////////////////////////////////////////////////////////////
////////////////////////////////////////////////////////////////////////////////////////////////////////////////////////////////////
>
>
>
>
>
>
>
****************************************************************************************************************************************
VECTOR / VENGEANCE / VORTEX / VECTOR / VENGEANCE / VORTEX / VECTOR / VENGEANCE / VORTEX / VECTOR / VENGEANCE / VORTEX / VECTOR / VENGEANCE / VO
****************************************************************************************************************************************
>
>
The                     right                     shoe                     for                     the                     right                     athlete
========================================================================================================================================
//
//
//
//
//
//
//
//
//
//
1986 marked a milestone in the history of running that today we take for granted.
Runners had begun asking for shoes that addressed more specific needs and Nike
//                      responded with the V-Series, three shoes for three different
//                      types of runner.
° °° ° °° ° °° ° °° ° °° ° °° ° °° ° °° ° °° ° °° ° °° ° °° ° °° ° °° ° °° ° °° ° °° ° °° ° °° ° °° ° °° ° °°
-_-_-_-_-_-_-_-_-_-_-_-_-_-_-_-_-_-_-_-_-_-_-_-_-_-_-_-_-_-_-_-_-_-_-_-_-_-_-_-_-_-_-_-_-_-_-_-_-_-_-_-_-_-_
° °° ° °° ° °° ° °° ° °° ° °° ° °° ° °° ° °° ° °° ° °° ° °° ° °° ° °° ° °° ° °° ° °° ° °° ° °° ° °° ° °° ° °°
-_-_-_-_-_-_-_-_-_-_-_-_-_-_-_-_-_-_-_-_-_-_-_-_-_-_-_-_-_-_-_-_-_-_-_-_-_-_-_-_-_-_-_-_-_-_-_-_-_-_-_-_-_-_
° °° ° °° ° °° ° °° ° °° ° °° ° °° ° °° ° °° ° °° ° °° ° °° ° °° ° °° ° °° ° °° ° °° ° °° ° °° ° °° ° °° ° °°
-_-_-_-_-_-_-_-_-_-_-_-_-_-_-_-_-_-_-_-_-_-_-_-_-_-_-_-_-_-_-_-_-_-_-_-_-_-_-_-_-_-_-_-_-_-_-_-_-_-_-_-_-_-_
///////////////////////////////////////////////////////////////////////////////////////////////////////////////
                                                                                        The Vortex for normal runners,
                                                                                        the Vengeance for competitive runners
                                                                                        and the Vector for over-pronating runners.
////////////////////////////////////////////////////////////////////////////////////////////////////////////////////////////////////
{error} >>>>>>>>>>>>>>>>>>>>>>>>                                                                      Each shoe came with an instructi
{error} >>>>>>>>>>>>>>>>>>>>>>>>                                                                      that not only explained the indiv
{error} >>>>>>>>>>>>>>>>>>>>>>>>                                                                      features, but gave advice on how
{error} >>>>>>>>>>>>>>>>>>>>>>>>
>
These shoes not only began the segmentation of the running market,
they set the standard for it that still applies today.
                        Nike pays tribute to these innovators by putting them back on the trail they blazed.
>
>
V-SERIES
//                      V-SERIES
//                      V-SERIES
//                      V-SERIES
//                      V-SERIES
V-SERIES
//                      V-SERIES
//                      V-SERIES
//                      V-SERIES
```

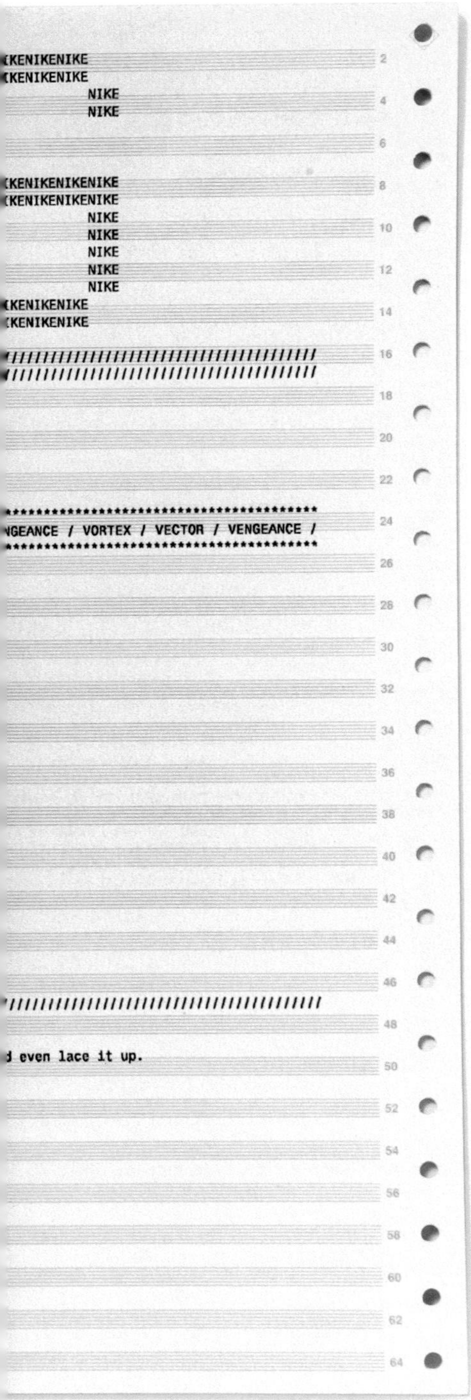
NIKE
NIKE
NIKE
NIKE
NIKE
NIKE
NIKE
VORTEX / VECTOR / VENGEANCE /

–
–
–
Contemporary
Brochures
Catalogues
Documents
–
–
–
–
–
–
–
–
–

Description:
The V-Series range was originally released by Nike in the 1980s as a 'technologically advanced running shoe'. Design group Spin, under the creative directorship of Tony Brook, was invited by the sportswear giant to make 'appropriate promotional materials to support its re-release'.
–
Rather than produce the traditional brochure, Spin produced a dynamic piece of communication that was placed in stores and retail outlets, to be picked up by the public. Brook describes their thinking: 'The folding continuous data paper and the ASCII art translations/illustrations of the shoes were used to reflect the technology of the era when the shoes were originally released.'
–
–
–
–
–
–

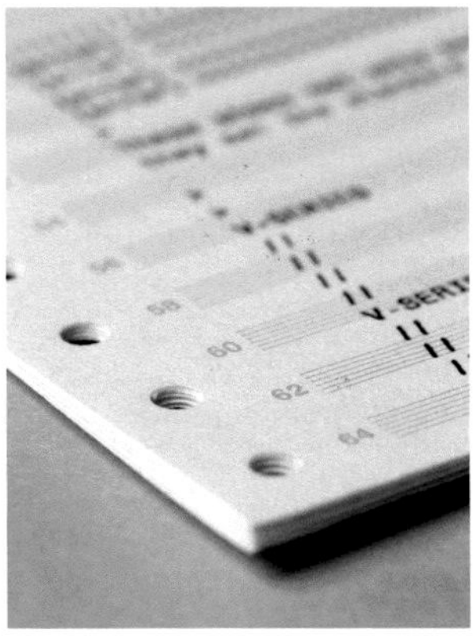

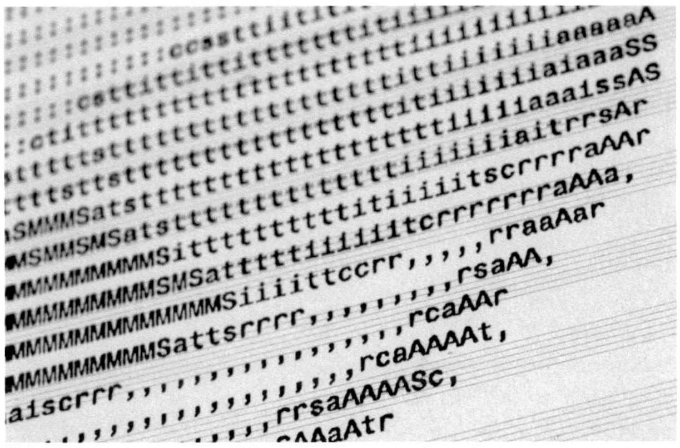

–
–
–
Contem
Broc
Cat
Doc
–
–
–
–
–
–
–
–
–

Title:
Ping-Pong: A Telling
–
Origin:
The Netherlands
–
Client:
Ping-Pong
–
Designer:
Lonne Wennekendonk
–
Dimensions:
214mm x 159mm
8.4" x 6.2"
–
–
–
–
–
–

TM
ping-pong a telling

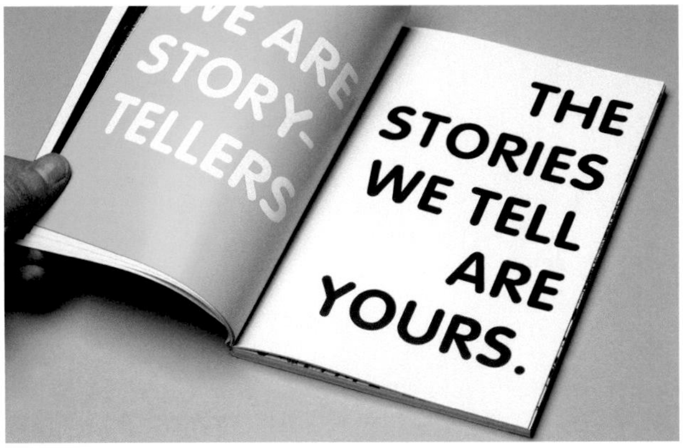
WE ARE
STORY-
TELLERS
THE
STORIES
WE TELL
ARE
YOURS.

–
–
–
–
–
–
–
–
–

Description:
Ping-Pong is a graphic design agency based in Rotterdam. It creates visual identities for corporate clients. The group invited writer Meghan Ferrill to write about its work and asked Rotterdam designer Lonne Wennekendonk to design a brochure to promote the agency to new clients. The document combined Ferrill's text and Ping-Pong's extensive portfolio of eye-catching work.
–
As Wennekendonk explains: ‘Meghan divided her text into three chapters. I wanted this to become visible in the design. That's why I made each chapter visually different, but also because Ping-Pong create different looks for different clients – they don't repeat themselves. The design brings the story to life, and the story brings the design to life. The subtitle, *Consider This*, refers to the book's contents – consider this book of ideas.’
–
–
–
–
–
–

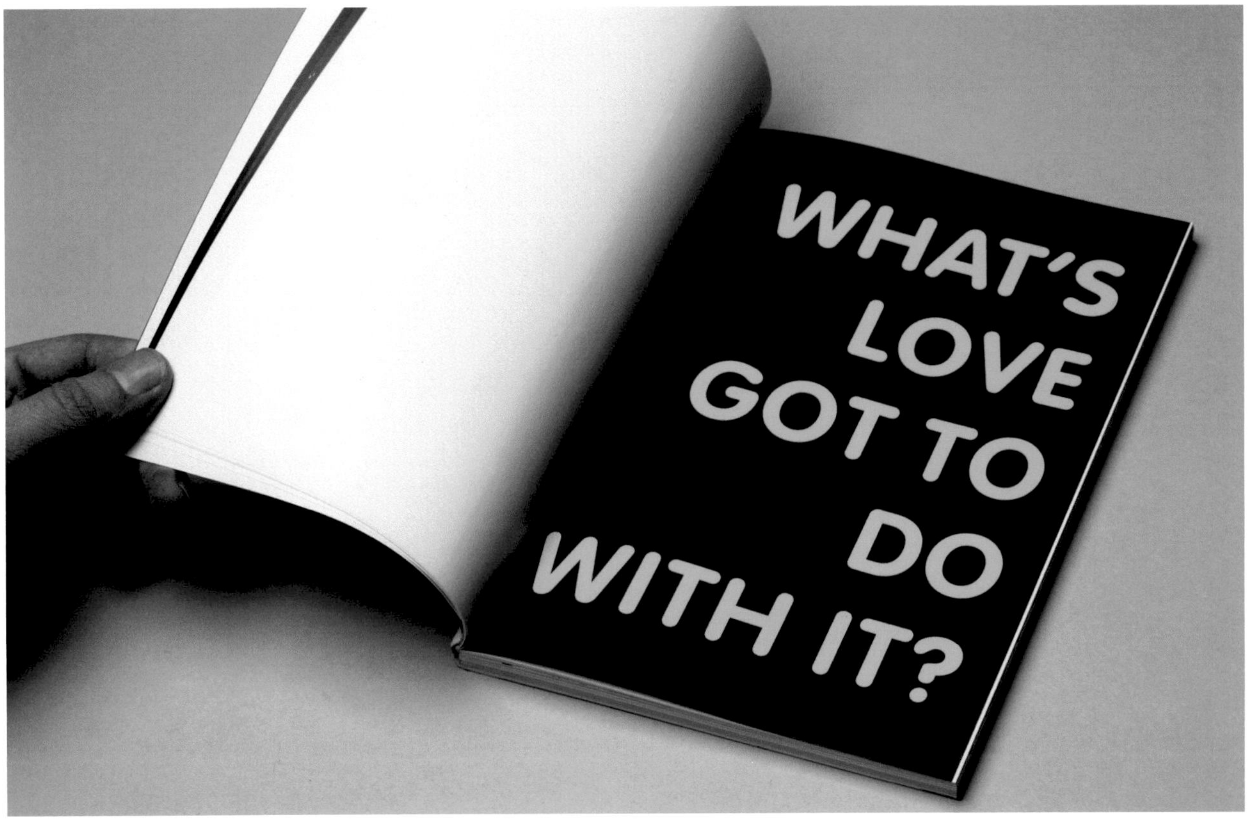
WHAT'S
LOVE
GOT TO
DO
WITH IT?

WE ARE
PROSPECTORS
WE DIG
FOR GOLD.
YOURS.

Contem
Broc
Cat
Doc

Title:
Anni Kuan

Origin:
USA

Client:
Anni Kuan

Studio:
Sagmeister Inc.

Dimensions:
407mm x 288mm
16" x 11.3"

Description:
Having as a client someone who is also your boyfriend or girlfriend does not always guarantee good work. But in the case of Stefan Sagmeister's project for his girlfriend, the fashion designer Anni Kuan, the results are brilliantly and joyously successful.

When Kuan briefed Sagmeister to design a promotional item for her fashion brand, she made only one stipulation: it mustn't cost more that the promo postcards she was currently mailing out. Displaying the ingenuity and chutzpah that have made him one of the most famous graphic designers in the world, Sagmeister created a 'newspaper' for the cost of a postcard. As he explains: 'The idea of doing all these newspaper items came completely out of her tiny budget. Before we took over her graphics, she sent out a four cent postcard to all her buyers. Someone mentioned this Korean newsprint place in New York. They print a 32-page paper for the price of a postcard.'

Sagmeister's newsprint aesthetic has become part of Anni Kuan's identity. He relishes the tight limitations: 'It has to be on newsprint, maximum two colours and then only red, orange and blue; it has to look good in a rough half-tone dot, and it should be different from previous mailings, since the mailing list stays roughly the same.'

The cellophane-bound documents have been rapturously received by people on Kuan's mailing list, the buyers she sells her clothes to, and graphic designers ('not on her mailing list but potential customers'), who have come to know her label by seeing Sagmeister's mailers in design award books.

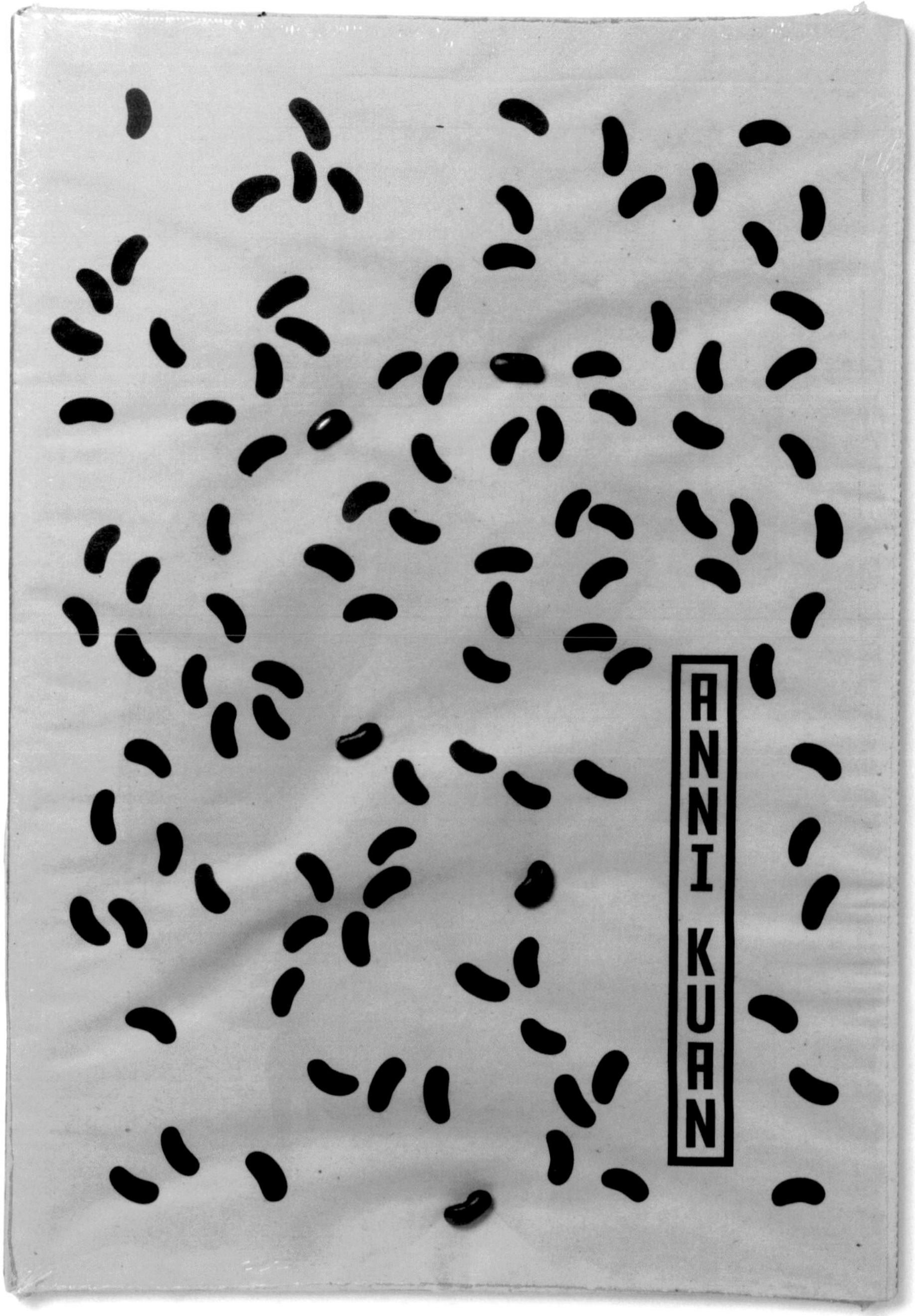
ANNI KUAN

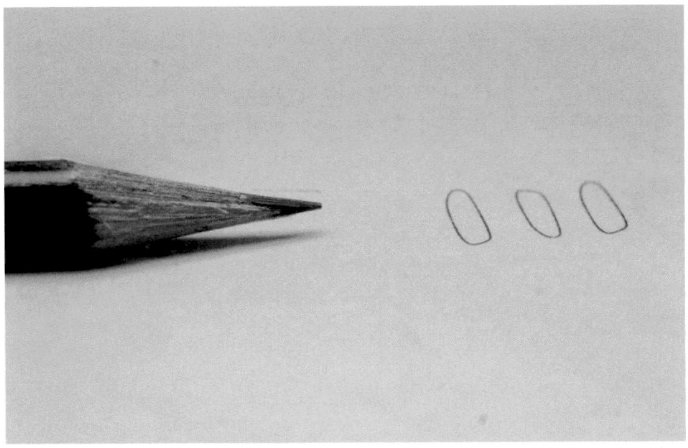

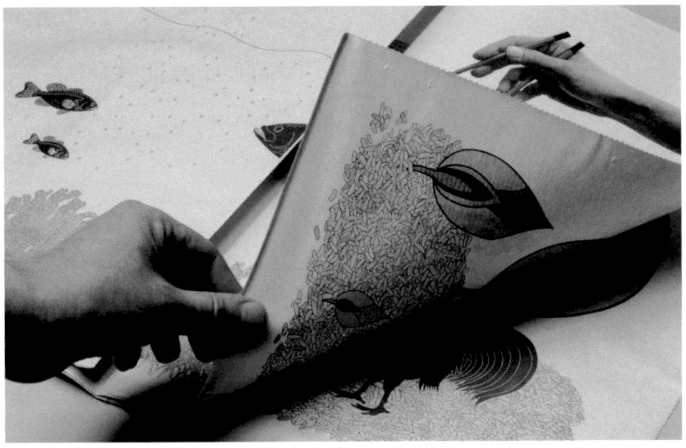

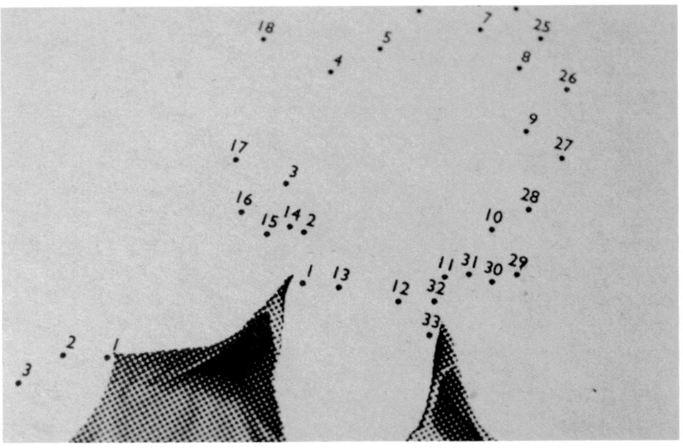

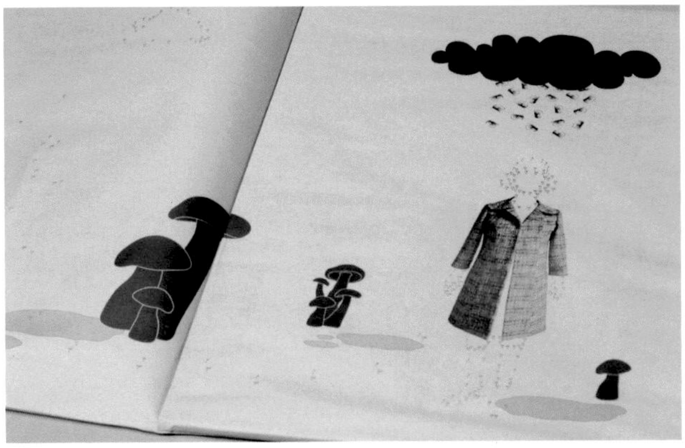

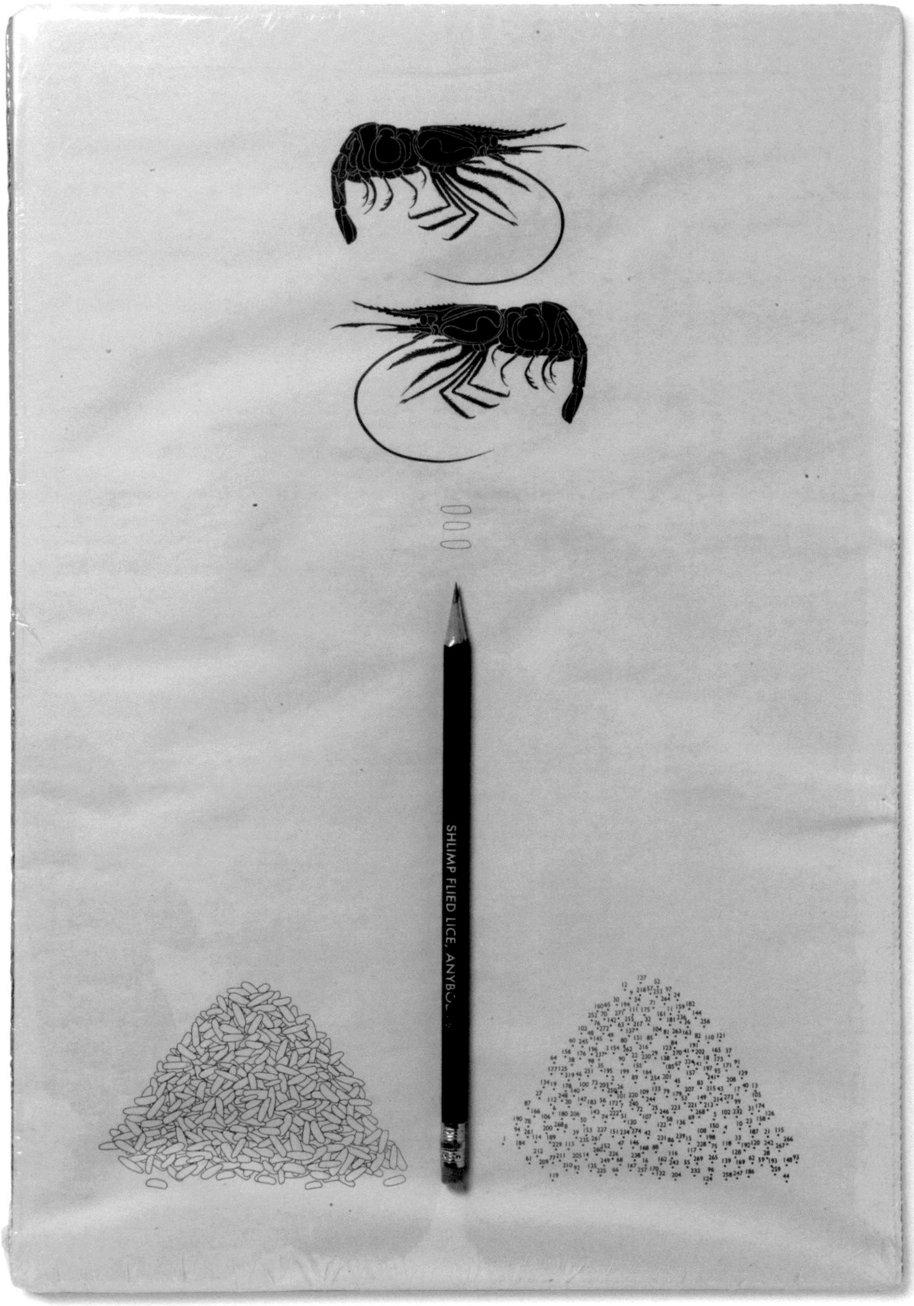
SHLIMP FLIED LICE, ANYB

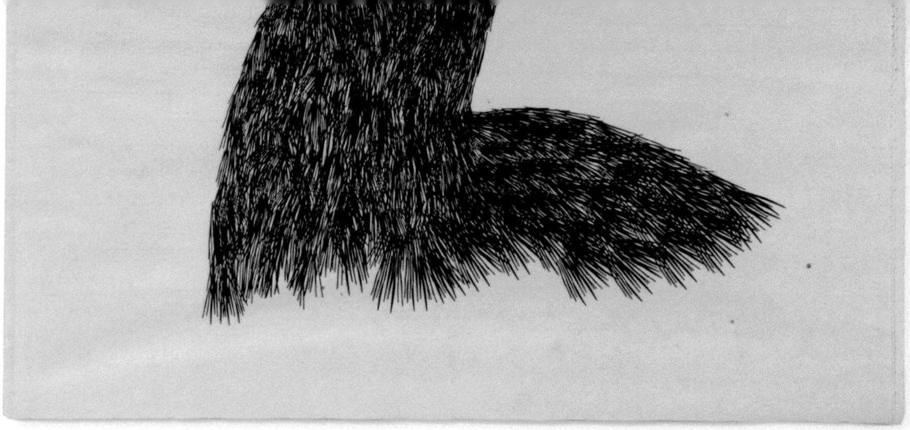

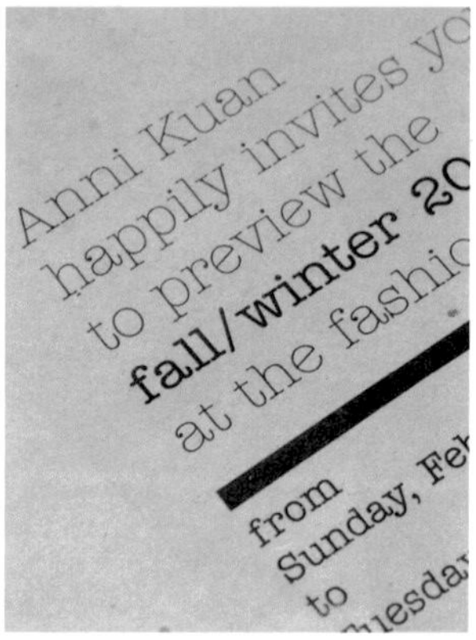
Anni Kuan
happily invites yo
to preview the
fall/winter 20
at the fashio
from
Sunday, Feb
to

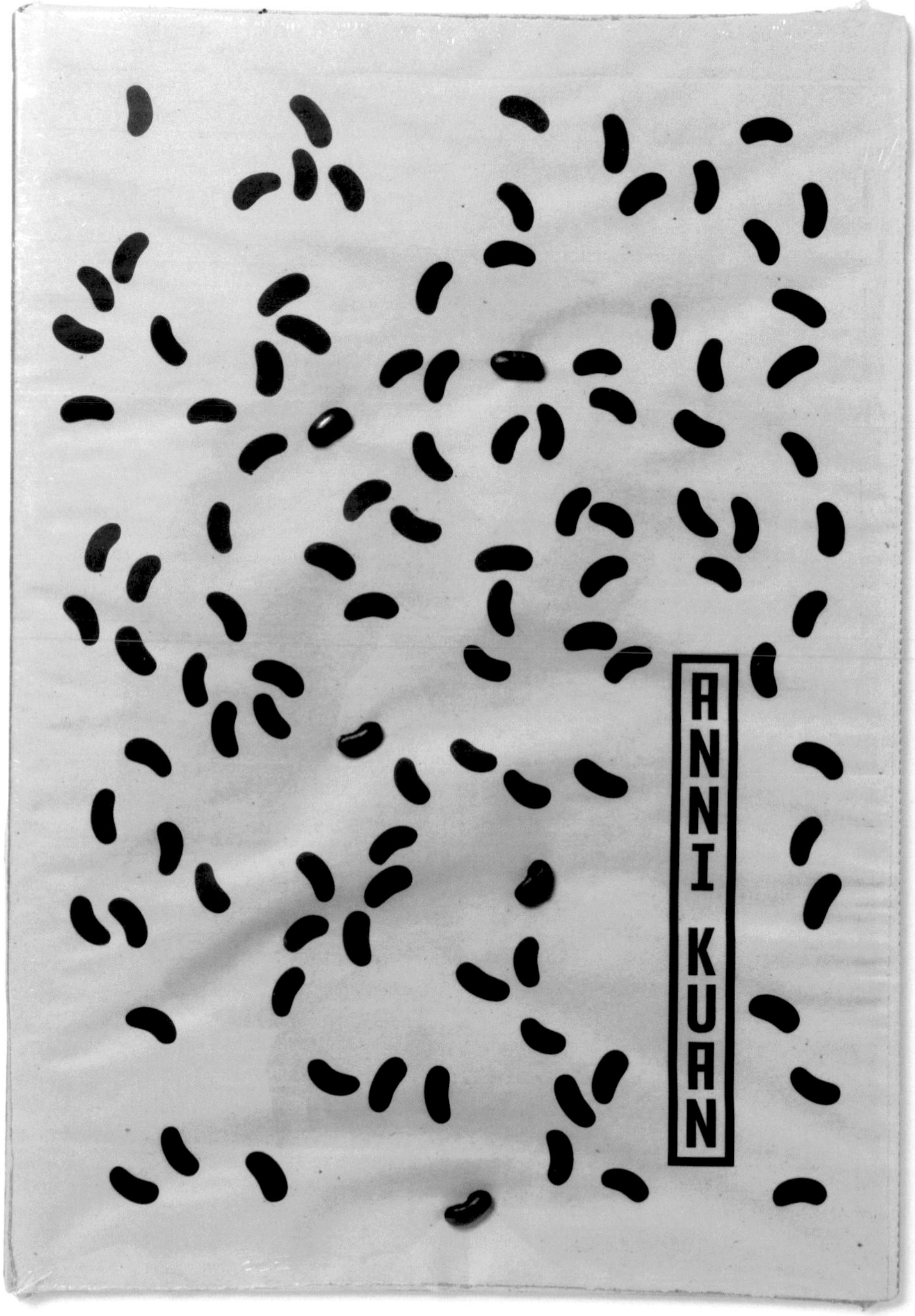
ANNI KUAN

mat
erial

MATERIAL LUXURIES ARE BEST ENJOYED IN SMALL DOSES

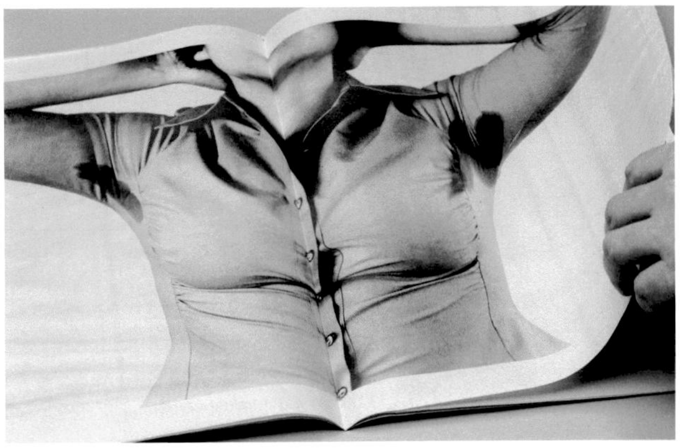

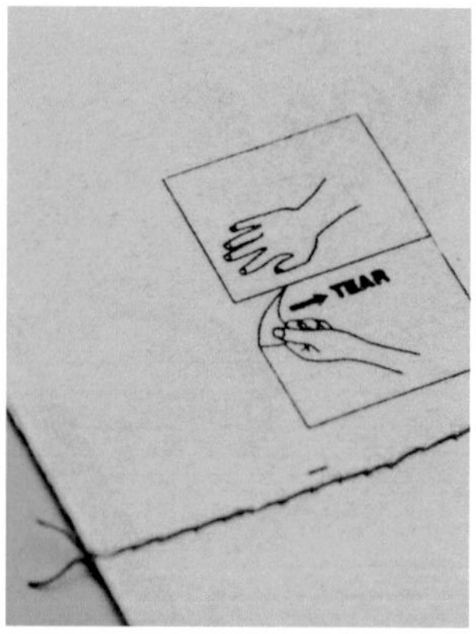
TEAR

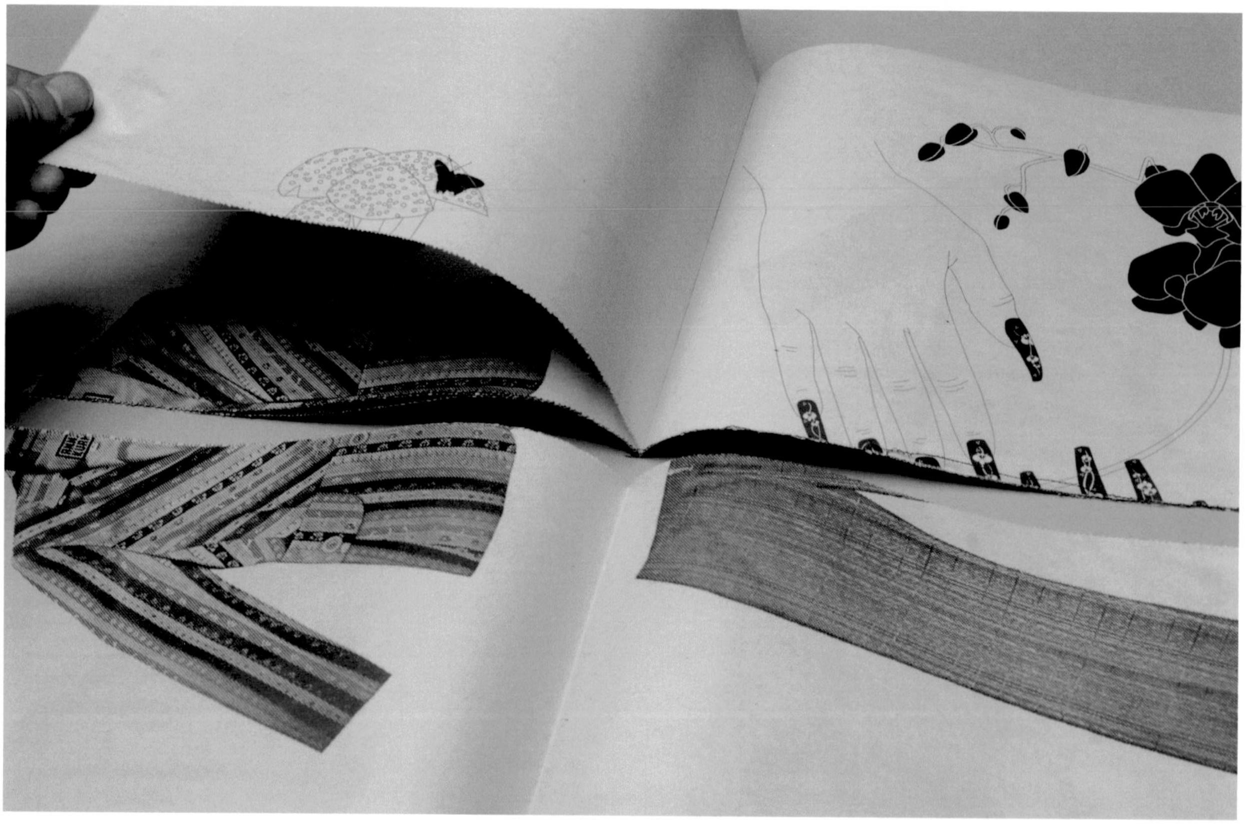

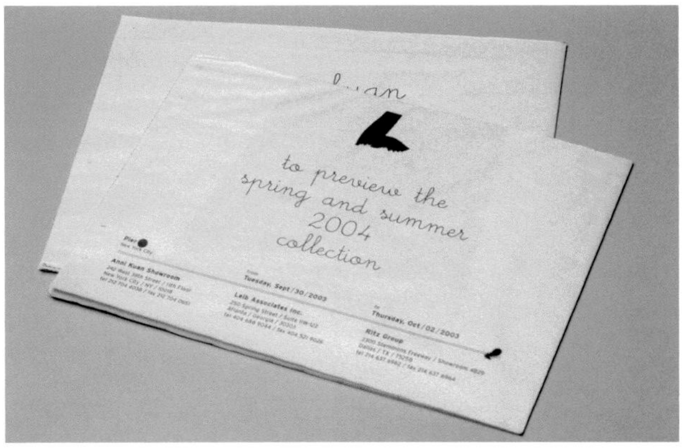
to preview the
spring and summer
2004
collection
Anni Kuan Showroom
Tuesday, Sept/30/2003
Leib Associates Inc.
Thursday, Oct/02/2003
Ritz Group

Contem
Broc
Cat
Doc

Title:
A Stolen Moment – Gregor Neuerer

Origin:
Germany

Client:
Gregor Neuerer

Studio:
Keller Maurer Design

Dimensions:
330mm x 240mm
13" x 9.4"

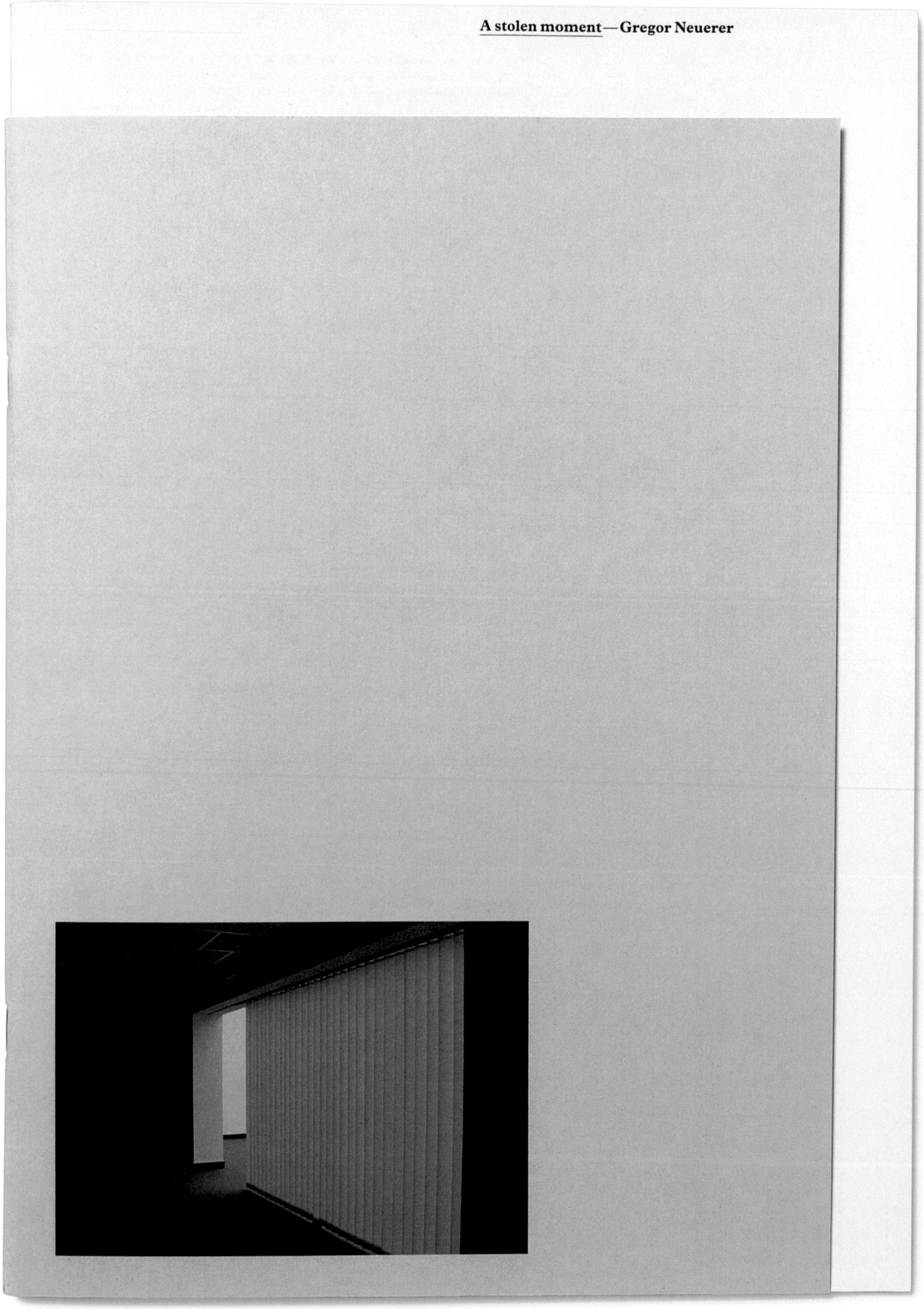
A stolen moment—Gregor Neuerer

–
–
–

Contemporary
Brochures
Catalogues
Documents

–
–
–
–
–
–
–
–
–

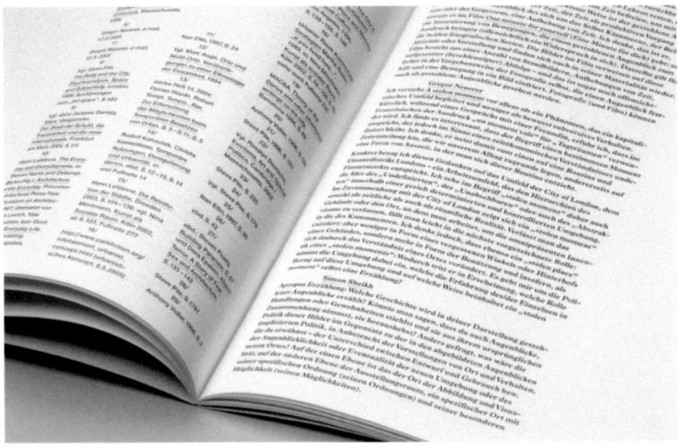

Gregor Neuerer

Description:
For the exhibition 'A Stolen Moment' in Innsbruck in 2005 Austrian artist Gregor Neuerer invited Munich-based design studio Keller Maurer (Martina Keller and Marcus Maurer) to design a catalogue comprising illustrations of three artworks, an installation and text in German and English.

–

Keller Maurer's first act was to 'separate everything'. As Marcus Maurer explains: 'We sectioned off pictures, text, installation views and the two languages. Secondly, we arranged all content sequentially. Thirdly, we derived the design format, paper stock and page plan from that order. And fourthly, by arranging everything at the base of each page, and on top of each other, we developed a system that designed itself.'

–

The catalogue appears to be two documents fused together: 'Yes, it's really two formats', confirms Maurer. 'We wanted to create the feeling that someone had collected all this material and stuck it into a file. Also by using "two formats" we were able to print the title of the catalogue on page 7, a purely text page.'

–

Three paper stocks were used: all the four-colour material was printed on an A0 sheet of glossy coated stock (for enhanced reproduction); all text pages containing black-and-white views of the installation were reproduced on two A0 sheets of uncoated paper; the cover used a heavier, uncoated, coloured stock, the sort of material commonly found in offices, thus emphasizing the intriguing 'vernacular' nature of Neuerer's art. The fonts used were Plantin Bold and Neue Helvetica Medium.

–
–

–
–
–
Contem
Broc
Cat
Doc
–
–
–
–
–
–
–
–
–
Title:
Marc Quinn – Flesh
–
Origin:
UK
–
Client:
Irish Museum of
Modern Art
–
Studio:
Stephen Coates
–
Dimensions:
340mm x 245mm
13.4" x 9.6"
–
–
–
–
–
–

Marc Quinn Flesh

–
–
–

Contemporary
Brochures
Catalogues
Documents

–
–
–
–
–
–
–
–
–

Seated Figure (Bull)
2004
Bronze, black patina
179.5 x 93 x 87.5 cm
Courtesy Mary Boone
Gallery (New York)
xii
xiii

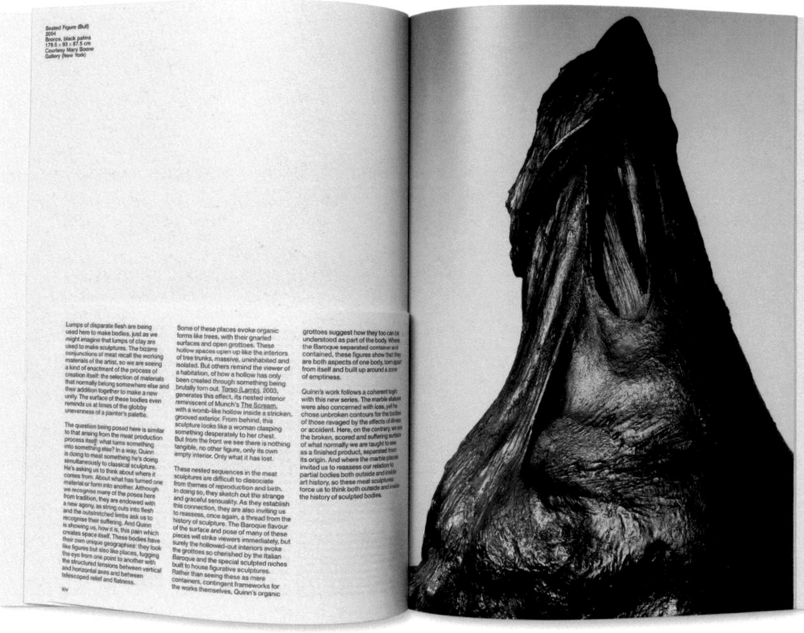

Marc Quinn Flesh

Description:
British artist Marc Quinn had concluded that the design of his previous catalogues, although intelligently done, came between the viewer and his artwork. For his new catalogue he wanted the artworks – dramatic life-size castings in black bronze of animal carcasses – to speak for themselves as large photographic reproductions.

–

'The schedule was very tight', explains designer Stephen Coates. 'The art works were made specially for the show. They were fabricated in Spain, flown to London for photography, then on to Dublin for installation. The essays couldn't be written until the writers had visited the studio to see the artworks, so the texts would be arriving at the last possible moment. The solution of not integrating the images and texts was partly pragmatic.'

–

Even the choice of binding was determined by practical decisions as much as by aesthetic ones: 'With the scale and the subject of some of the works', observes Coates, 'we were taken with the idea that they were partly obscured/revealed by the text inserts – as half-width horizontal or vertical sections. Because of the inserts, the most suitable binding option available was perfect binding. Sandwich-gluing the bound book between thick boards gave it the required heft and provided another option for keeping text and image separate by printing the title only on the exposed spine, where the stripe of red is the only colour in the whole piece.'

–
–
–
–
–

–
–
–
Contem
Broc
Cat
Doc
–
–
–
–
–
–
–
–
–

Title:
Merlin Carpenter
Nueva Generación
–
Origin:
UK
–
Client:
Merlin Carpenter
–
Studio:
Non-Format
–
Dimensions:
297mm x 220mm
11.7" x 8.7"
–
–
–
–
–
–

Carpenter
Nueva

–
–
–
–
–
–
–
–
–

Description:
Merlin Carpenter is a British painter who has exhibited in Europe and the USA. To accompany a solo show in Madrid in 2004, Non-Format, the London-based designers of this book, created a striking and unstereotypical catalogue.
–
Carpenter requested a catalogue that would display his paintings and feature two essays, one of which was written by himself. Through discussion with the artist the idea emerged of a document constructed in two layers. Non-Format suggested French-folding the pages, with the essays on the outer and the images on the inner. The folded edges were perforated to allow readers to open them easily.
–
Carpenter liked the idea that a decision had to be taken whether or not to rip open the pages. It was hoped that visitors to the exhibition might buy two copies: one to keep intact, the other to open.
–
–
–
–
–
–

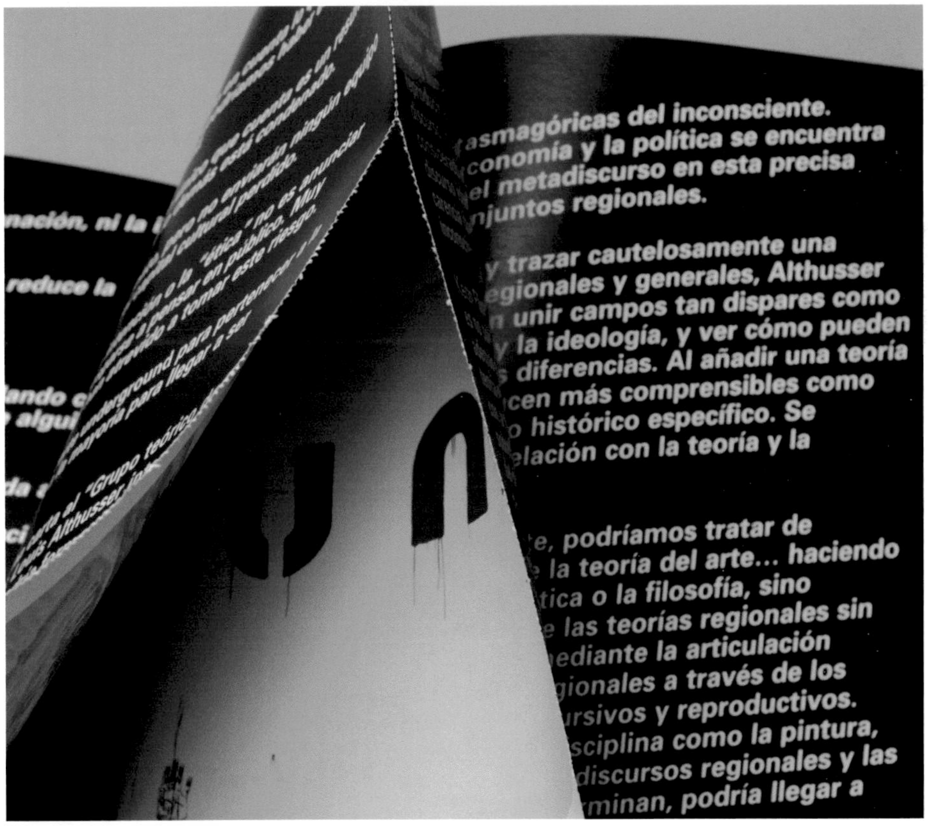
tasmagóricas del inconsciente.
conomía y la política se encuentra
el metadiscurso en esta precisa
njuntos regionales.
y trazar cautelosamente una
egionales y generales, Althusser
n unir campos tan dispares como
y la ideología, y ver cómo pueden
s diferencias. Al añadir una teoría
cen más comprensibles como
o histórico específico. Se
elación con la teoría y la
te, podríamos tratar de
e la teoría del arte... haciendo
tica o la filosofía, sino
e las teorías regionales sin
ediante la articulación
gionales a través de los
rsivos y reproductivos.
sciplina como la pintura,
discursos regionales y las
rminan, podría llegar a

miu miu

Conte
Broc
Cat
Doc

Title:
Circular 13: The Magazine of the Typographic Circle

Origin:
UK

Client:
The Typographic Circle

Studio:
Lippa Pearce

Dimensions:
333mm x 237mm
13.1" x 9.3"

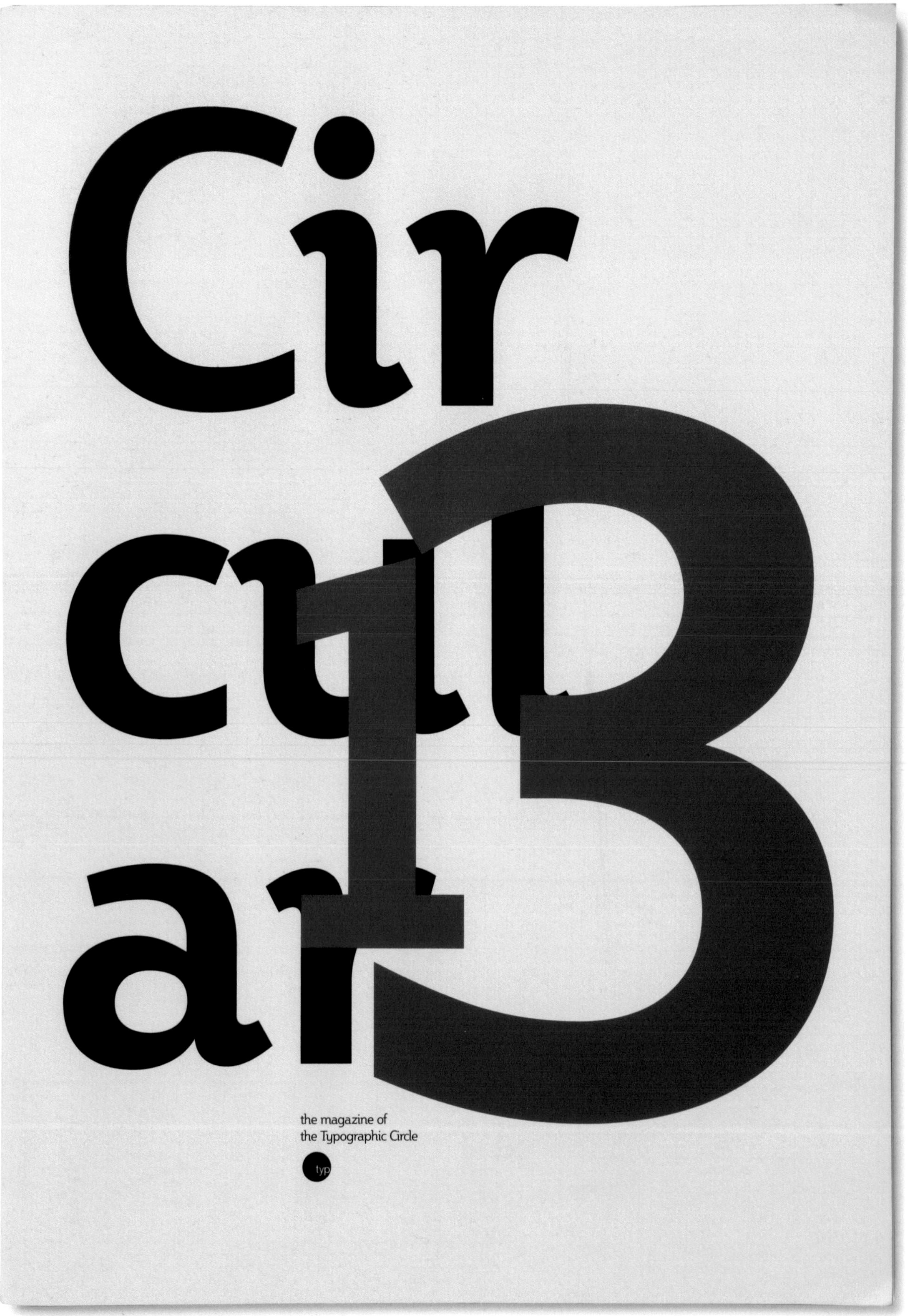
Cir
cul
ar
13
the magazine of
the Typographic Circle
typ

N

02_03

Description:
The Typographic Circle is a distinctive landmark on the UK design and typographic scene. Formed about 30 years ago by advertising typographers as the Type Directors Club, it was intended to unite practitioners in the art of typography. Today membership is open to anyone with an interest in the subject.

The Circle holds talks by leading designers, including such figures as Stefan Sagmeister, David Carson, Chip Kidd and Ken Garland. It also publishes its own journal, *The Circular*, which is free to members but can be bought by non-members.

Circular 13 was designed by graphic designer Dominic Lippa, a founder member of London design group Lippa Pearce – an award-garlanded practice with a substantial body of thoughtfully crafted work. Lippa has created a *tour de force* of typographic expressiveness. His unbound document mixes papers stocks, fonts and printing techniques yet retains a potent stylistic unity not always found in similarly experimental publications. He uses the typeface Plume and a mix of stocks, including Monadnock PC100 148gsm for the cover and a selection of GF Smith creative papers.

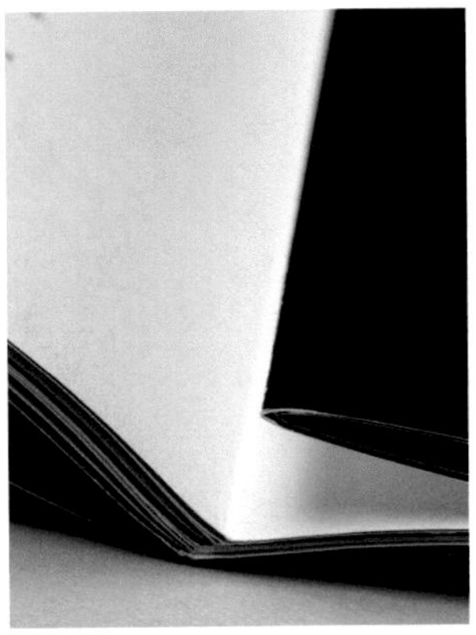

50_51

Page 098

Contem
Broc
Cat
Doc

Title:
21 Grams

Origin:
UK

Client:
Icon

Studio:
Ranch Associates

Dimensions:
215mm x 243mm
8.5" x 9.6"

Description:
This stylish brochure accompanied the UK release of the film *21 Grams*, directed by Alejandro González Iñárritu, famous for his earlier movie *Amores Perros*. With its intriguing perforated cover, the document was designed by London-based studio Ranch Associates. It was distributed to members of the press at screenings and by mail.

According to Ranch founder Paul Jenkins, the brief was simply to create a stunning brochure that reflected the film. The title, *21 Grams*, refers to the amount of weight you lose when you die. 'When you rip open the perforated cover,' Jenkins explains, 'the detached piece that gets left behind is meant to symbolize that missing weight – perhaps it's the weight of your soul!'

Photographs of the cast (which includes Sean Penn, Naomi Watts and Benicio Del Toro) are printed 4-colour CMYK onto green paper stock, a trademark Ranch technique. 'Yes, I'm very keen on printing onto coloured stocks,' notes Jenkins, 'but this is the furthest we have pushed it. By printing onto a very strong colour, it creates a fantastic effect, and it's fun because you never quite know what you're going to get until you see the proofs.'

21
GRAMS

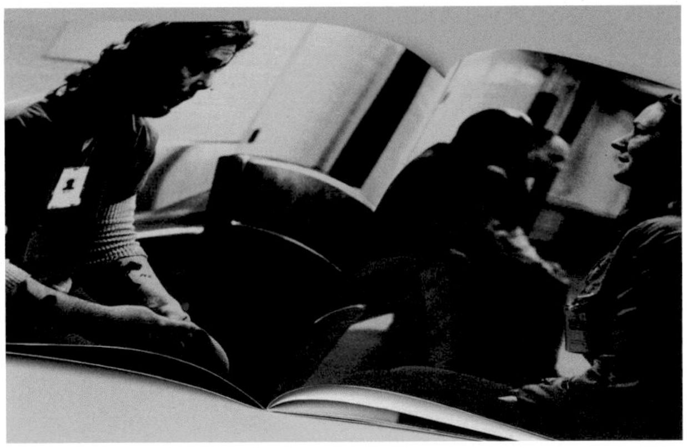

Title:
Attitudes

Origin:
Spain

Client:
Audi

Designers:
David Torrents
Ana Gasulla

Dimensions:
235mm x 194mm
9.2" x 7.6"

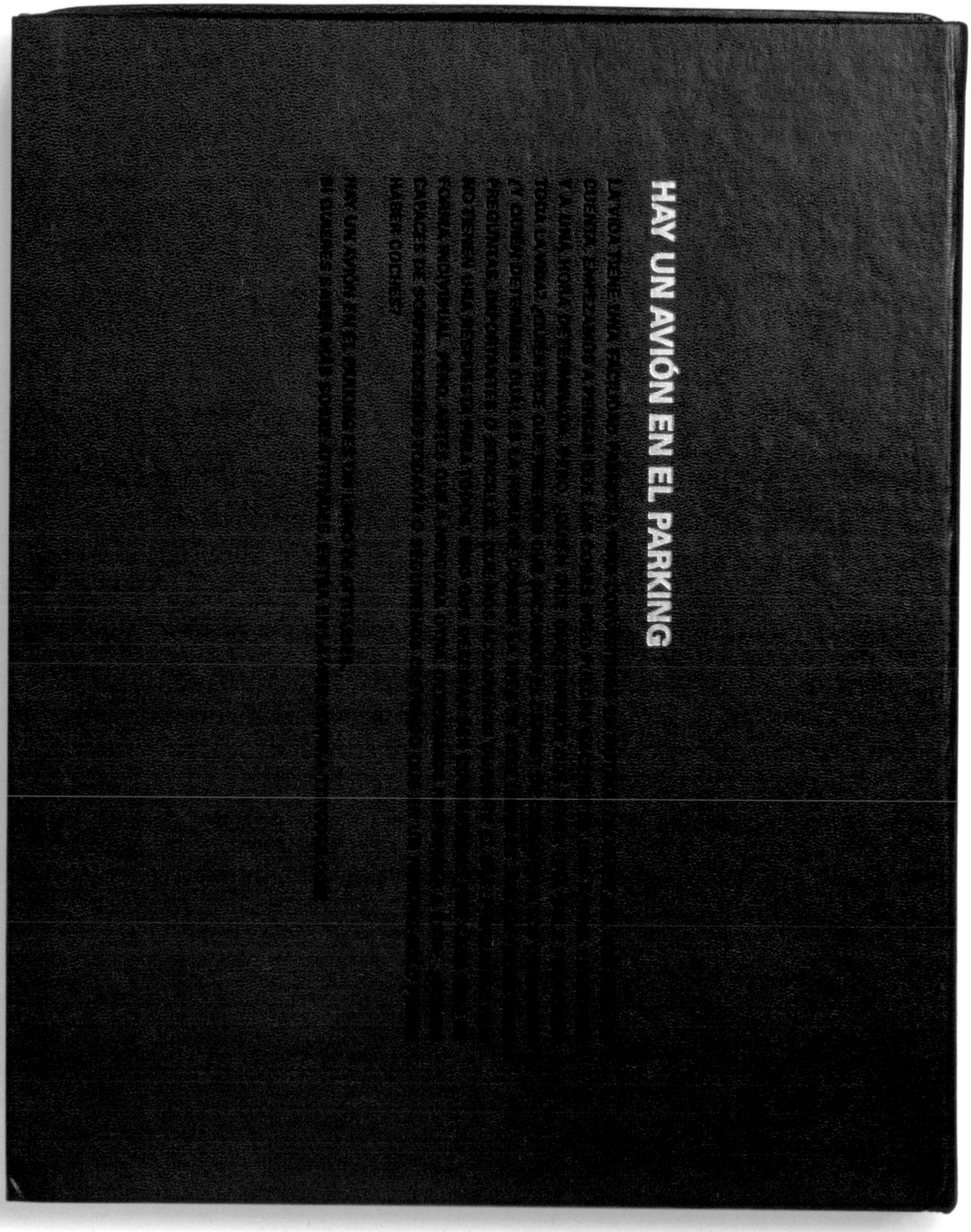
HAY UN AVIÓN EN EL PARKING

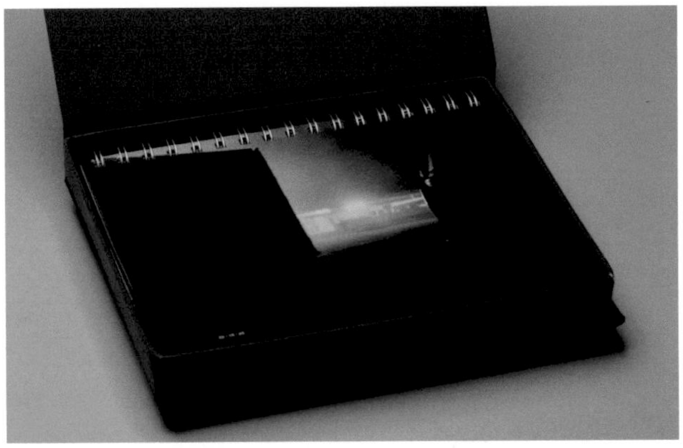

Description:
For their client, the car-maker Audi, Barcelona-based designers David Torrents and Ana Gasulla created a brochure in a box. The brief was to produce a 'book of facts' expressing the attitudes of the Audi brand. But the designers had other ideas. 'We wanted to show something more,' explains Torrents, 'and so we convinced the client to make a book about the people who might one day buy an Audi.'

–

The target audience was defined as '30–60 years old, open-minded, potential Audi buyers.' Torrents and Gasulla set about creating a document that depicted real people in domestic settings, in offices, on the street and in real-life situations. 'We photographed lots of people taking decisions which might change their lives.'

–

The spiral-bound brochure contains emotive, reportage-style photography, sometimes coupled with sharp, modern, diagrammatic graphics, thus creating a strong impression of entering a world of real people with real preoccupations. The document, with its uncoated paper stock, avoids the normal glitzy tropes associated with car brochures.

–

As Torrents notes: 'Audi was surprised and pleased.'

–
–
–
–
–
–

HAY UN AVIÓN EN EL PARKING

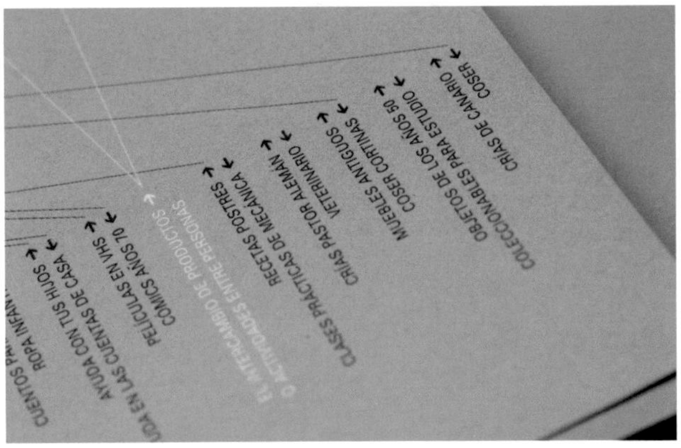
COSER
CRIAS DE CANARIO
OBJETOS DE LOS AÑOS 50
COSER CORTINAS
MUEBLES ANTIGUOS
VETERINARIO
RECETAS POSTRES
COMICS AÑOS 70

Contem
Broc
Cat
Doc

Titles:
Gerard Byrne –
Books, Magazines
and Newspapers
Peter Friedl –
Four or Five Roses
Nicolas Bourriaud –
Post production

Origin:
Germany

Client:
Lukas & Sternberg

Studio:
Markus Weisbeck/surface

Dimensions:
170mm x 108mm
6.7" x 4.2"

GERARD BYRNE
BOOKS, MAGAZINES, AND NEWSPAPERS
LUKAS & STERNBERG, NEW YORK 009

PETER FRIEDL
FOUR OR FIVE ROSES
LUKAS & STERNBERG, NEW YOR

NICOLAS BOURRIAUD
POSTPRODUCTION

–
–
–

Contemporary
Brochures
Catalogues
Documents

–
–
–
–
–
–
–
–
–

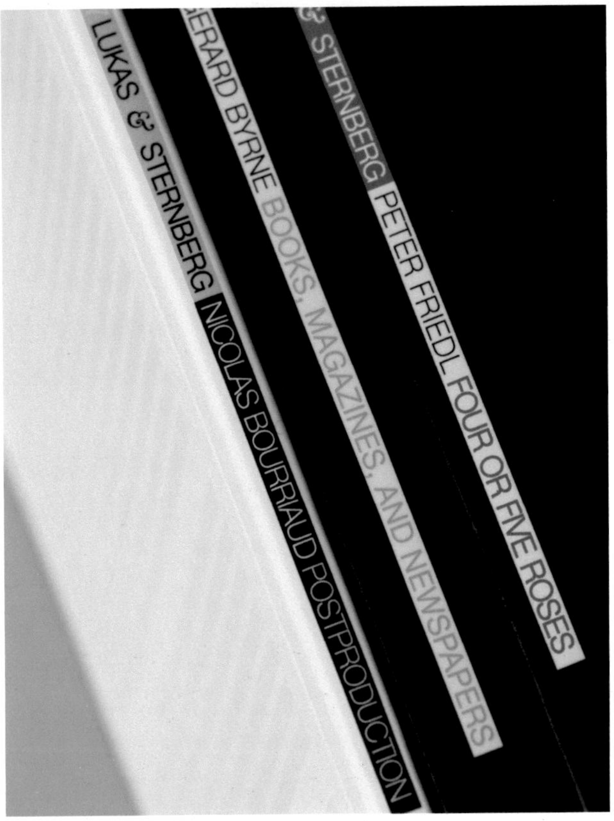
LUKAS & STERNBERG NICOLAS BOURRIAUD POSTPRODUCTION
ERARD BYRNE BOOKS, MAGAZINES, AND NEWSPAPERS
& STERNBERG PETER FRIEDL FOUR OR FIVE ROSES

Description:
These examples are from a series of 12 pocket-sized paperbacks ('Pocketbooks') published by Lukas & Sternberg, New York. The series began with Liam Gillick's *Five or Six*, and more editions are planned. The distinctive and coolly precise graphic appearance of the range is the work of German designer Markus Weisbeck, of Surface.

–

'The idea of the gloss varnish on the cover', explains Weisbeck, 'is to exactly mirror the text on the first page. It means that the author, in a way, controls the look of the cover.'

–

To accompany the series Weisbeck has produced a clear and precise style manual to ensure graphic uniformity and production consistency. It includes the following instructions:
Font/Headlines:
45 Helvetica Light, 10pt;
56 Helvetica Roman, 10pt;
Line spacing 11.5pt.
Word spacing -10;
Print specification/cover:
Format 110mm x 170mm.
Four-sided.
Colour 2/0 coloured.
Paper: 300 G Image Printing paper matt coated/wood-free.
Matt lamination, partial print varnish.
Font/logo: 45 Helvetica Light 8.5pt.
Line spacing 11.5pt.
Word spacing -10.

GERARD BYRNE
BOOKS, MAGAZINES, AND NEWSPAPERS

–
–
–
–
–
–

Conte
Bro
Cat
Doc

Title:
Migrating Identity – Transmission/ Reconstruction

Origin:
The Netherlands

Client:
SEB Foundation

Studio:
Sander Boom

Dimensions:
240mm x 160mm
9.4" x 6.3"

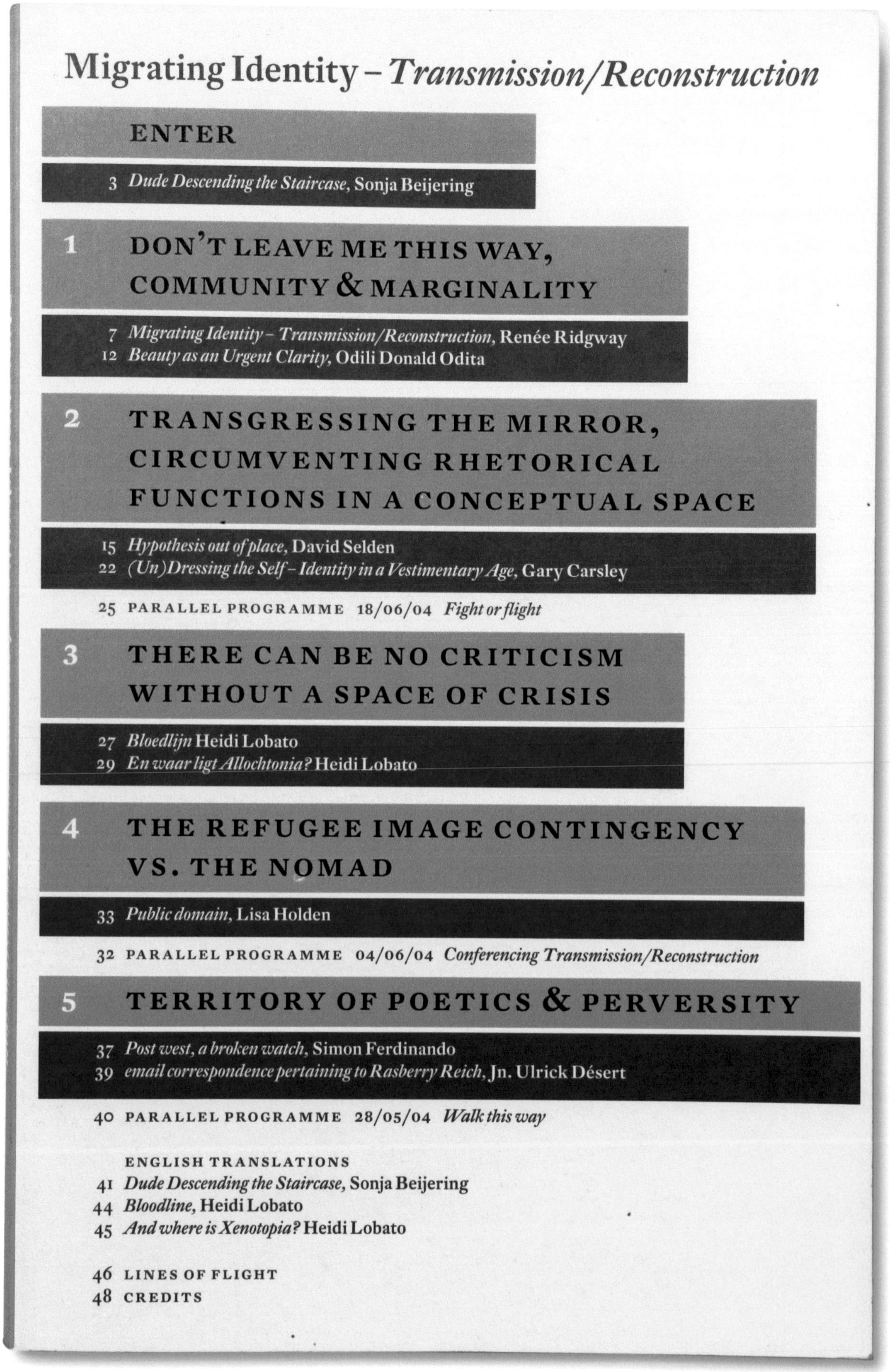

Migrating Identity – *Transmission/Reconstruction*

–
–
–
Contemporary
Brochures
Catalogues
Documents
–
–
–
–
–
–
–
–
–

Description:
The Netherlands, with its rich visual arts heritage (how many great Dutch writers can you name?), produces a limitless supply of graphic talent. Sander Boom is one of a seemingly endless stream of intelligent and fastidious young Dutch designers emerging onto the contemporary scene.
–
Boom studied at the Willem de Kooning Academie in Rotterdam. He now lives and works in Amsterdam. He says: 'Affinity with the client plays an important role in my work. I prefer working on projects that have relevance in the social and cultural field. Though I am familiar with "new media", most of my work is in classical print.'
–
The catalogue for the exhibition 'Migrating Identity –Transmission/ Reconstruction' exudes an identifiably Dutch aesthetic sensibility: understated yet at the same time assertive. The perfect-bound document makes good use of fluoro-orange ink on the cover, and the fold-out pages on the inside create a dynamic canvas for the photography. A clever mix of stock (uncoated for text, coated for photography) creates an appealing visual experience.
–
As well as designing the exhibition, Boom designed all the supporting materials: invitation, film titles, advertising and website.
–
–
–
–
–
–

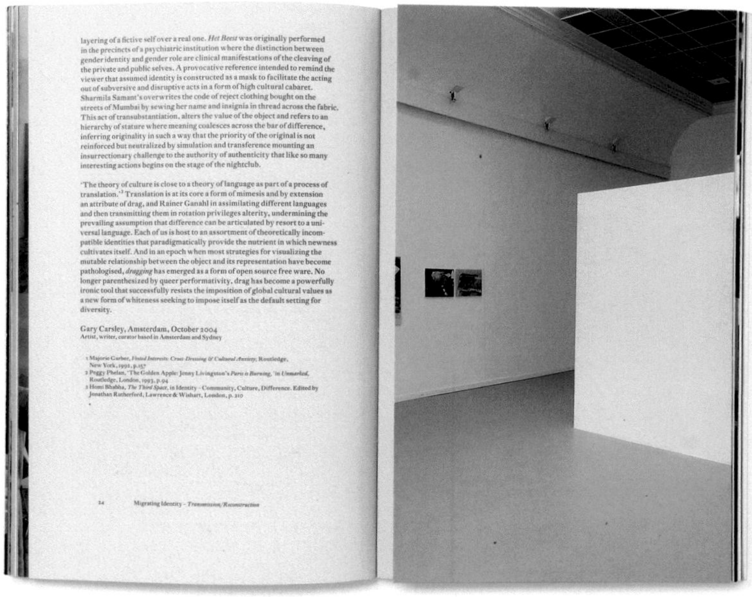
layering of a fictive self over a real one. Het Beest was originally performed in the precincts of a psychiatric institution where the distinction between gender identity and gender role are clinical manifestations of the cleaving of the private and public selves. A provocative reference intended to remind the viewer that assumed identity is constructed as a mask to facilitate the acting out of subversive and disruptive acts in a form of high cultural cabaret. Sharmila Samant's overwrites the code of reject clothing bought on the streets of Mumbai by sewing her name and insignia in thread across the fabric. This act of transubstantiation, alters the value of the object and refers to an hierarchy of stature where meaning coalesces across the bar of difference, inferring originality in such a way that the priority of the original is not reinforced but neutralized by simulation and transference mounting an insurrectionary challenge to the authority of authenticity that like so many interesting actions begins on the stage of the nightclub.
'The theory of culture is close to a theory of language as part of a process of translation.'[3] Translation is at its core a form of mimesis and by extension an attribute of drag, and Rainer Ganahl in assimilating different languages and then transmitting them in rotation privileges alterity, undermining the prevailing assumption that difference can be articulated by resort to a universal language. Each of us is host to an assortment of theoretically incompatible identities that paradigmatically provide the nutrient in which newness cultivates itself. And in an epoch when most strategies for visualizing the mutable relationship between the object and its representation have become pathologised, dragging has emerged as a form of open source free ware. No longer parenthesized by queer performativity, drag has become a powerfully ironic tool that successfully resists the imposition of global cultural values as a new form of whiteness seeking to impose itself as the default setting for diversity.
Gary Carsley, Amsterdam, October 2004
Artist, writer, curator based in Amsterdam and Sydney
1 Majorie Garber, Vested Interests: Cross-Dressing & Cultural Anxiety, Routledge, New York, 1992, p.157
2 Peggy Phelan, 'The Golden Apple: Jenny Livingston's Paris is Burning,' in Unmarked, Routledge, London, 1993, p.94
3 Homi Bhabha, The Third Space, in Identity - Community, Culture, Difference. Edited by Jonathan Rutherford, Lawrence & Wishart, London, p. 210
24 Migrating Identity – Transmission/Reconstruction

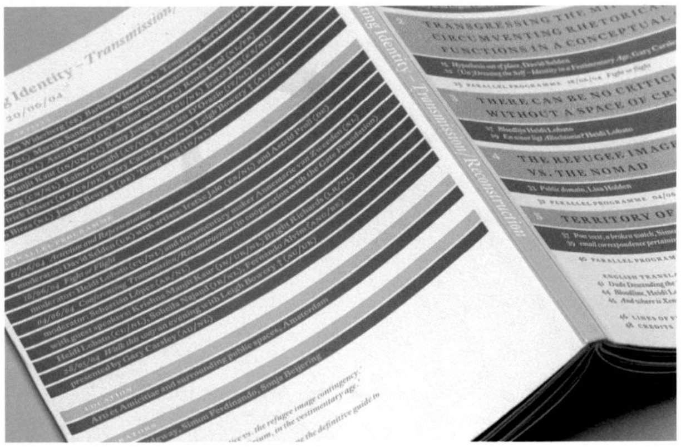

THERE CAN BE NO CRITICISM WITHOUT A SPACE OF CRISIS

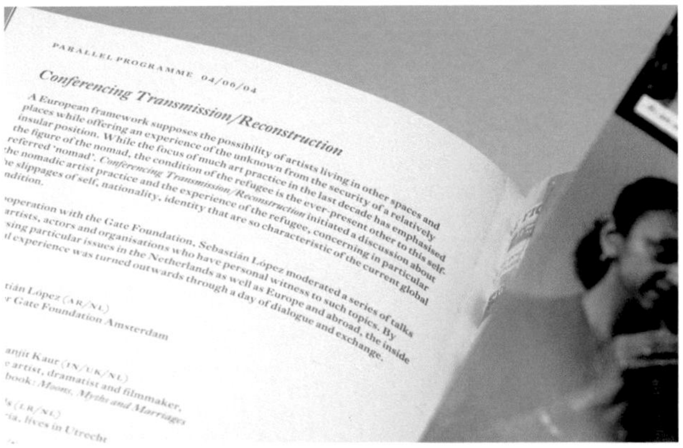
PARALLEL PROGRAMME 04/06/04
Conferencing Transmission/Reconstruction

Contem
Broc
Cat
Doc

Title:
Urgent Painting Catalogue

Origin:
France

Client:
Musée d'Art Moderne
de la Ville de Paris

Studio:
Labomatic

Dimensions:
230 x 160mm
9" x 6.3"

–
–
–

Contemporary
Brochures
Catalogues
Documents

–
–
–
–
–
–
–
–
–

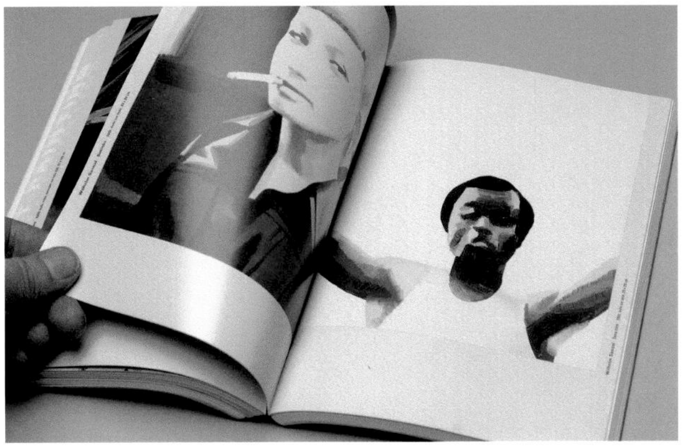

Description:
Parisian design studio Labomatic was commissioned to create a catalogue for a group show called 'Urgent Painting' at the Musée d'Art Moderne de la Ville de Paris. 'There was no specific brief,' explains Labomatic, 'rather a series of conversations with the museum's curators, Hans-Ulrich Obrist, Laurence Bossé and Julia Garimorth, on the various complex political issues surrounding contemporary painting.'

–

Labomatic proposed making a 'book-object' based on a sequence of text/art/text, flanked on either side by two series of blurred images. 'These images were an impertinent, tongue-in-cheek reply to the too hip title of the show. We blurred the paintings, as if we saw them from a very fast train window.'

–

Labomatic explains the rationale behind the document's distinctive use of transparent binding: 'We wanted the blurred images to be seen all at once. We wanted to show the layers of the page sections as layers of paint on a canvas, and we wanted to give the feeling that the book was glued with paint. This didn't quite work because we couldn't find coloured glue. Also, plastic isn't a material normally associated with painting, which even today remains a "classical" medium.'

–
–
–
–
–
–

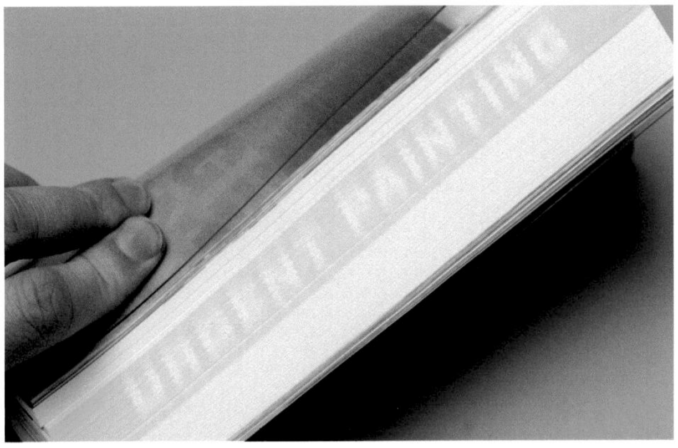
URGENT PAINTING

Title:
British Fashion Council Report of Activities 2001–2002

Origin:
UK

Client:
British Fashion Council

Studio:
Egelnick and Webb

Dimensions:
295mm x 186mm
11.6" x 7.3"

British Fashion Council
Report of Activities 2001-2002

BFC Princess of Wales Charitable Trust

The fourth BFC Princess of Wales Charitable Trust scholarship was won by four students: John Joseph Mooney, Carli Simone Pearson and Patrick Soderstam, each of whom was awarded a fee scholarship and Graeme Raeburn, who was awarded an expenses allowance to complement the fee scholarship he had received from his college.

The scholarship was set up in memory of the Princess of Wales' contribution to the fashion industry, and provides an annual scholarship for a graduate from a British Fashion Design college who, for financial reasons, would otherwise be unable to take up that place. Founder members of the Trust are: Arcadia Group, Coats Viyella, Conde Nast Publications, Marks & Spencer, National Magazine Company and the Pentland Group; the Trustees are Anna Harvey, Anne Tyrrell and John Wilson.

Other Activities in Brief

The London Fashion Week Advisory Committee, chaired by Anne Tyrrell, considers first time applications from designers wishing to exhibit at London Fashion Week or wishing to be included on the show schedule. It also considers applications for New Generation Designer sponsorship.

The International and UK Buyers Committee has met during the year to make input to the organising of London Fashion Week.

The Press Committee, chaired by Anna Harvey (Vogue International), includes editors or fashion editors of the principal daily newspapers and trade and consumer press and gives feedback to the BFC on London Fashion Week and the British Style Awards.

Designer Fact File, written for the BFC in 1997 by Caroline Coates, continues to be widely used as an essential reference book for those setting up a designer company - copies are available from the BFC at 5 Portland Place.

The BFC Secretariat handles a wide range of enquiries from the public, students and the industry.

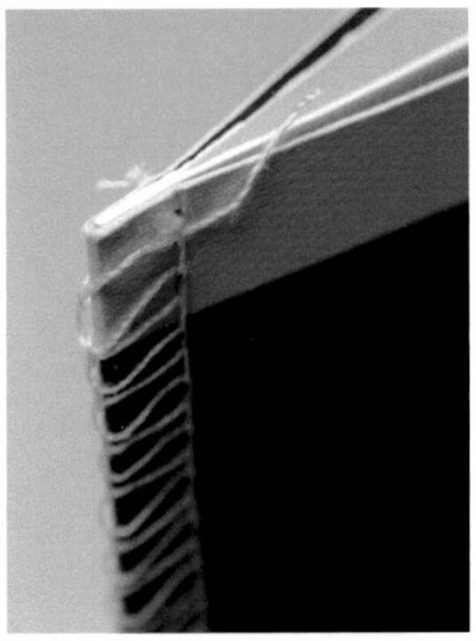

Description:
'We were shown the previous year's report,' recalls designer Toby Egelnick, 'which was two colours and very austere-looking, in black and silver. We were given a tight budget and told that if we could produce a new report, then the job would go live.'
–
Egelnick and partner Malcolm Webb set about creating a stylish document that reflected the creativity and vibrancy of the British fashion industry. 'Our idea was to maintain a "straight" text layout,' notes Egelnick, 'so as not to upset the key supporters – MDs of big fashion retailers, for example – but coupling this with a more modern and lively layout of the images. The idea was a "collection" of images, arranged in an overlapping layout that looked like a scrapbook collection from the year sewn into the spine.'
–
The London-based duo restricted themselves to two colours, but by mixing the ink channels they managed to produce a range of hues, which prevented the document from looking cheap and low-budget. The paper stock was chosen for its resemblance to fabric and was donated by manufacturer Arjo Wiggins. The stitched spine necessitated borrowing an overlocker from the fashion designer next door to the designer's studio, and the hire of her student placement.
–
–
–
–
–
–

–
–
–
Contem
Broc
Cat
Doc
–
–
–
–
–
–
–
–
–
Title:
Flashback: Twenty-Five Years on Starwhite
–
Origin:
USA
–
Client:
Fox River Paper
–
Studio:
Thirst
–
Dimensions:
305mm x 229mm
12" x 9"
–
–
–
–
–
–

FlashBack
Twenty-five years on Starwhite

80 Gene Simmons stuck his tongue out at the idea of the American idol.
In 2005 Mr. Simmons came out from behind the white makeup
uest judge of American Idol on the Fox Network.
80#T Flash Blue Smooth 4/c process over 4/c

Twenty-five

Starwhite Tiara
Starwhite Archiva
Starwhite Sirius
Starwhite Flash

Description:
Paper manufacturers, with their self-evident need to show off the graphic capabilities of the various paper stocks they produce, are among graphic design's most generous and encouraging patrons. In *Flashback*, a sleek and seductively presented document, Rick Valicenti and his team of collaborators at Thirst road-test the possibilities inherent in manufacturer Fox River's Starwhite range of weights and finishes.

–

Valicenti adopts the theme of retrospection to celebrate 25 years of Starwhite. He uses every technique in the graphic designer's lexicon as he contrasts images and data from 1980 (when Starwhite first appeared) with images and data from 2005: Priscilla Presley sits opposite her daughter Lisa Marie Presley – both Queens of Pop, their reigns separated by a quarter of a century; the young bodybuilder Arnold Schwarzenegger sits opposite the besuited Governor of California; an elegant graphic map shows the redistribution of world population over the past 25 years.

–

The result is a sumptuous document: a hymn of praise to the art of good design, fine printing and high-grade paper stock.

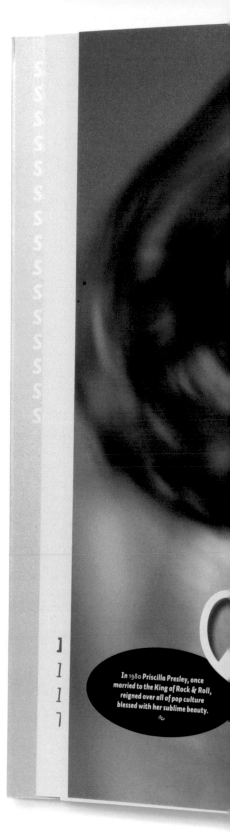
In 1980 Priscilla Presley, once married to the King of Rock & Roll, reigned over all of pop culture blessed with her sublime beauty.

80#T Tiara Hi-Tech 4/c process + 1 match color over 4/c + 1*
Queen
Queen
Lisa Marie once married her very own King of Pop and reigned supreme in all tabloid media. Who will bow to this queen in 2005?

Fast Forward
Twenty-five more years...

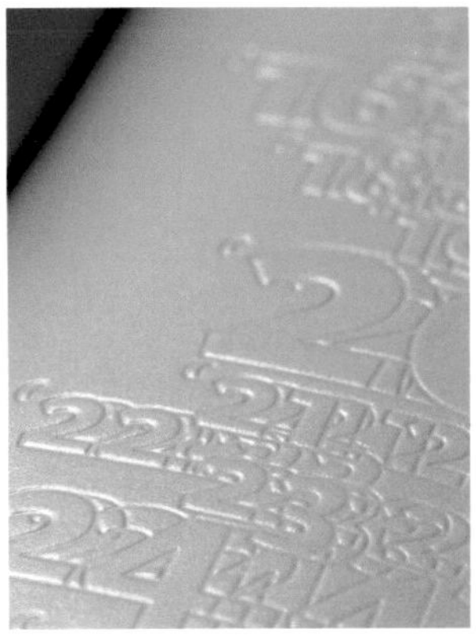

–
–
–
Conte
Broc
Cat
Doc
–
–
–
–
–
–
–
–
–

Title:
Inter
–
Origin:
Japan
–
Client:
Institute of Advanced
Media Arts & Science
(IAMAS)
–
Studio:
Kent Shimizu
IAMAS Annual 2000
Committee
–
Dimensions:
150mm x 150mm
5.9" x 5.9"
–
–
–
–
–
–

INTER

IAMAS

–
–
–
–
–
–
–
–
–
–
–
–
–
–
–
–
–
–

Description:
IAMAS is an art and media school in Ogaki City, Gifu prefecture, in the middle of mainland Japan. It focuses on research, developing new forms of creativity and merging information technology with the arts. It consists of two schools: the Institute of Advanced Media Arts and Sciences, founded in 1996, and the International Academy of Media Arts and Sciences, which opened in 2001. There are 20 students in each year of the course. The Academy is a vocational college and accepts 30 students each year.
–
Since its establishment IAMAS has actively pursued overseas links. Many members of the teaching staff and numerous students come from abroad. Additionally, many foreign artists and researchers visit the school, which explains why much of its promotional literature is in English.
–
As a record of the activities of the IAMAS graduates in 2000, designer Kent Shimizu created a striking white, textured hinged box, containing a DVD and a small, square, perfect-bound booklet. Four words – ‘change’, ‘lace’, ‘act’ and ‘view’ – are connected with the prefix ‘inter’, which is the title of the document. The use of intertwining lines as a recurring decorative motif on the DVD and on the booklet cover alludes to the notion of interlacing, a central theme of this ‘annual report’.
–
–
–
–
–
–

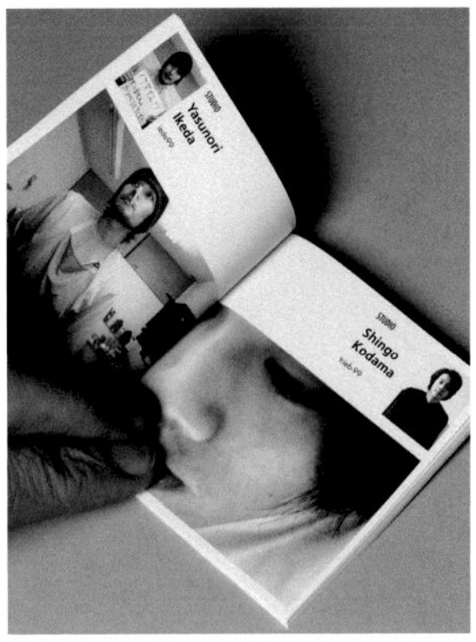
Yasunori
Ikeda
Shingo
Kodama

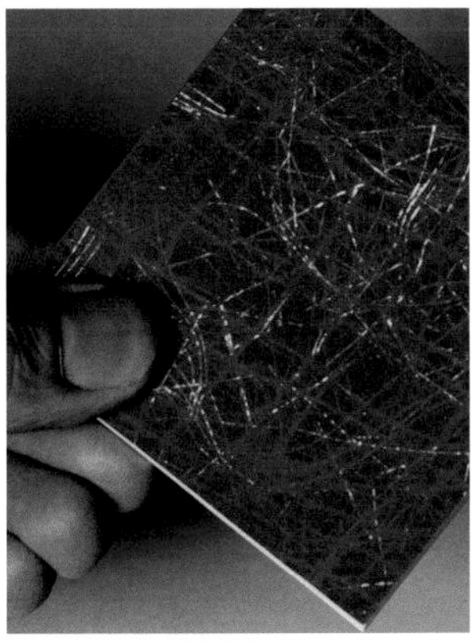

–
–
–
Contem
Broc
Cat
Doc
–
–
–
–
–
–
–
–
–

Title:
Année du Brésil en France
–
Origin:
France
–
Client:
Association Française d'Action Artistique
–
Designer:
Philippe Apeloig (assisted by Ellen Zhao)
–
Dimensions:
297mm x 222mm
11.7" x 8.7"
–
–
–
–
–
–

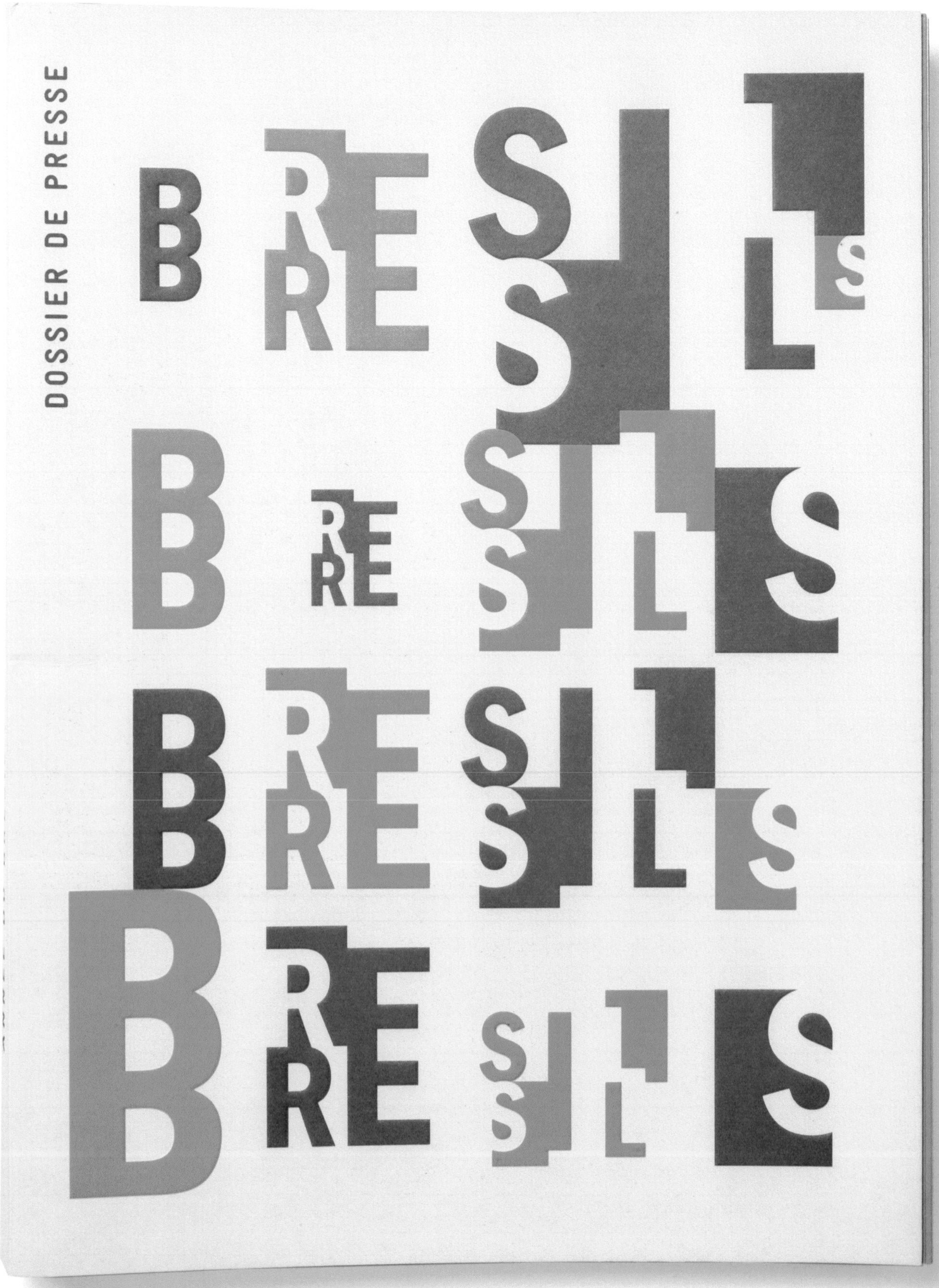
DOSSIER DE PRESSE

–
–
–
Contemporary
Brochures
Catalogues
Documents
–
–
–
–
–
–
–
–
–

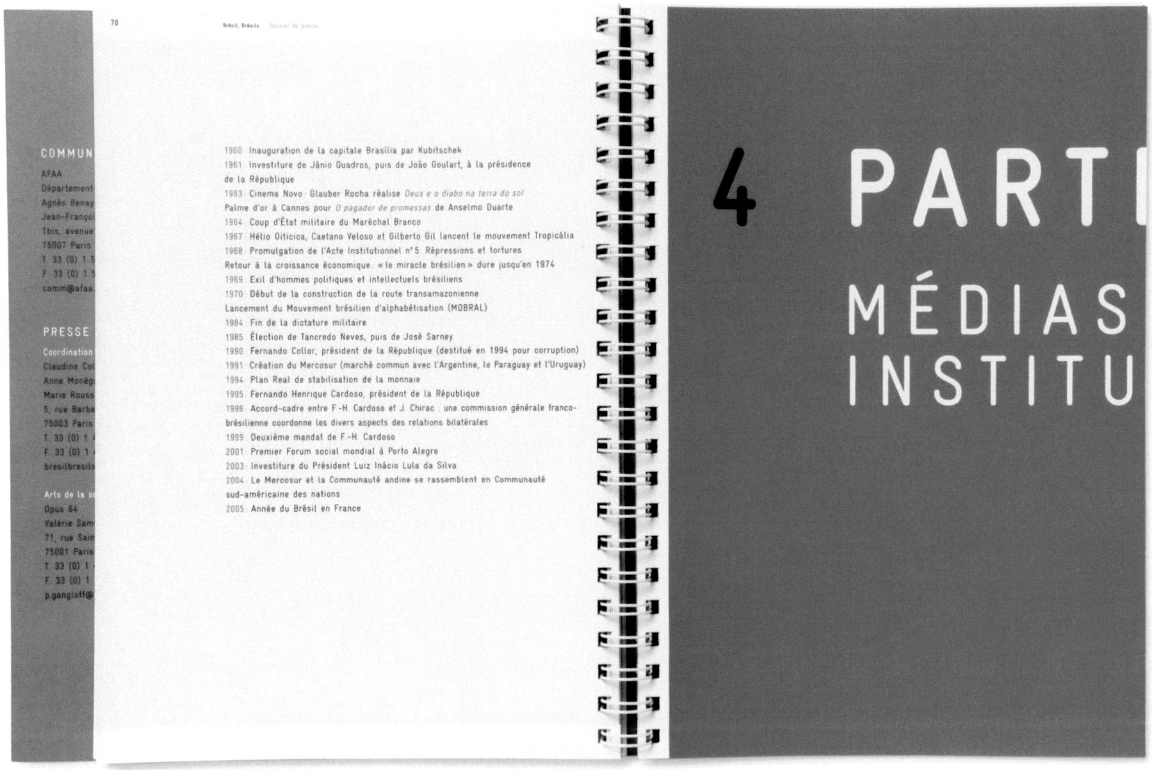
1960 Inauguration de la capitale Brasília par Kubitschek
1961 Investiture de Jânio Quadros, puis de João Goulart, à la présidence de la République
1963 Cinema Novo Glauber Rocha réalise *Deus e o diabo na terra do sol*
Palme d'or à Cannes pour *O pagador de promessas* de Anselmo Duarte
1964 Coup d'État militaire du Maréchal Branco
1967 Hélio Oiticica, Caetano Veloso et Gilberto Gil lancent le mouvement Tropicália
1968 Promulgation de l'Acte Institutionnel n°5 Répressions et tortures
Retour à la croissance économique « le miracle brésilien » dure jusqu'en 1974
1969 Exil d'hommes politiques et intellectuels brésiliens
1970 Début de la construction de la route transamazonienne
Lancement du Mouvement brésilien d'alphabétisation (MOBRAL)
1984 Fin de la dictature militaire
1985 Élection de Tancredo Neves, puis de José Sarney
1990 Fernando Collor, président de la République (destitué en 1994 pour corruption)
1991 Création du Mercosur (marché commun avec l'Argentine, le Paraguay et l'Uruguay)
1994 Plan Real de stabilisation de la monnaie
1995 Fernando Henrique Cardoso, président de la République
1996 Accord-cadre entre F.-H. Cardoso et J. Chirac : une commission générale franco-brésilienne coordonne les divers aspects des relations bilatérales
1999 Deuxième mandat de F.-H. Cardoso
2001 Premier Forum social mondial à Porto Alegre
2003 Investiture du Président Luiz Inácio Lula da Silva
2004 Le Mercosur et la Communauté andine se rassemblent en Communauté sud-américaine des nations
2005 Année du Brésil en France
4
PARTI
MÉDIAS
INSTITU

ANNÉE DU BRÉ

Description:
The Paris-based graphic designer Philippe Apeloig occupies a unique place in contemporary European design. He combines typographic clarity and typographic pattern-making with breathtaking aplomb. His work, with its palette of strong colours and confident typography, is always readily distinguishable among the visual hubbub of contemporary graphic design.
–
Apeloig's spiral-bound press pack *Brésil, Brésils* was designed to promote the Year of Brazil in France (L'Année du Brésil en France) in 2005. It is a bravura display of his signature style. His use of French folding allows text to be wrapped around the fold. The cover uses seemingly random blocks of lettering – embossed for added effect – that are at once abstract and legible. The cover uses only three colours: the green and yellow of Brazil and a Gallic blue.
–
As with all Apeloig's work, this document is impeccably printed, exquisitely laid out and typographically sophisticated.
–
–
–
–
–
–

Conte
Broc
Cat
Doc

Title:
Edmund de Waal
–
Origin:
UK
–
Client:
Blackwell, The Arts and Crafts House
–
Studio:
Pentagram
–
Dimensions:
240mm x 240mm
9.4" x 9.4"

Description:
Pentagram partner Angus Hyland was invited to create a catalogue showcasing the work of the highly regarded ceramicist Edmund de Waal. Hyland's sensitive, unobtrusive design and Graham Murrell's atmospheric photography capture De Waal's Japanese-inspired porcelain beautifully. The setting is Blackwell, a house designed by the architect M. H. Baillie Scott (1865–1945) in the Arts and Crafts style (a precursor of Art Nouveau) and located in the Lake District, an area of outstanding natural beauty long associated with British literature and art.
–
The square-format catalogue makes use of a mix of paper stocks from paper manufacturer Howard Smith and deploys a variety of page sizes to create a gentle feeling of discovery. According to Hyland: 'Each spread is like entering a new space though a half-open door. It is quite literally a journey through a historic house, and each room in turn reveals surprises. I used a mix of paper stocks to suggest a sense of craft, appropriate to Edmund's beautiful work.'
–
De Waal's apprentices are given a section of their own at the back of the document. 'A kind of mini-catalogue as appendix', explains Hyland.

Edmund de Waal A line around a shadow

Contem
Broc
Cat
Doc

Title:
The Institute for Words & Pictures

Origin:
USA

Client:
CalArts

Designers:
Zak Kyes with Tahli Fisher

Dimensions:
171mm x 104mm
6.7" x 4.1"

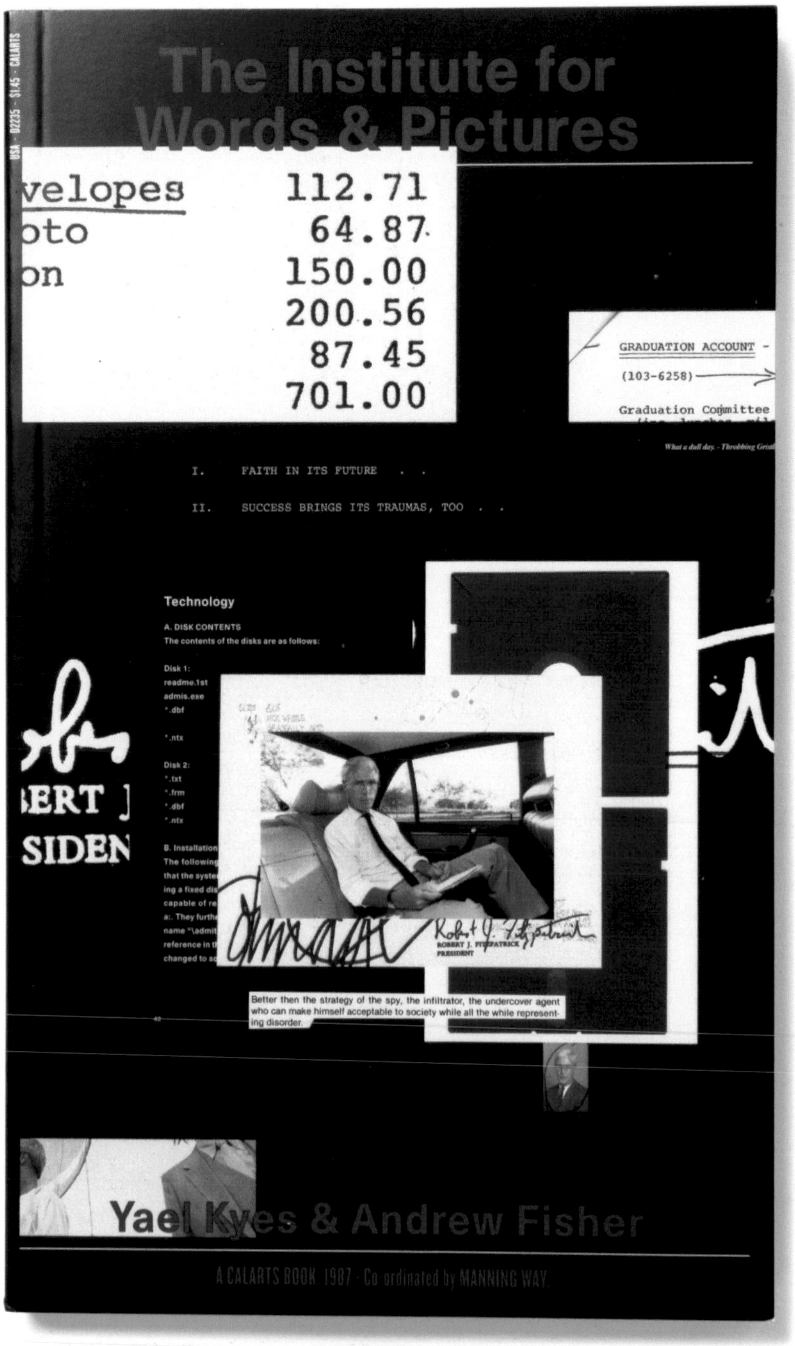
The Institute for Words & Pictures
velopes 112.71
oto 64.87
on 150.00
200.56
87.45
701.00
GRADUATION ACCOUNT
(103-6258)
Graduation Committee
I. FAITH IN ITS FUTURE
II. SUCCESS BRINGS ITS TRAUMAS, TOO
Technology
A. DISK CONTENTS
The contents of the disks are as follows:
Better then the strategy of the spy, the infiltrator, the undercover agent who can make himself acceptable to society while all the while representing disorder.
Yael Kyes & Andrew Fisher
A CALARTS BOOK 1987 Co ordinated by MANNING WAY

Notes & Memories;

No more of this shit.
CalArts Graduation 2005

–
–
–
Contemporary
Brochures
Catalogues
Documents
–
–
–
–
–
–
–
–
–
Description:
This might just be the most interesting publication featured in this book. It has an air of mystery about it. It claims to be 'designed and co-authored' by the pseudonymous sounding Yael Kyes and Andrew Fisher, and bears the imprint of CalArts. But it's not clear what it is about or what its purpose is. It closely resembles a 1960s' counter-culture journal. The fact that it comes with a badge saying 'No more of this shit' reinforces its maverick status.
–
In a hard-to-read paragraph on the back cover the following text appears: '4.15.05 – Dear Reader, This book is a rare artefact of the dreams and traumas that surrounded CalArts during the 1980s. The Institute for Words & Pictures was mysteriously cancelled at press in March of 1987. The project was abandoned and the original materials were eventually lost. In 2005 an envelope containing most of the lost book pages was found when the building occupied by the printer was demolished. Some pages remain missing. Uncovered after eighteen years, the images in this book tell strange tales; revered and refuted, poetry and fiction, mysteries, detectives and true crimes alike. The first, long delayed, imprint of this lost volume is published in honour of CalArts' 35th graduating class.' So now we know.
–
–
–
–
–
–

Notes & Memories;
CalArts Graduation May 20th 2005

void this page

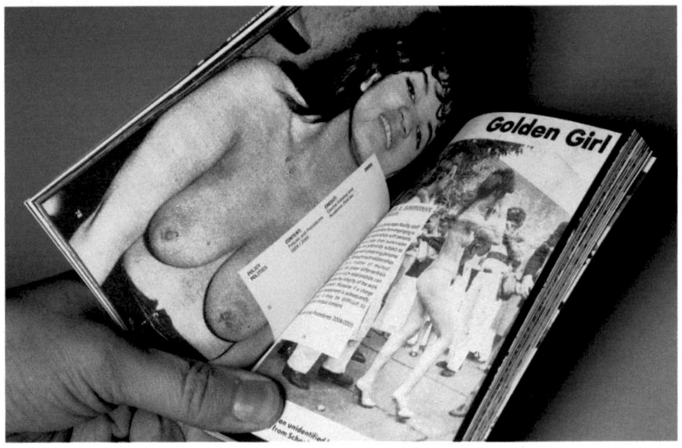
Golden Girl

Conte
Broc
Cat
Doc

Title:
Crop

Origin:
USA

Client:
Corbis

Studio:
Segura Inc.

Dimensions:
600mm x 480mm
23.6" x 18.9"

Description:
Chicago-based Segura Inc. is widely regarded as one of the pre-eminent US design groups. Founder Carlos Segura is a significant presence on the contemporary design and type scene. The group has received numerous awards for its ground-breaking work for Corbis, the giant image library. Segura Inc.'s first task was to rebrand the entire company, starting with their logo. 'We then did the Corbis Crop series, eight in total,' explains Carlos Segura. 'Corbis had many years of bad habits under their belt. Their perception in the market-place, from a "creative's" perspective, was dismal. Our challenge was to change that. Not an easy task when you are speaking to what I believe is a very sophisticated target audience.'

Segura's response was to create materials that would not only tackle Corbis's competition, 'but also', as Segura explains, 'compete with the onslaught of sensory input we get all day. There is very little room to "carve" out a place in our "experience". We all remember the best car, the best movie, the best computer, the best "experience". And we wanted to be in that league.'

All eight Crop catalogues are striking examples of graphic invention. Using sheer size (Corbis catalogues are big) and dramatic layouts, Segura successfully re-engineered the perception of Corbis among cynical designers. Did he find it liberating or intimidating to be working on material that would be assessed critically by his peers? 'Liberating', he says, without hesitation.

13 premier photojournalists

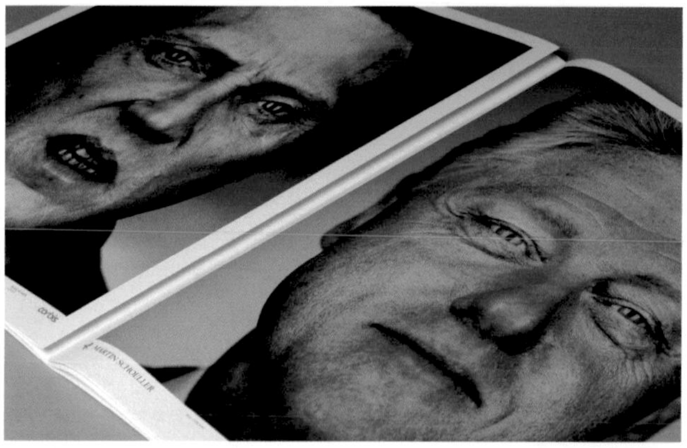

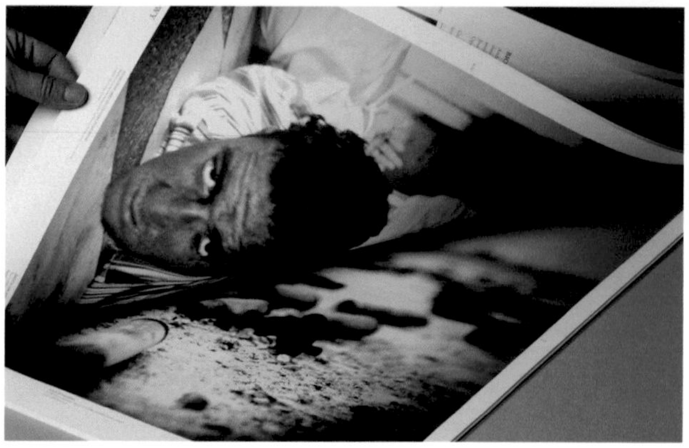

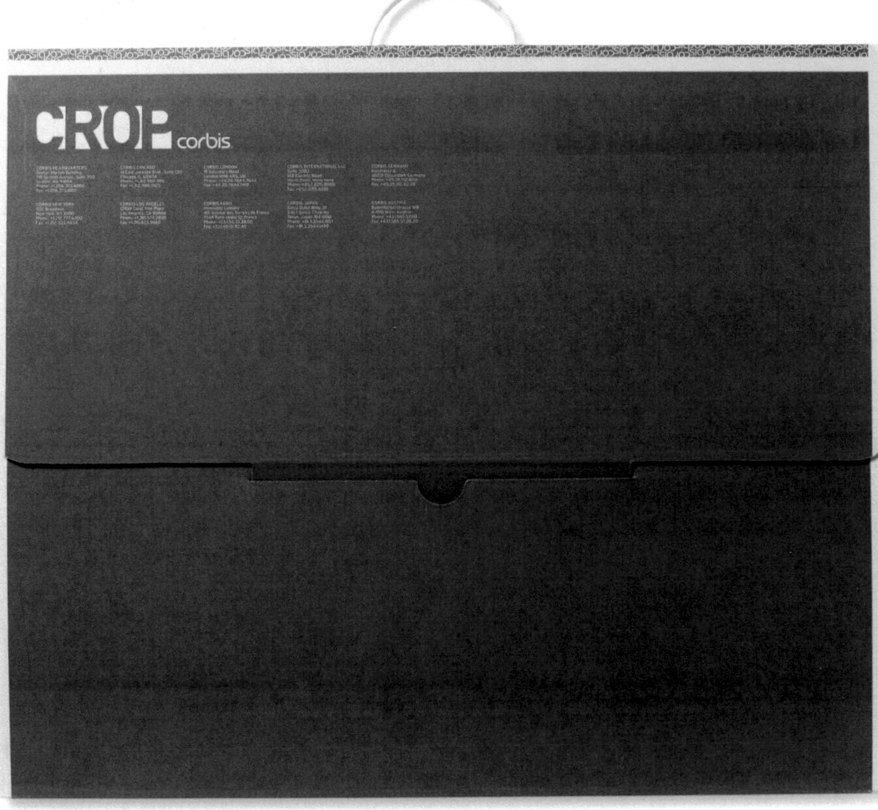
CROP corbis

Conte
Broc
Cat
Doc

Title:
De Theatercompagnie
–
Origin:
The Netherlands
–
Client:
De Theatercompagnie
–
Studio:
Experimental Jetset
–
Dimensions:
210mm x 148mm
8.3" x 5.8"

Description:
De Theatercompagnie is an Amsterdam theatre group, which recently invited Experimental Jetset to design its graphic identity. Experimental Jetset decided to carry out the commission in a 'few successive steps, rather than to design everything at once. That's why we focused foremost on the graphic design of the posters for [the theatre's] first play of 2005, an adaptation of the epic *Gilgamesh*.'
–
The brochure for *Gilgamesh* is a two-sided A2 poster, folded to an A5 booklet. While one side of the sheet displays all the relevant information, arranged as separate pages, the other side is a typographic poster displaying the name of the play, the name of the theatre group and two phrases ('Death is blind', 'just as blind as we are') from the play. The brochure uses folding techniques Experimental Jetset had previously developed in their work for the Stedelijk Museum CS.
–
The work is a fine example of the studio's robust typographic style: extensive use of large point sizes, lower-case lettering, a limited palette of strong colours and a marked absence of photographic content. It is classically Dutch, but with the group's distinctive flavour.

compagnie
theater
tehuur
compagnie
tehuur
tehuur
tehuur
theater
tehuur
tehuur
tehuur
tehuur
tehuur

theater
tehuur
tehuur

gilgamesj
de theater
compagnie
gilgamesj
compagnie
theater
25 januari
26 maart 05

seizoen
005
006
de theater
compagnie

www.
theater
compagnie
.nl

dood
blind
net
zo
blind
als
wij
de theater
compagnie
gilgamesj

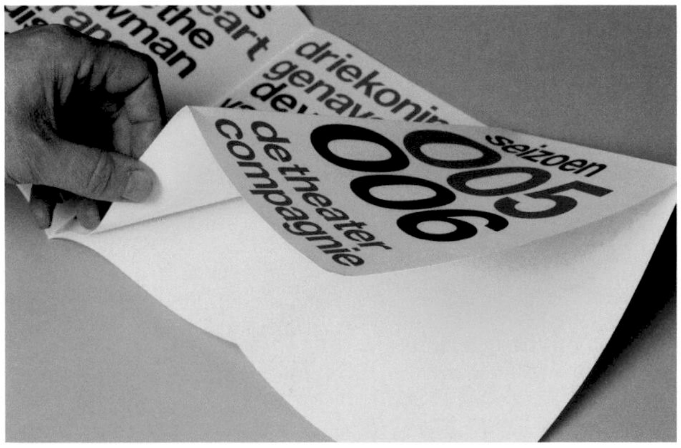
seizoen
005
006
de theater
compagnie

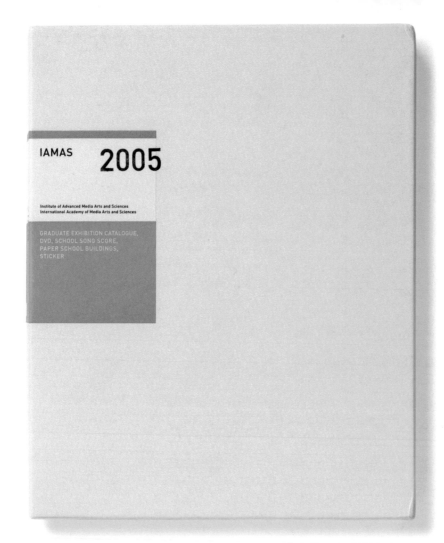
IAMAS
2005
Institute of Advanced Media Arts and Sciences
International Academy of Media Arts and Sciences
GRADUATE EXHIBITION CATALOGUE,
DVD, SCHOOL SONG SCORE,
PAPER SCHOOL BUILDINGS,
STICKER

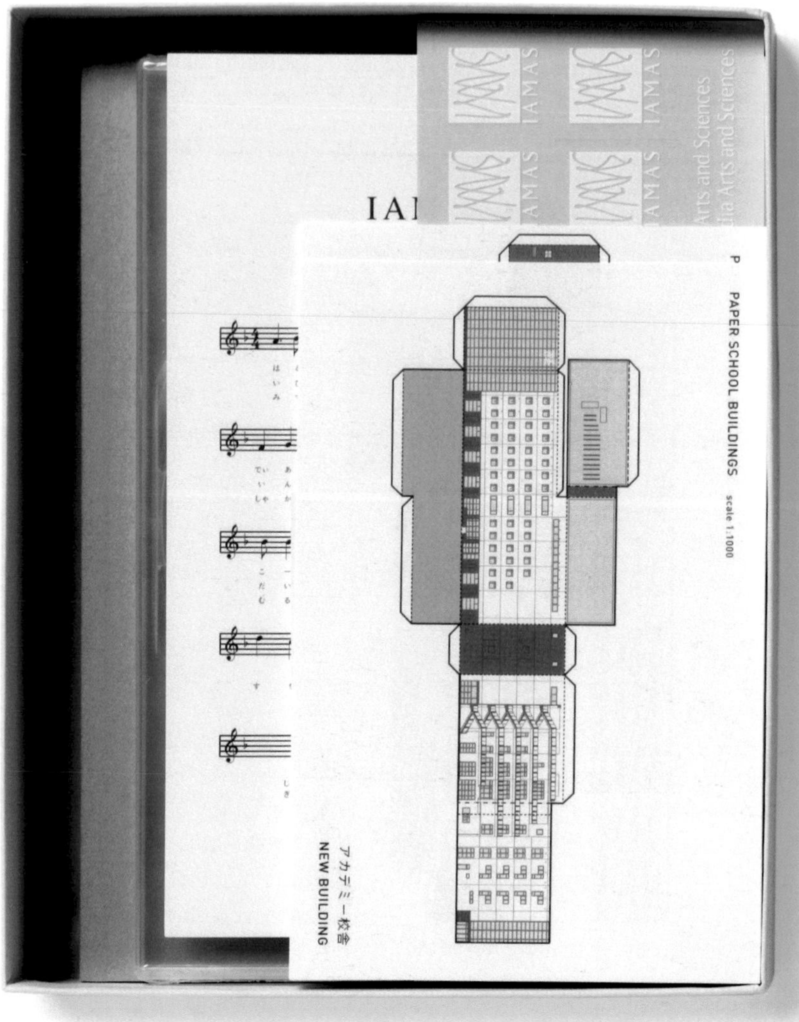
PAPER SCHOOL BUILDINGS
scale 1:1000
アカデミー校舎
NEW BUILDING

Title:
IAMAS 2005

–

Origin:
Japan

–

Client:
Institute of Advanced Media Arts & Science (IAMAS)

–

Designers:
Shoko Ito
Aiko Inada
Hiroko Terawaki
Yosuke Nakanishi
Chiaki Noji
Ken'ichi Hagihara

–

Dimensions:
197mm x 148mm
7.7" x 5.8"

Description:
The designers were briefed to create a catalogue and DVD for the IAMAS 2005 graduate exhibition. The document was also required to act as an annual report cataloguing events at this Japanese art and media school during 2004.

–

Rather than design the customary brochure with CD attached, they used a box – a 'toy box' – with a lift-off lid and containing numerous novelty items intended to provide graduates with mementoes of their time at IAMAS. These included a perfect-bound graduate exhibition catalogue, a DVD, the school song as sheet music, a strip of rub-down logos, printed plans of various school buildings to be cut out and folded into models, stickers, and a smaller concertina-formatted booklet.

–

The design team was under strict budget controls. To minimize costs they used sturdy white boxes already in the school's possession. To reduce outgoings further, the designers applied two colour stickers to each box, and then stamped the date of the project on each box by hand.

IAMAS
ANNUAL
2005
PAPER SCHOOL BUILDINGS

IAMAS
2005
IAMAS
Institute of Advanced Media Arts and Sciences
International Academy of Media Arts and Sciences
GRADUATE EXHIBITION CATALOGUE,
DVD, SCHOOL SONG SCORE,
PAPER SCHOOL BUILDINGS,
STICKER
2005

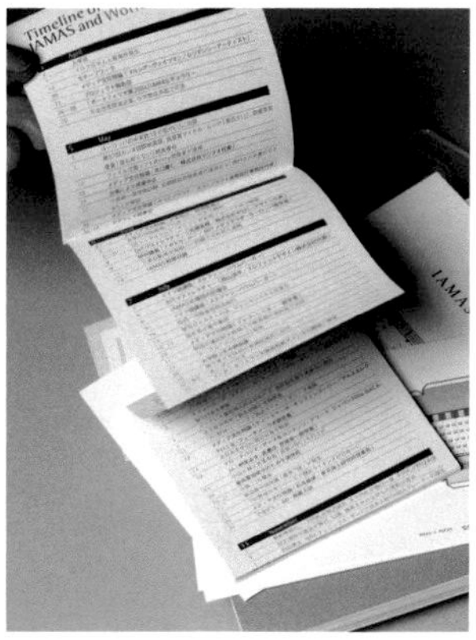

–
–
–
Contem
Broc
Cat
Doc
–
–
–
–
–
–
–
–
–
Title:
School Buildings: The State of Affairs
–
Origin:
Switzerland
–
Client:
Birkhauser – Publishers for Architecture
–
Designers:
Alberto Vieceli
Tania Prill
Kristina Milkovic
–
Dimensions:
300mm x 231mm
11.8" x 9.1"
–
–
–
–
–
–

Schulhausbau
Der Stand der
Dinge
Hochbaudepartement der Stadt Zürich
Eidgenössische Technische Hochschule Zürich/ETH Wohnforum
Schul- und Sportdepartement der Stadt Zürich
Pädagogische Hochschule Zürich
Der Schweizer Beitrag im internationalen Kontext
School Buildings
The State of
Affairs
The Swiss Contribution in an International Context
BIRKHÄUSER

112
d
Erweiterung Quartierschule Scherr
Scherr Neighbourhood School, extension
Zürich-Oberstrass, Switzerland
Patrick Gmür, Zürich
Die Halle/the hall
Buntes Innenleben
A Colourful Interior

50
51

–
–
–

Contemporary
Brochures
Catalogues
Documents

–
–
–
–
–
–
–
–
–

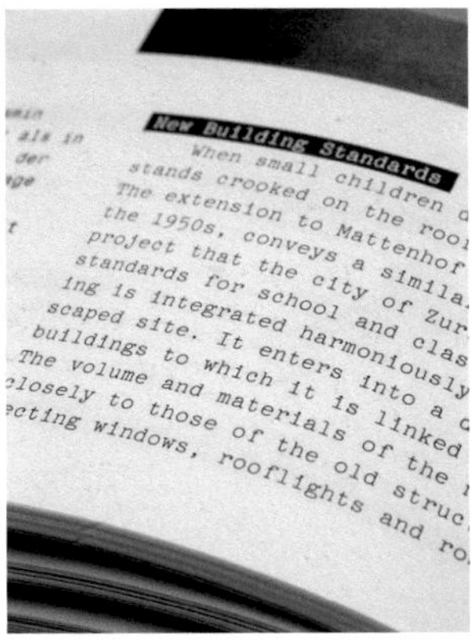
New Building Standards

Description:
Swiss designers Alberto Vieceli, Tania Prill and Kristina Milkovic have produced an elegant catalogue to accompany an exhibition of school architecture held in Zurich. The book features 31 projects and buildings from Switzerland and other European countries. The document is described as an 'independent reference work'.

–

The designers have created a volume that turns a potentially dull subject into a lively and engaging one. The catalogue undoubtedly succeeds as a 'reference work' – it contains diagrams, schematics and plans – but it also functions as an accessible and readable document, with none of the graphic design pedantry normally associated with this sort of semi-official publication.

–

The document, although conventionally bound, uses a mix of paper stocks and jumps between mono images, full-colour images, pages of letterforms, computer-generated illustrations and some unexpected, child-like layouts. The designers make bold use of Cooper Black to create a compelling document.

–
–
–
–
–
–

–
–
–
Contem
Broc
Cat
Doc
–
–
–
–
–
–
–
–
–
Title:
The Open University Brand Design Guidelines
–
Origin:
UK
–
Client:
The Open University
–
Studio:
North
–
Dimensions:
302mm x 210mm
11.9" x 8.3"
–
–
–
–
–
–

The Open University
Brand Design Guidelines

–
–
–

Contemporary
Brochures
Catalogues
Documents

–
–
–
–
–
–
–
–
–

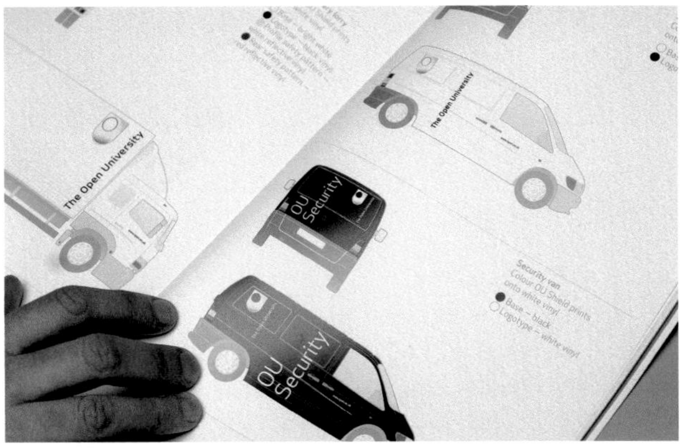

The Open University
The Open University
OU Security
OU Security

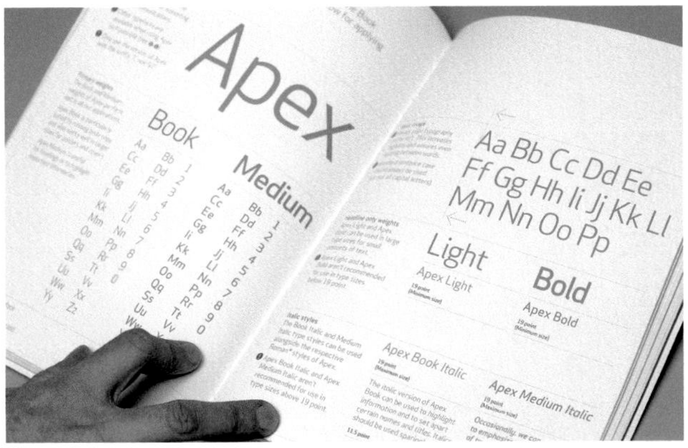

Apex
Book
Medium
Aa Bb Cc Dd Ee
Ff Gg Hh Ii Jj Kk Ll
Mm Nn Oo Pp
Light
Apex Light
Bold
Apex Bold
Apex Book Italic
Apex Medium Italic

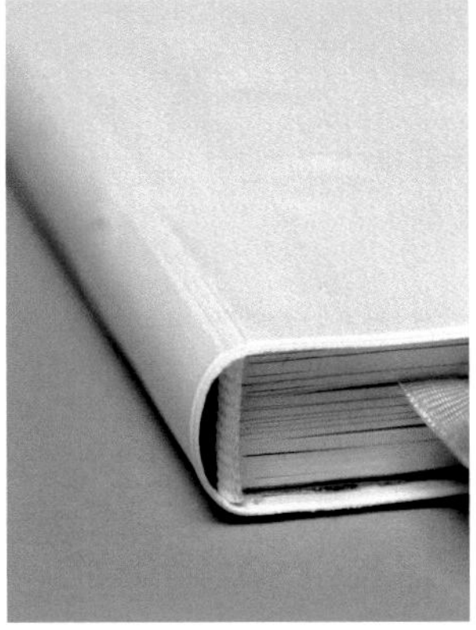

3.3 The Shield and colour
The Shield works well against all but four of the colours in the OU Colour Palette. The exceptions are OU Blue, OU Beige, Mid Grey and Light Grey, which are too similar in tone causing the Shield to lose definition and clarity.
Colour Shield
Greyscale Shield
Monotone Shield
OU Blue
OU Beige
OU Mid Grey
OU Light Grey

Description:
The Open University is one of the great success stories in modern education. It is the UK's only university dedicated to 'distance learning'. The OU has around 150,000 undergraduates and more than 30,000 postgraduate students. Nearly all OU students are part-time; many work during the day and study remotely in their spare time. The university was founded in the 1960s, and its first students enrolled in 1971.

–

North was commissioned to create an identity manual that covered every aspect of the university's brand identity, from business cards to vehicle liveries, from publications to merchandise. The manual has an embossed PVC cover (for durability); it uses CMYK plus one special colour, and 1,000 copies were produced.

–

The OU employs around 200 in-house designers, as well as regularly commissioning numerous external agencies. With this number of people involved in producing communication materials it is essential to have a practical document providing clear guidelines. The clarity and thoroughness with which this document is executed provide a master class in information design.

–
–
–
–
–
–

–
–
–
Contem
Broc
Cat
Doc
–
–
–
–
–
–
–
–
–

Title:
Mirage
–
Origin:
UK
–
Client:
Mirage
–
Studio:
Multistorey
–
Dimensions:
296mm x 210mm
11.6" x 8.3"
–
–
–
–
–
–

MIRAGE

Description:
Mirage is a stand-alone fashion boutique in London. Design duo Multistorey were invited to produce a promotional brochure for the shop that would, for financial reasons, last longer than one season.

'We decided to explore the visual interpretation of a mirage, the hot sun and the trick of light', notes designer Rhonda Drakeford. 'We styled the fashion shoot using clothing from the shop that had strong shapes that would look good in silhouette. A powerful circular backlight was used and kept in shot to create the silhouetted clothes. This gave us the opportunity to show clothing, but in a way that did not reveal details such as colour, which meant the brochure could be used for more than one season.'

'The photography was then printed onto translucent tracing-paper stock, and the pages were positioned with the backlight lined up on the same point each time. The central card-weight section was printed with an abstract image of a sun made from layered coloured trace that had been scanned on a flatbed scanner. The centre of this sun was lined up with the backlight from the fashion images, creating the illusion of being the actual light source for the images.'

MIRAGE

–
–
–
Conte
Broc
Cat
Doc
–
–
–
–
–
–
–
–
–

Title:
Swiss Design 2004 – Innovation
–
Origin:
Switzerland
–
Client:
Swiss Federal Office of Culture
–
Studio:
Elektrosmog,
with Alex Trüb
–
Dimensions:
290mm x 216mm
11.4" x 8.5"
–
–
–
–
–
–

Swiss Design
2004
Innovation –
Textes sur ce thème
Innovation –
Texts on the topic
Lars Müller Publishers
ISBN 3-03778-044-4
8.04 2000 120047
Herausgegeben vom Bundesamt für Kultur
Publié par l'Office féderal de la Culture
Issued by the Swiss Federal Office of Culture

Seite/Page/Page 133
Sandrine Pel
Seite/Page/Page 139

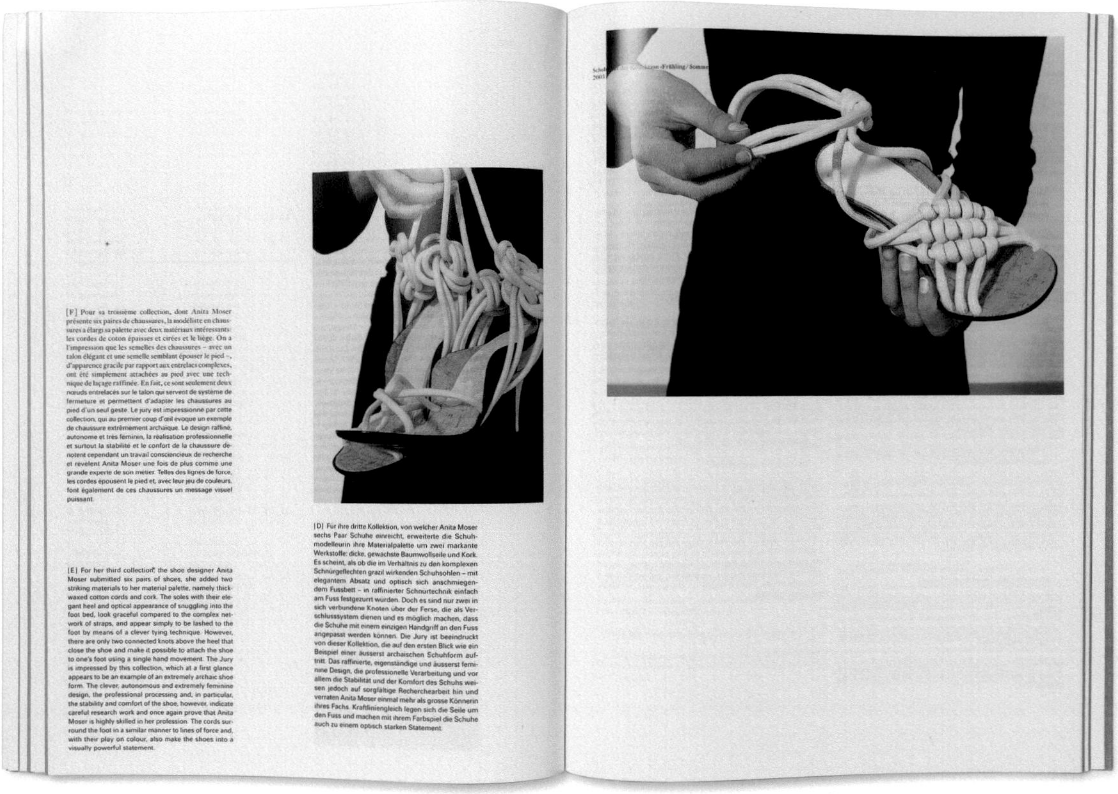

Laurent Benner
Marceline Berchtold
Franziska Burkhardt
Patricia Collenberg
Zuzana Ponicanova
Frédéric Dedelley

Description:
This handsome catalogue is for the annual Swiss Federation Design Competition, showcasing the prize-winning works and their designers. The design is by young Swiss design duo Elektrosmog (Valentin Hindermann and Marco Walser), working with Alex Trüb. Trüb's graphic work is featured as one of the prize-winners.

The 216-page catalogue (with six cover pages) is printed in three languages (German, French and English), and boasts a matt cover (Piano Jet 320g/m2) and coated text pages (Luxo Art 115 g/m2). Fonts used: DTL Fleishmann and Univers.

Contem
Broc
Cat
Doc

Title:
La fémis

Origin:
France

Client:
La fémis

Designer:
Philippe Apeloig

Dimensions:
210mm x 149mm
8.3" x 5.9"

L'ATELIER SCÉNARIO 2005
L'A TE LIER
SCÉ NA RIO
La femis

INITIATION AU CINÉMA
LES FONDAMENTAUX DE LA RÉALISATION
INI TIA TION
AU
CINÉ MA
La femis

L'ATELIER SCÉNARIO 2006
L'A TE LIER
SCÉ NA RIO
La femis

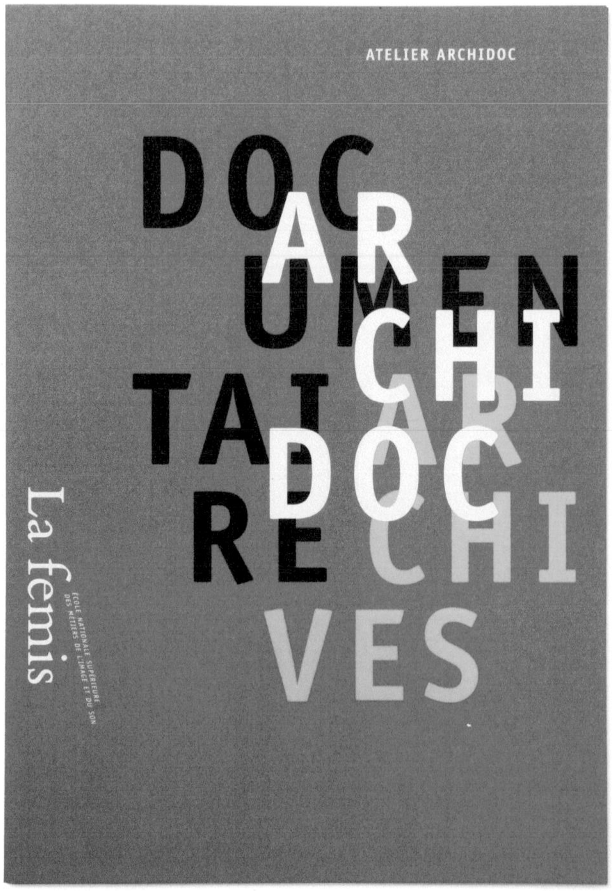
ATELIER ARCHIDOC
DOC UMEN TAI RE
AR CHI DOC
AR CHI VES
La femis

Description:
La fémis is a school in Paris, teaching cinematic and audio-visual arts. Set up in 1984, it is now more properly known as the Ecole Nationale Supérieure des Métiers de l'Image et du Son. Among other things, it offers training in the writing and developing of documentaries, and training courses for each stage in the making of a film. It offers workshops, master classes and seminars in all aspects of film and audio-visual education.

–

Paris-based designer Philippe Apeloig has created a suite of stylish literature for the school. Eschewing imagery of any kind, he has developed a typography-led approach, which imparts a look of serious, pedagogical intent. Using his signature device of overlapping type, Apeloig creates his own master class in typographic purpose and aesthetic poise.

–
–
–
–
–
–

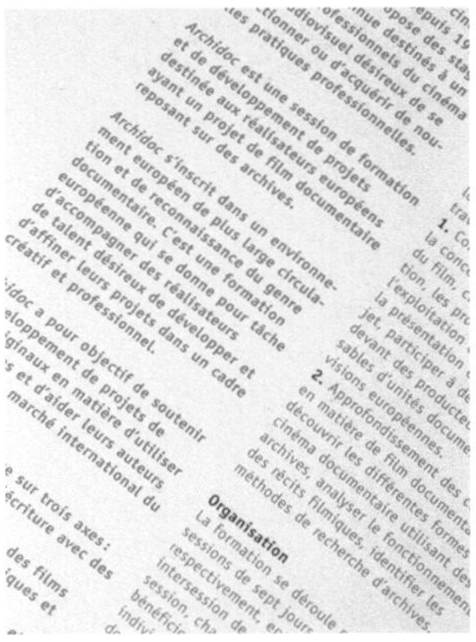

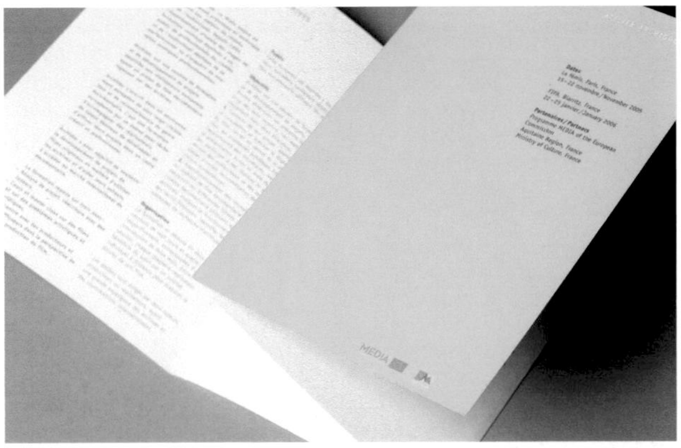

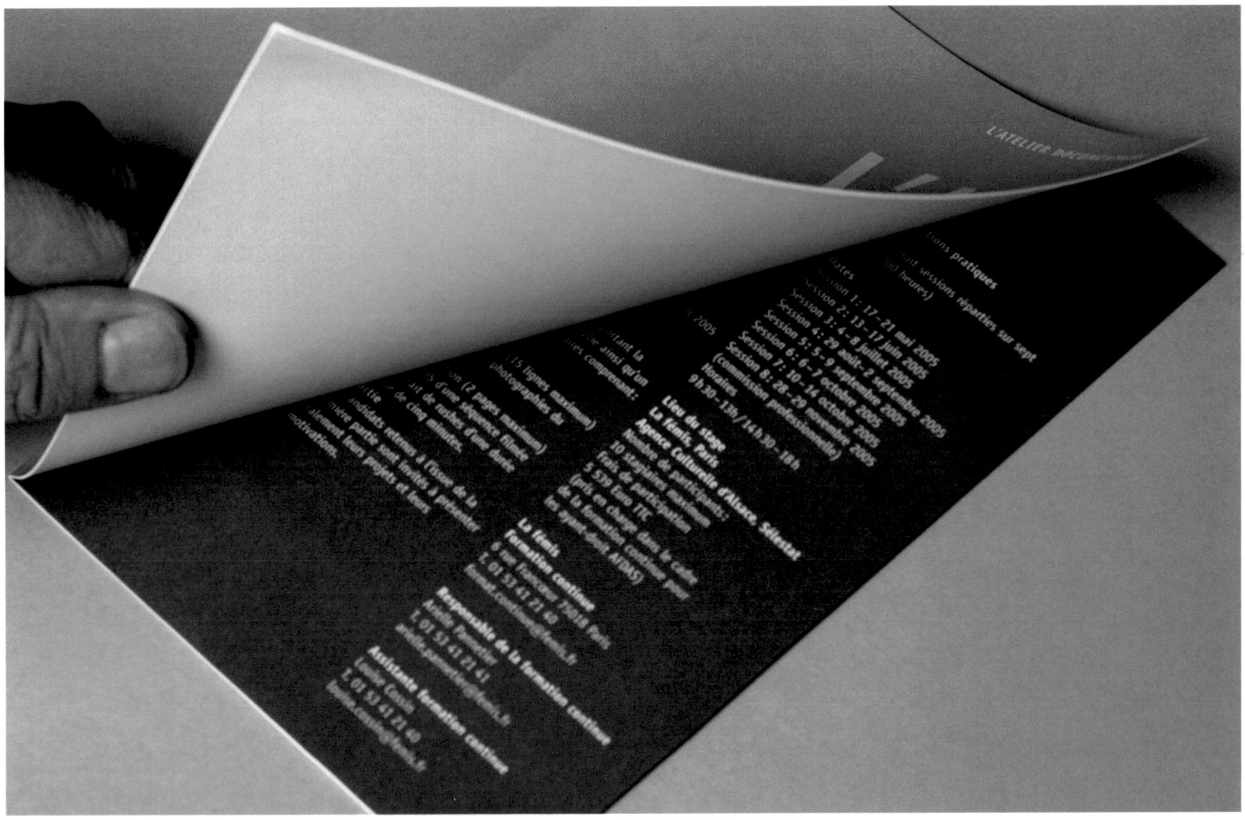

–
–
–
Contem
Broc
Cat
Doc
–
–
–
–
–
–
–
–
–

Title:
High Noon, High Nature, High Light
–
Origin:
The Netherlands
–
Client:
Self-initiated, with Johannes Schwartz
–
Studio:
Experimental Jetset
–
Dimensions:
330mm x 230mm
13" x 9"
–
–
–
–
–
–

HIGH
LIGHT
HIGH
BOLD
High Light / High Bold
ABCDEFGHIJKLMNOPQRSTUVWXYZ
abcdefghijklmnopqrstuvwxyz
A project by Johannes Schwartz
Graphic design by Experimental Jetset
Printed by drukkerij robstolk (r)
In the same series: **High Noon** (2003) and **High Nature I, II, III** (2004)
High Light / High Bold was published on the occasion of the exhibition **Principle Junk** that took place in February 2005 at PAKT in Amsterdam.
The exhibition **Principle Junk** has been realised in cooperation with Herman Verkerk (EventArchitecture).
Copyright (c) 2005 Johannes Schwartz
D
E
I
J
K
O

HIGH
NOON

HIGH
NATURE I
High Nature I, II, III
Three natural conditions.
A project by Johannes Schwartz.
High Nature I, II, III
Graphic design by Experimental Jetset.
Printed by drukkerij robstolk.
In the same series: **High Noon** (2003).
High Nature I, II, III was published on the occasion of the exhibition **Boys 97** that took place in January 2004 at Foam (Amsterdam Museum of Photography).
The exhibition **Boys 97** has been realised in cooperation with Herman Verkerk (EventArchitecture).
Copyright (c) 2004 Johannes Schwartz.

–
–
–
–
–
–
–
–
–

HIGH
BOLD

Description:
High Noon, *High Nature* and *High Light* form a trio of publications produced as a creative collaboration between photographer Johannes Schwartz and Dutch design trio Experimental Jetset. *High Noon* was published in 2003, and as Experimental Jetset explain: ‘When we designed *High Noon*, it was never our intention to start a whole series. But when Johannes approached us in 2004, to ask if we wanted to design a publication for an upcoming exhibition, we decided to stick with the “High”, and to continue the format. And so we designed *High Nature*.’
–
High Nature is a booklet that, when folded out, separates into three different elements; *High Light*, the third instalment, was published on the occasion of ‘Principle Junk’, an exhibition that took place in February 2005 at the PAKT art space in Amsterdam, in co-operation with architect Herman Verkerk.
–
All three documents contain examples of Experimental Jetset’s confident style: see-through elements, visual games, booklets doubling as posters, and unexpected inserts, bound together by their customary refined typography.
–
–
–
–
–
–

HIGH
NATURE I

Contem
Broc
Cat
Doc

Title:
Various catalogues
–
Origin:
France
–
Client:
Ultralab and Magda Danysz Gallery
–
Studio:
Labomatic
–
Dimensions:
215mm x 160mm
8.5" x 6.3"

Description:
Labomatic is a Paris-based group of graphic designers. Their sister group Ultralab comprises some of the members of Labomatic, plus others. It was established to explore the field of contemporary arts.
–
A series of low-budget booklets was produced to showcase both the collective and solo work of Ultralab. Each document is designed differently, but the size of the booklet remains the same, giving consistency to the group's published output. The need to split the group's commercial commissions from its art-based work is explained by Labomatic: 'We have to keep our commercial work and our art projects separate to avoid confusion. In France you can't live under the same name in two boxes at once.'
–
Magda Danysz owns the gallery that represents the group. For the past three years Labomatic have designed her seasonal invitations and books.

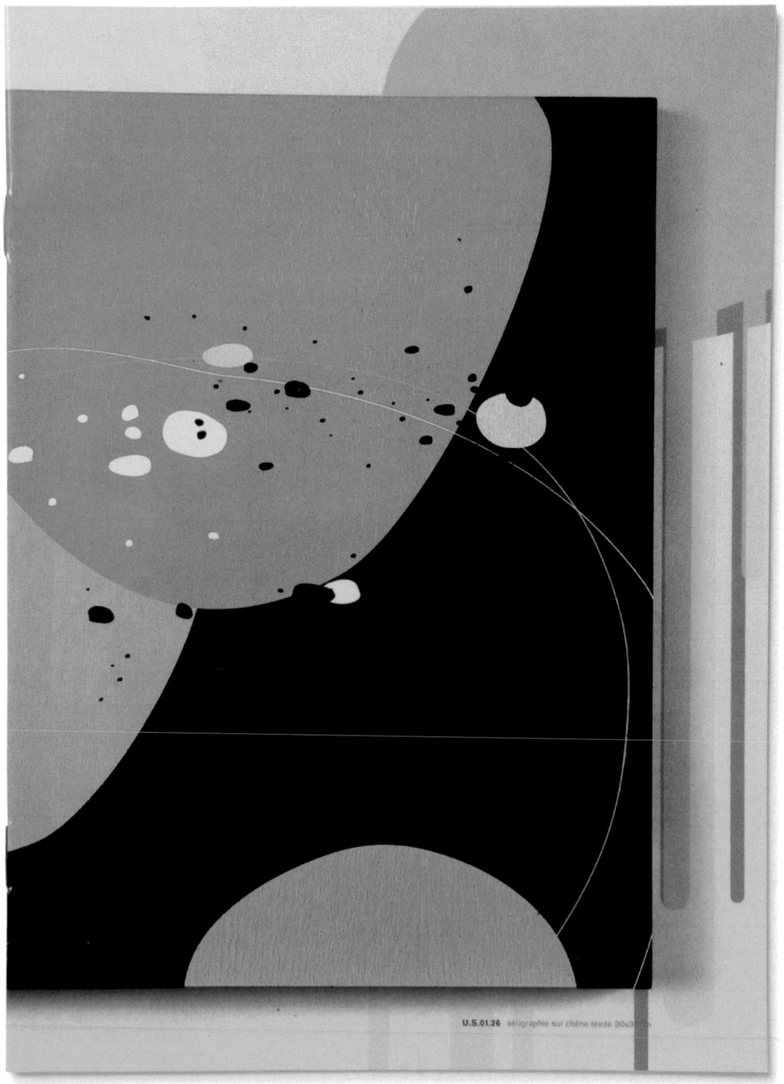

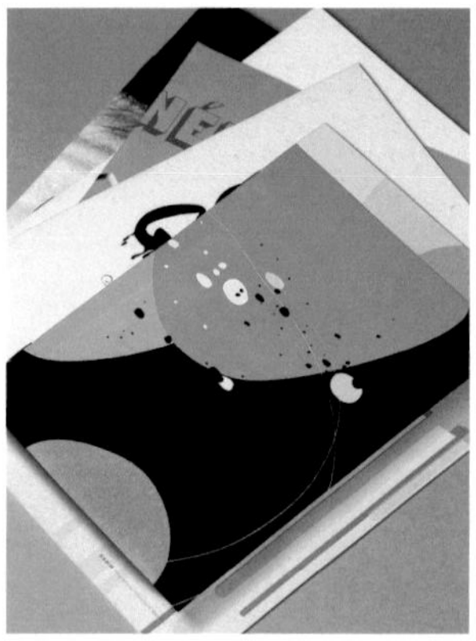

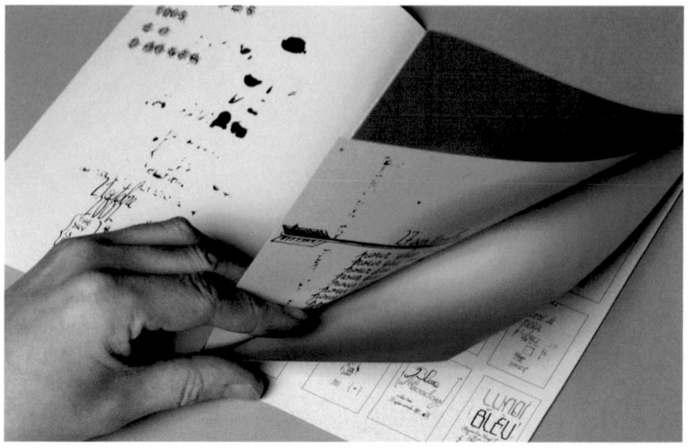

GOSIA
GALAS
Journal / 2001-2002

NÉRATION
.2001

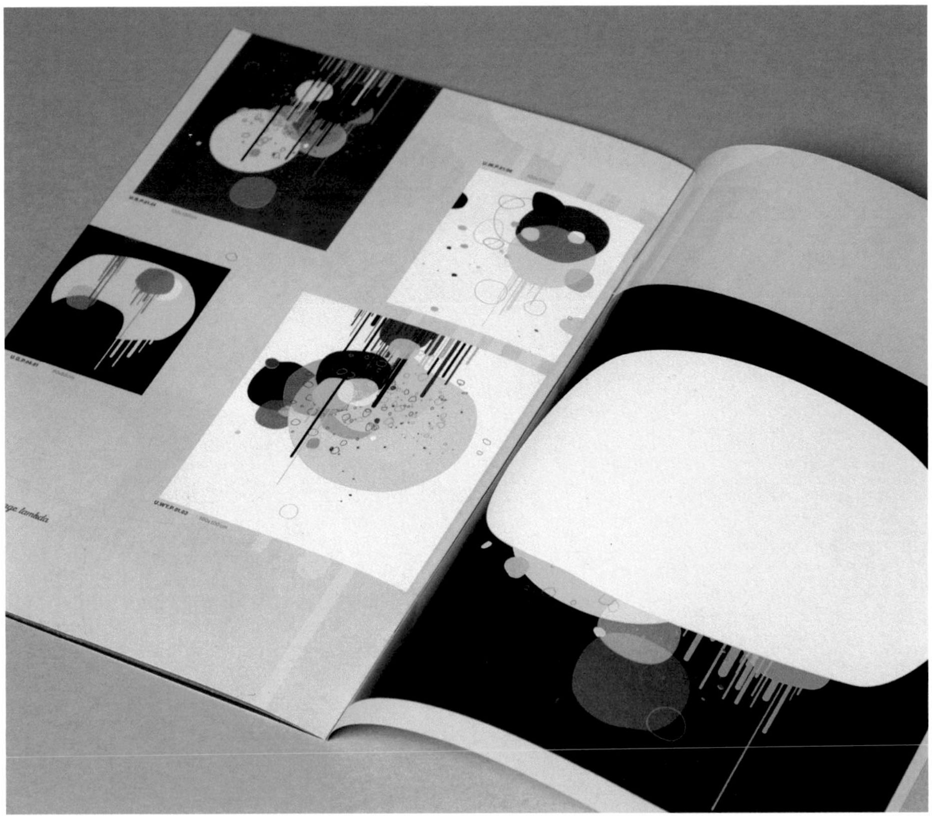

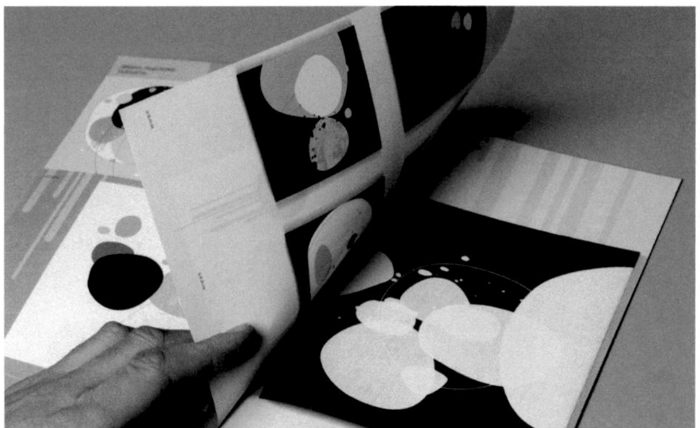

Conte
Broc
Cat
Doc

Title:
Animals

Origin:
UK

Client:
Haunch of Venison

Studio:
Spin

Dimensions:
277mm x 204mm
10.9" x 8"

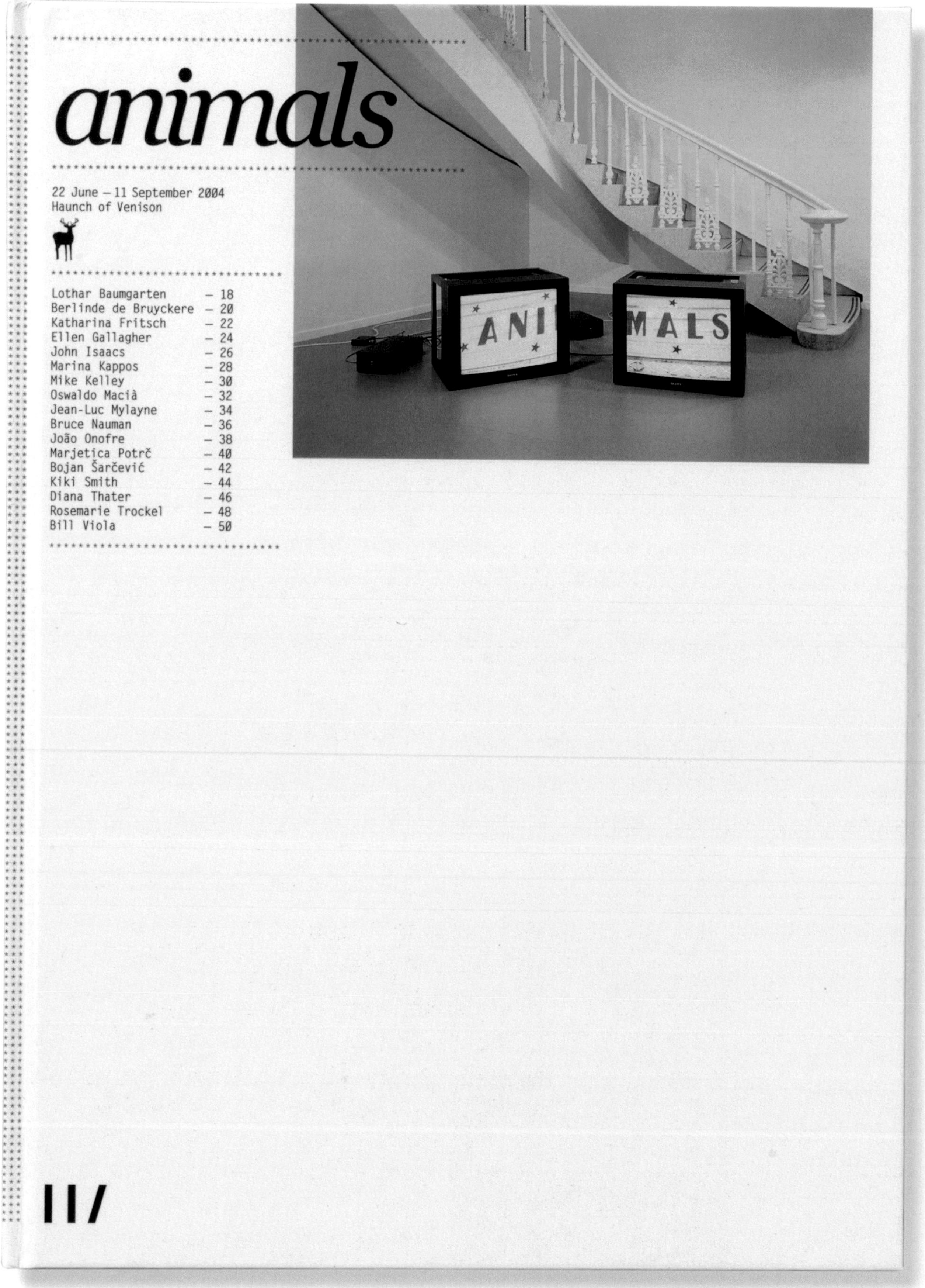
animals
22 June – 11 September 2004
Haunch of Venison
Lothar Baumgarten – 18
Berlinde de Bruyckere – 20
Katharina Fritsch – 22
Ellen Gallagher – 24
John Isaacs – 26
Marina Kappos – 28
Mike Kelley – 30
Oswaldo Macià – 32
Jean-Luc Mylayne – 34
Bruce Nauman – 36
João Onofre – 38
Marjetica Potrč – 40
Bojan Šarčević – 42
Kiki Smith – 44
Diana Thater – 46
Rosemarie Trockel – 48
Bill Viola – 50
ANI
MALS

Contemporary
Brochures
Catalogues
Documents

katharina fritsch

Animals – Haunch of

reprinted with the kind permission
of the author and Routledge.
ISBN No: 0-9540671-8-5

Description:
The Haunch of Venison is one of London's foremost galleries for modern and contemporary art. Centrally based, it hosts regular exhibitions by leading international artists. 'Animals' was an investigation into the ways artists have used animals in their work.

–

A hardback catalogue was designed by Spin. 'The theme of the exhibition fed directly into our solution', explains creative director Tony Brook. 'The fonts allude to both the Victorian humanization of animals (serif) and the contemporary use of animals for experiments (Monospace). The decorative aspects also relate to the Victorian and contemporary scientific idea.'

–

Bound within the elegant catalogue sits a smaller, mainly text-based document. 'This is part of the same thinking,' notes Brook, 'blending a Victorian journal with a scientific notebook. Our decision on format depends on our concept. Art catalogues usually involve a degree of negotiation, with us trying to squeeze as much as possible out of the budget. Hardback catalogues tend to be used for more established artists, an idea we try not to pay too much heed to.'

–
–
–
Contem
Broc
Cat
Doc
–
–
–
–
–
–
–
–
–

Title:
Phenoman
–
Origin:
USA
–
Client:
FIA art group/Publikum
–
Studio:
Karlssonwilker
–
Dimensions:
600mm x 307mm
23.5" x 12.1"
–
–
–
–
–
–

ПУБЛИКУМ
PUBLIKUM
ФЕНОМАН: карлсонвилкер
PUBLIKUM KALENDAR
2005
NEW VISIONS
IN VISUAL COMMUNICATIONS
karlssonwilker
VS
СРБИЈА
12 DANA U SRBIJI
12 DAYS IN SERBIA
Adventures in Real Time Design
with many colors inside!
www.artkalendar.com
PHENOMAN: karlssonwilker
PUBLIKUM CALENDAR
2005

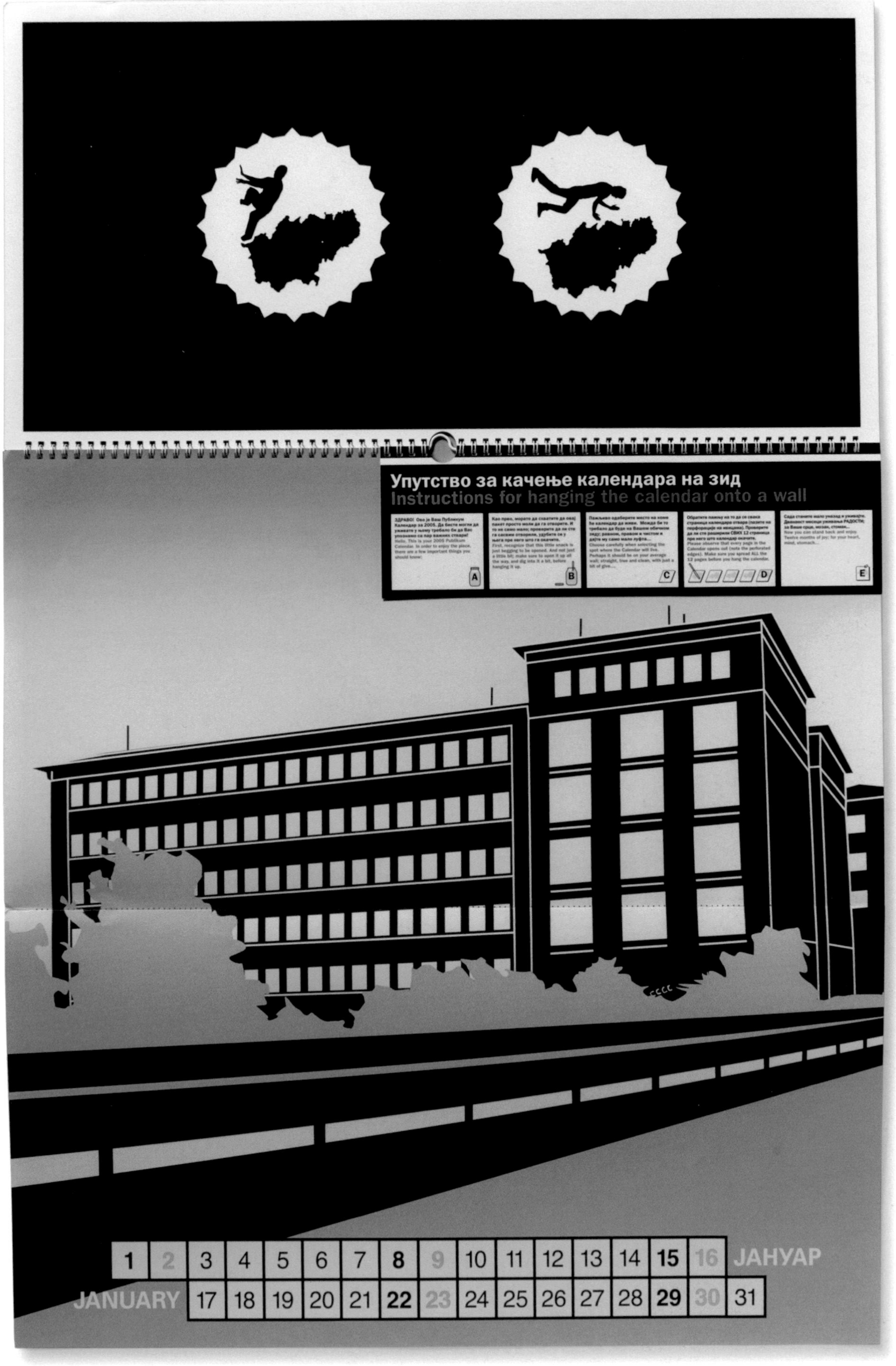
Упутство за качење календара на зид
Instructions for hanging the calendar onto a wall
A
B
C
D
E
1 2 3 4 5 6 7 8 9 10 11 12 13 14 15 16 JAHYAP
JANUARY 17 18 19 20 21 22 23 24 25 26 27 28 29 30 31

Description:
Hjalti Karlsson and Jan Wilker are a New York duo with an audacious portfolio of visually articulate and intellectually engaging design work. Before setting up their own studio they both worked for Stefan Sagmeister, and something of their former employer's iconoclastic wit can be seen in their work.

–

For the past 13 years the FIA art group and the printers Publikum of Belgrade, Serbia, have staged a publishing and design event called Phenoman. Karlssonwilker explain: 'We were invited to do the project for the year 2005. We were offered a calendar, a book and an exhibition as our blank canvas, to produce a work that connects with Serbia. We said that if they'd fly us to Serbia, we'd take on the task. We wanted to breathe the Serbian air. Neither of us had any connections with Serbia.'

–

The pair travelled to Serbia for a 12-day visit. They took laptops and a digital camera, and 'investigated and observed Serbian visual culture'. Each day they created a fresh artwork, resulting in 12 pieces of work, which formed the 12 pages of the Phenoman calendar of 2005.

–

'This is one of our all-time favourite projects', they state. 'One of the reasons is that we felt that the people of Serbia were our clients – and how often does it happen that you design for a country and its citizens?'

1 2 3 4 5 6 7 8 9 10 11 12 13 14 15 АПРИЛ
APRIL 16 17 18 19 20 21 22 23 24 25 26 27 28 29 30

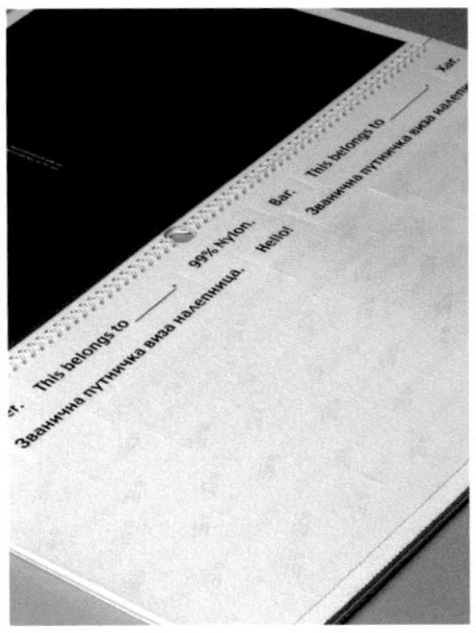
This belongs to ____. 99% Nylon. Bar. This belongs to
Званична путничка виза налепница. Hello!

100% Polyester. This belongs to ____. 99% Nylon. Bar. This belongs to
Cheers. Званична путничка виза налепница. Hello! Званична путничка виза
Ово не припада ____. No. Ово не припада ____. I love ____. Hi. I found
Хајде да то урадимо сутра. Не. Yes. Хајде да то урадимо сутра. Да. Go. Yes.
Вратићу се. Ти желиш ____. Branding. Вратићу се. Ти желиш ____. Talk to me.
Let's blame ____ for ____. Let's look for another ____. Louder. I am good.
Ја волим ____. Help! I want ____, too. Ја волим ____. Help! I want ____, too.
Awesome. Супер. Fantastic. Good morning. Especially for you. Let's just do this tomorrow.
You are ____. People are ____. Моји пријатељи ____ мене. Моји пријатељи ____ мене.
You are ____. This belongs to ____. I will be there. Jar. This belongs to
Cheers. Званична путничка виза налепница. Hvala. Званична путничка виза
Ово не припада ____. No. Ово не припада ____. I hate
Хајде да то урадимо сутра. Не. Yes. Хајде да то урадимо
Ти желиш ____. Ти желиш ____. I love Serbia.
for ____. Later. I live for
Awesome.

Hello!
I love

DAY NUMBER EIGHT
Rastavi da bi stvorio nešto drugo.
Disassemble to create something different.

Contem
Broc
Cat
Doc

Title:
CalArts flyers

Origin:
USA

Client:
Self-initiated

Studio:
Ed Fella

Dimensions:
431mm x 280mm
16.9" x 11"

Description:
American Ed Fella is a remarkable graphic designer. Self-taught, he started work in the commercial art studios of Detroit, where he worked quietly and conventionally until the age of 47, when he enrolled at the Cranbrook Academy of Art. There he became a pioneer of the new deconstructionist theories that revitalized visual communication in the 1980s and '90s. He is currently Professor of Graphic Design at California Institute of the Arts (CalArts).

To publicize his energetic programme of talks, lectures and exhibitions (he is in his 70s and, with self-deprecating wit, refers to himself as an 'exit-level designer') Fella prepares a mass of effervescent mini poster-flyers: neatly folded, they make compelling (and collectable) documentation that chronicles his activities.

Fella's work is characterized by highly illustrative typography; neither pure graphic design nor pure illustration, it is an invigorating amalgam of the two.

ART CENTER COLLEGE OF DESIGN
BOX 7197
CALIFORNIA
PASADENA
FROM
TO

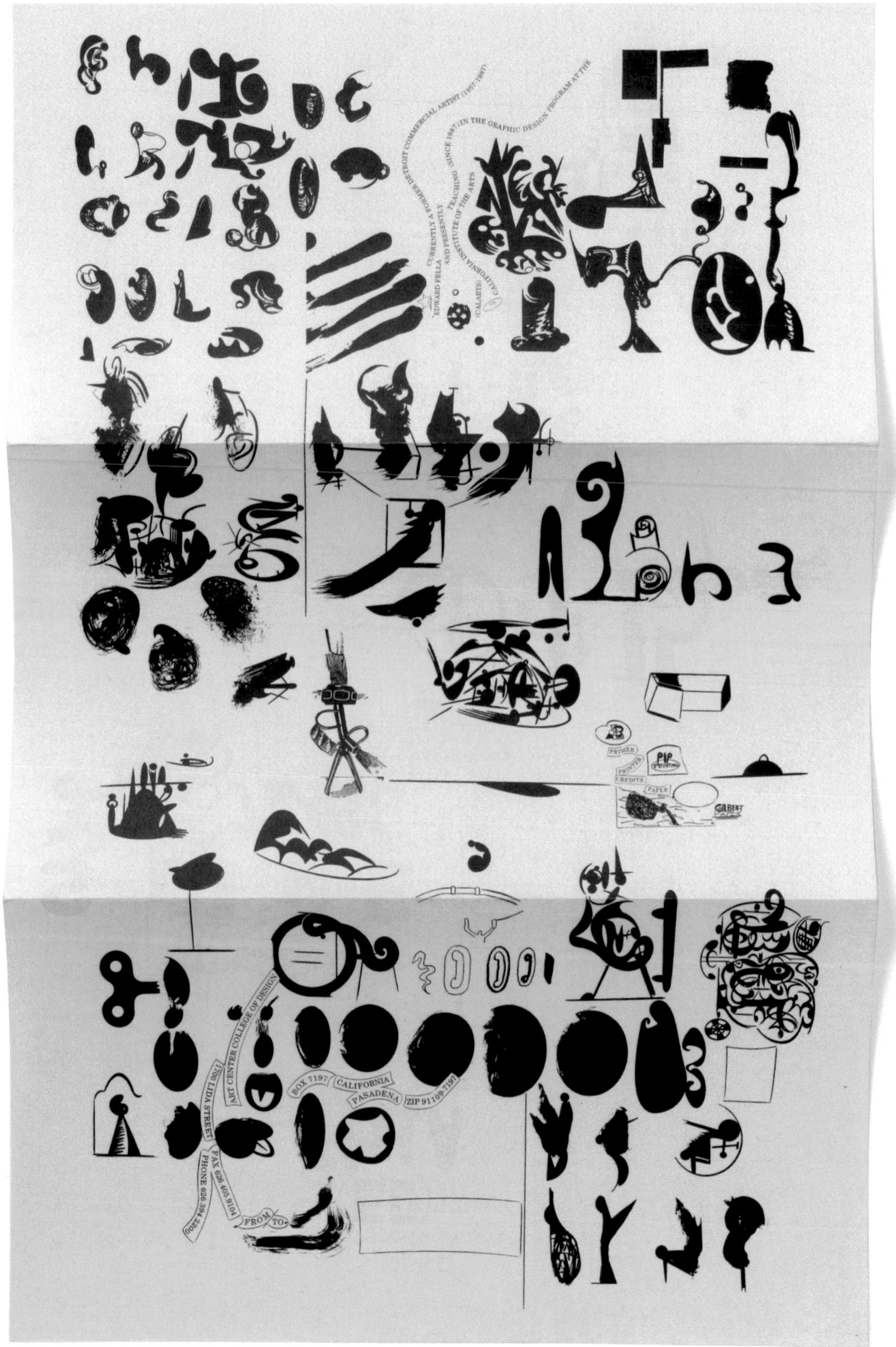
ART CENTER COLLEGE OF DESIGN
BOX 7197
CALIFORNIA
PASADENA
FROM
TO

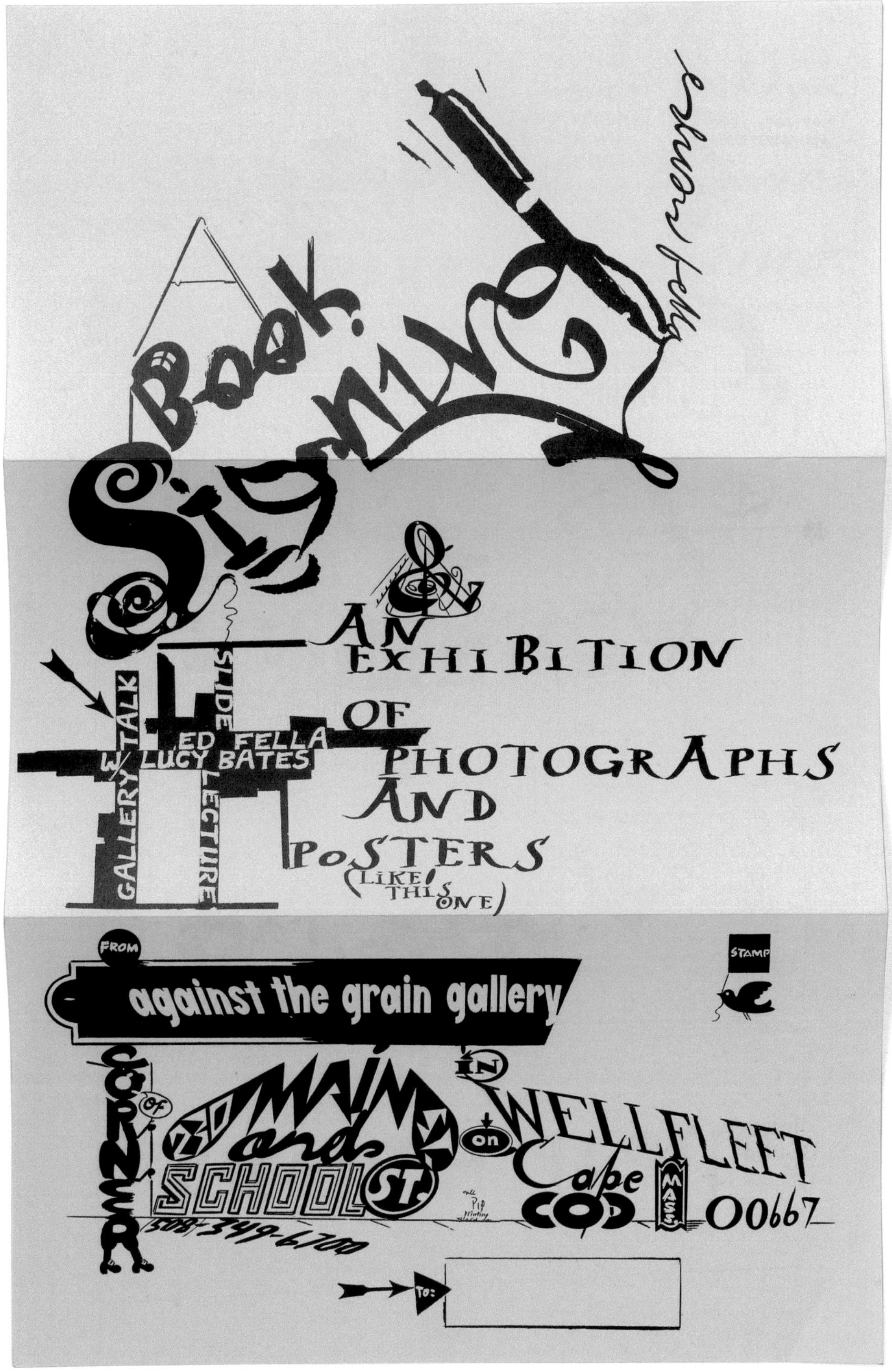
A Book Signing
edward fella
An Exhibition of Photographs and Posters (like this one)
Gallery Talk
Slide Lecture
Ed Fella w/ Lucy Bates
From
against the grain gallery
Stamp
Corner of 20 Main and School St.
in Wellfleet on Cape Cod Mass 00667
508-349-6700
To:

Sender
deliverer
Reciever

ed
Fella
SUBS

AMERICA

IMAGINE

–
–
–
Contem
Broc
Cat
Doc
–
–
–
–
–
–
–
–
–
Title:
Keith Tyson
–
Origin:
UK
–
Client:
Haunch of Venison
–
Studio:
Spin
–
Dimensions:
295mm x 420mm
11.6" x 16.5"
–
–
–
–
–
–

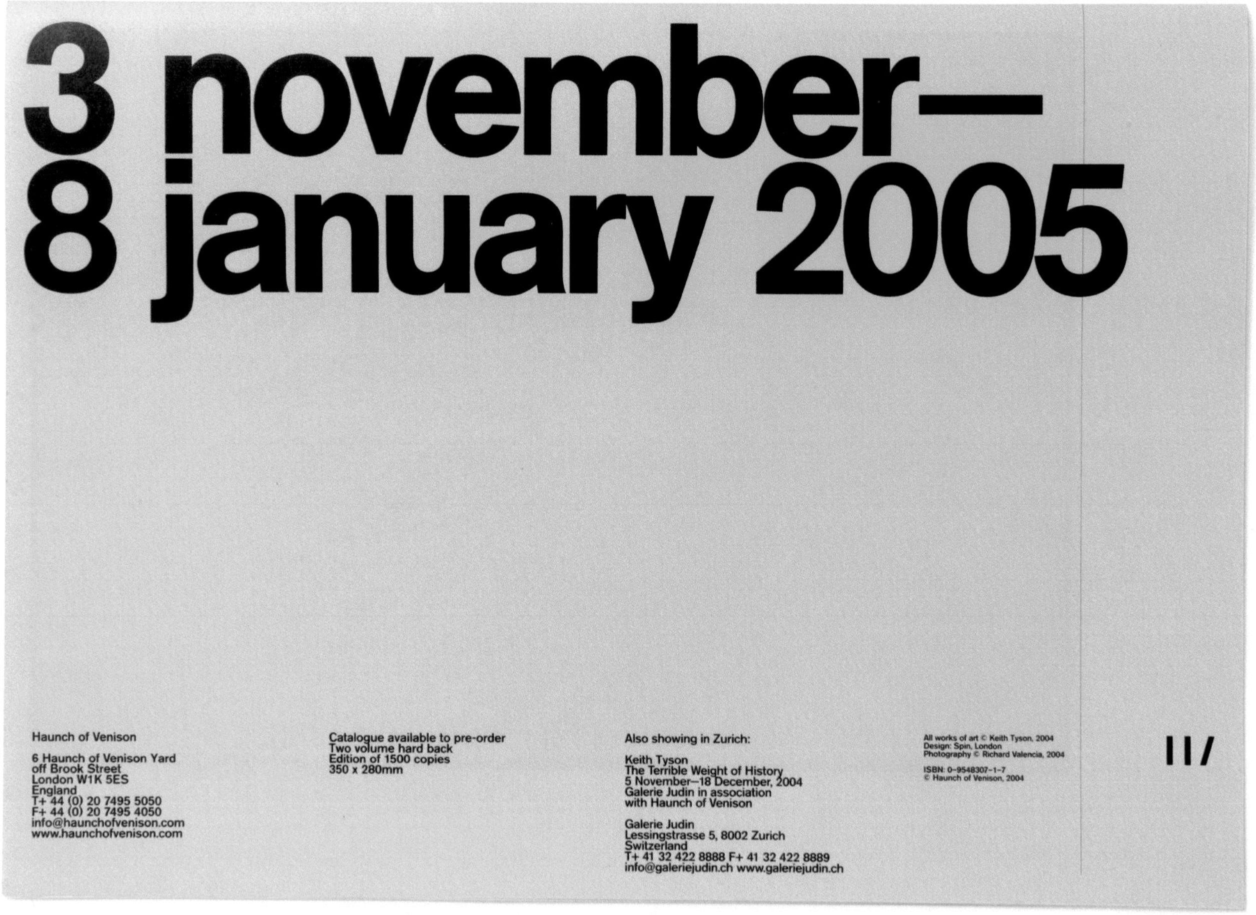
3 november—
8 january 2005
Haunch of Venison
6 Haunch of Venison Yard
off Brook Street
London W1K 5ES
England
T+ 44 (0) 20 7495 5050
F+ 44 (0) 20 7495 4050
info@haunchofvenison.com
www.haunchofvenison.com
Catalogue available to pre-order
Two volume hard back
Edition of 1500 copies
350 x 280mm
Also showing in Zurich:
Keith Tyson
The Terrible Weight of History
5 November–18 December, 2004
Galerie Judin in association
with Haunch of Venison
Galerie Judin
Lessingstrasse 5, 8002 Zurich
Switzerland
T+ 41 32 422 8888 F+ 41 32 422 8889
info@galeriejudin.ch www.galeriejudin.ch
All works of art © Keith Tyson, 2004
Design: Spin, London
Photography © Richard Valencia, 2004
ISBN: 0-9548307-1-7
© Haunch of Venison, 2004
II/

keith
tyson
geno/
pheno
paintings

Description:
In recent years London gallery Haunch of Venison has provided design studio Spin with numerous opportunities to create potent and evocative work. The studio's creative director, Tony Brook, describes the brief for an exhibition of the work of artist Keith Tyson: 'We were asked to create a strong identity for the event, plus a catalogue and advertising. We have a good understanding of what the gallery needs, and usually find our inspiration in some aspect of the artist's work. In Keith Tyson's case his work is incredibly complex and our response couldn't really hope to reflect it in any visual way, so we settled on a bold and graphically opinionated look that suggests something of the confidence Keith has.'

–

Does Brook find that he has to be 'respectful' towards the art he is asked to design for, or can he incorporate graphic thinking into the task? 'Depending on the client,' he notes, 'we might, for example, have no cropping of images, except as specific and agreed details. We might have no type on images except on covers and intros. There might be a request to have no text near an image, or a certain amount of space around it. Accurate reproduction is a high priority. Working for art galleries isn't really that dissimilar to working for a corporate client. I think in both cases you can use the guidelines to your advantage to create interesting work.'

–
–
–
–
–
–

3 november—
8 january 2005

–
–
–
Contem
Broc
Cat
Doc
–
–
–
–
–
–
–
–
–

Title:
Select. Arrange
–
Origin:
Switzerland
–
Client:
Vitra
–
Studio:
Cornel Windlin
–
Dimensions:
275mm x 212mm
10.8" x 8.3"
–
–
–
–
–
–

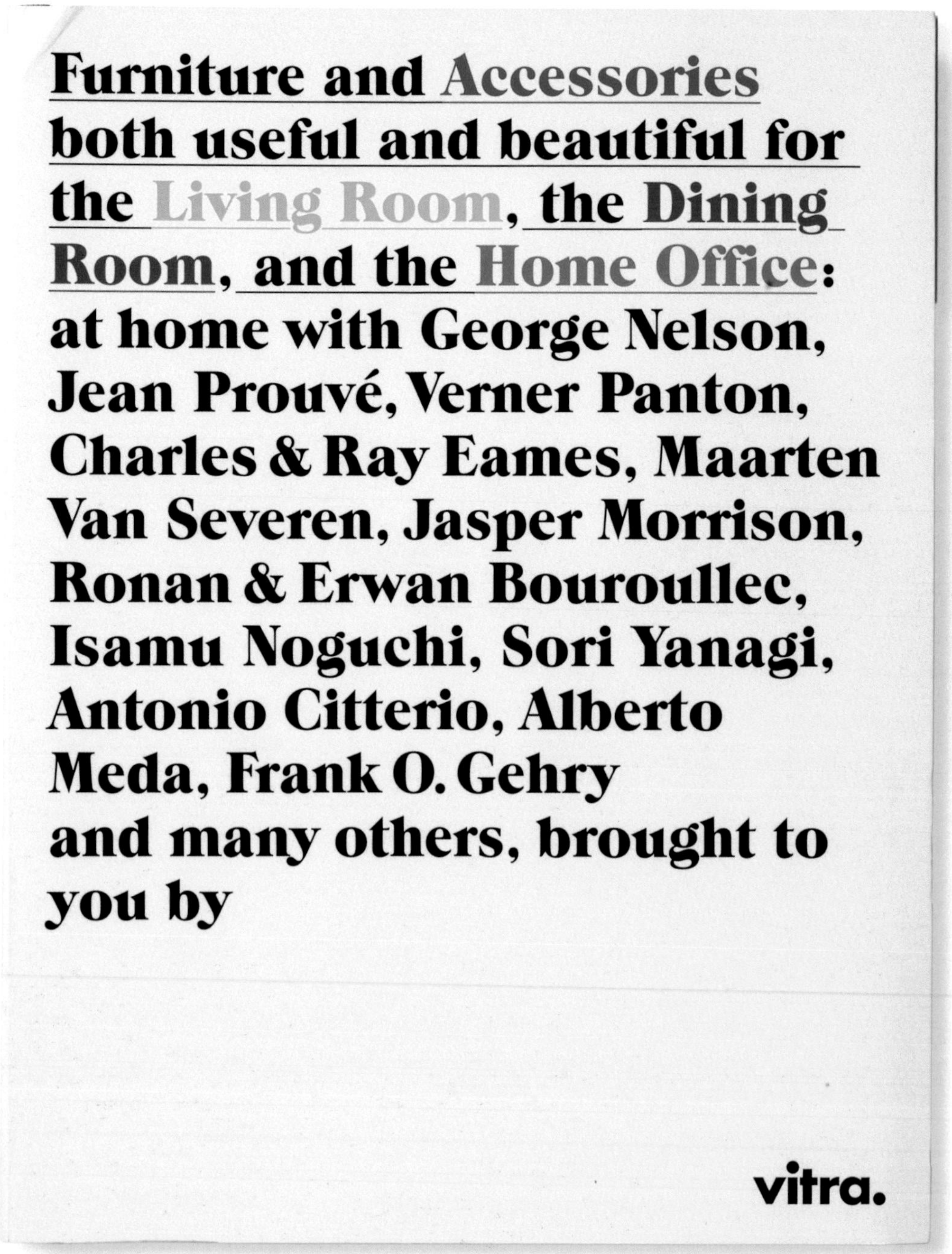
Furniture and Accessories
both useful and beautiful for
the Living Room, the Dining
Room, and the Home Office:
at home with George Nelson,
Jean Prouvé, Verner Panton,
Charles & Ray Eames, Maarten
Van Severen, Jasper Morrison,
Ronan & Erwan Bouroullec,
Isamu Noguchi, Sori Yanagi,
Antonio Citterio, Alberto
Meda, Frank O. Gehry
and many others, brought to
you by
vitra.

vitra.

vitra.
at home 2005 / English

arrange.
select.

–
–
–
–
–
–
–
–
–

GIMME
A
EAMES

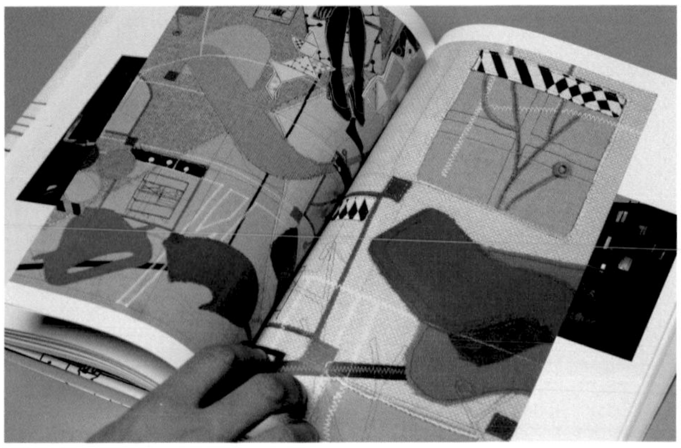

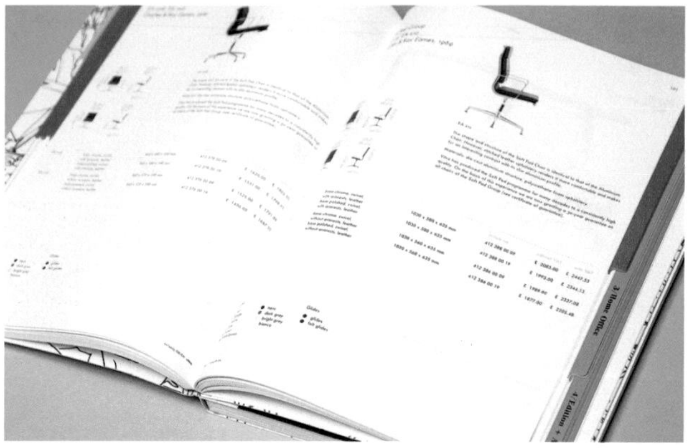

Description:
In 1988 Cornel Windlin moved from his native Switzerland to London, where he joined the studio of Neville Brody. He later followed in Brody's footsteps by becoming art director of *The Face*. He now runs his own Zurich-based studio.

–

Among Windlin's clients is Vitra, manufacturer of Modernist furniture for office and contract markets. The company recently decided to produce furniture for the home, and Windlin was invited to communicate this new venture to the public and to Vitra's dealers. Windlin's first act was to separate the two strands of Vitra: 'By completely separating the straight, "conventional" catalogue from the "inspirational" part', he notes, 'I gained more freedom to represent the product.'

–

Windlin also departed from the convention of always showing Modernist furniture in a clinical-looking setting. As he explains: 'I wanted to breathe life back into the world of perfect design, to present these design icons primarily as "nice pieces of furniture that you can live with, regardless of your lifestyle". I thought it was necessary to show that a nice place is not necessarily a dream home.'

–

'Typographically,' he states, 'I decided to continue with their existing choice of Futura, but to combine it with a new font that had more warmth and would provide contrast. Not being happy with the various Futuras on the market, we ended up designing a new, more geometric version.'

–
–
–
–

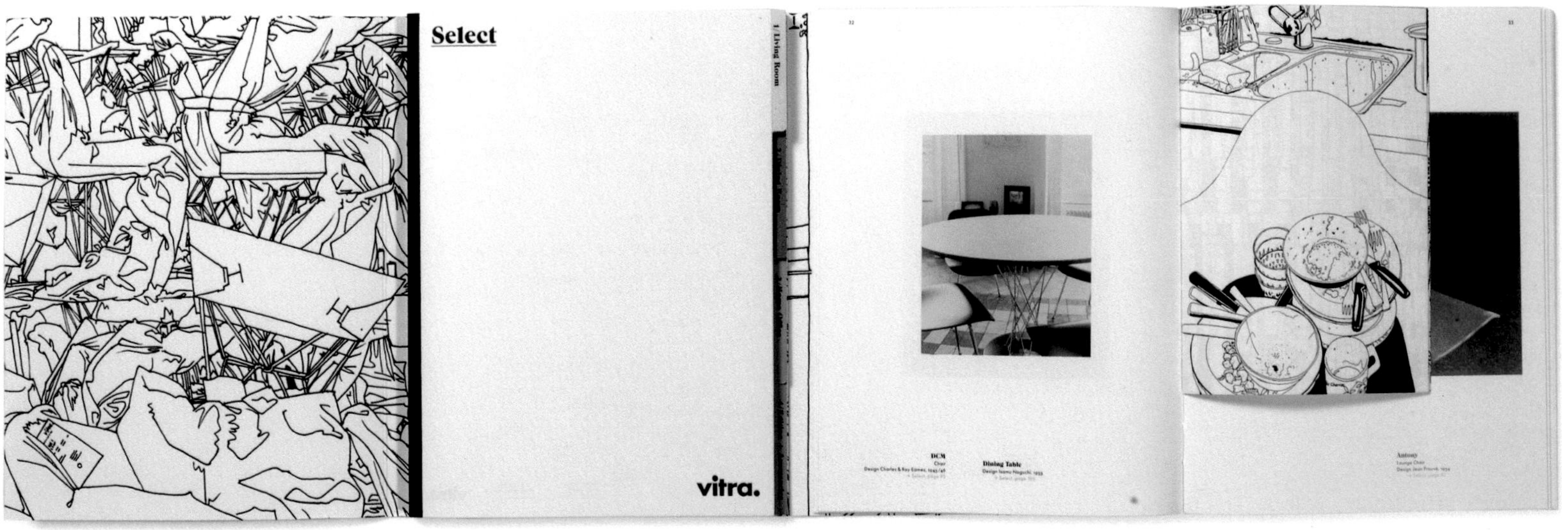
Select
1 Living Room
vitra.

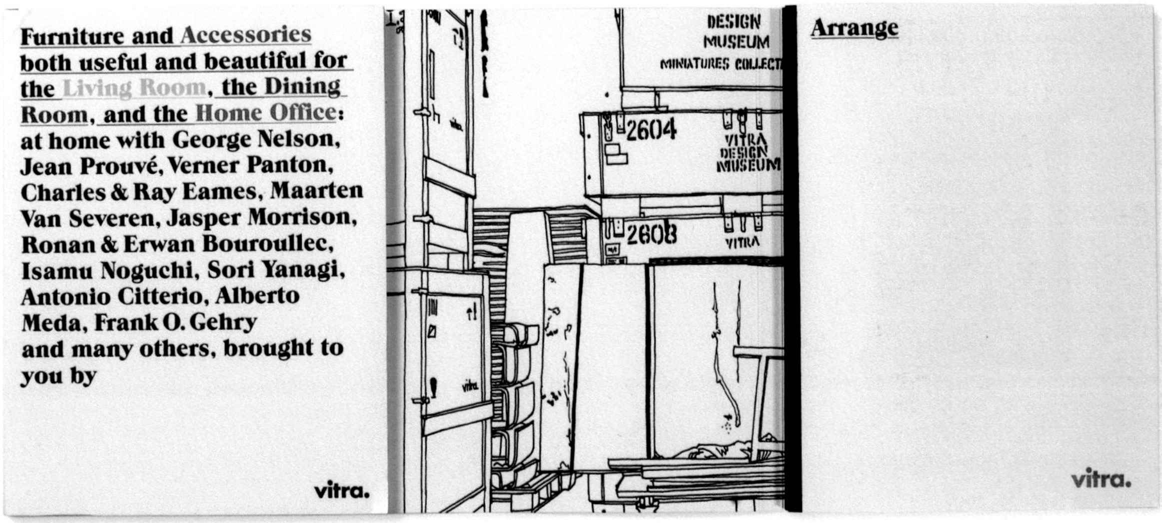
Furniture and Accessories both useful and beautiful for the Living Room, the Dining Room, and the Home Office: at home with George Nelson, Jean Prouvé, Verner Panton, Charles & Ray Eames, Maarten Van Severen, Jasper Morrison, Ronan & Erwan Bouroullec, Isamu Noguchi, Sori Yanagi, Antonio Citterio, Alberto Meda, Frank O. Gehry and many others, brought to you by
vitra.
DESIGN MUSEUM
2604
VITRA DESIGN MUSEUM
2608
VITRA
Arrange
vitra.

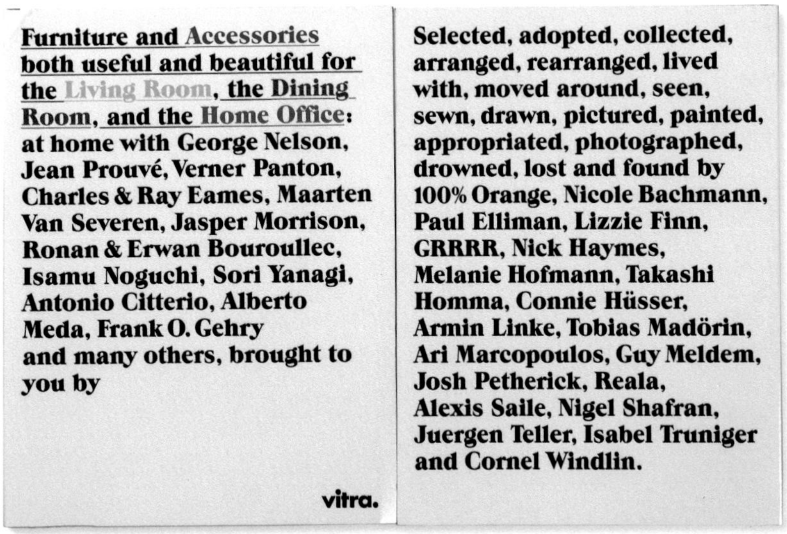
Furniture and Accessories both useful and beautiful for the Living Room, the Dining Room, and the Home Office: at home with George Nelson, Jean Prouvé, Verner Panton, Charles & Ray Eames, Maarten Van Severen, Jasper Morrison, Ronan & Erwan Bouroullec, Isamu Noguchi, Sori Yanagi, Antonio Citterio, Alberto Meda, Frank O. Gehry and many others, brought to you by
vitra.
Selected, adopted, collected, arranged, rearranged, lived with, moved around, seen, sewn, drawn, pictured, painted, appropriated, photographed, drowned, lost and found by 100% Orange, Nicole Bachmann, Paul Elliman, Lizzie Finn, GRRRR, Nick Haymes, Melanie Hofmann, Takashi Homma, Connie Hüsser, Armin Linke, Tobias Madörin, Ari Marcopoulos, Guy Meldem, Josh Petherick, Reala, Alexis Saile, Nigel Shafran, Juergen Teller, Isabel Truniger and Cornel Windlin.

Contem
Broc
Cat
Doc

Title:
Inspiration

Origin:
USA

Client:
Contractor Property Developers Company

Studio:
Werner Design Werks, Inc.

Dimensions:
241mm x 184mm
9.5" x 7.25"

INSPIRATION INSPIRATION
1215 Inspiration Parkway
Bayport, Minnesota 55003
ph: 651-556-4572
www.inspirationbayport.com
INSPIRATION

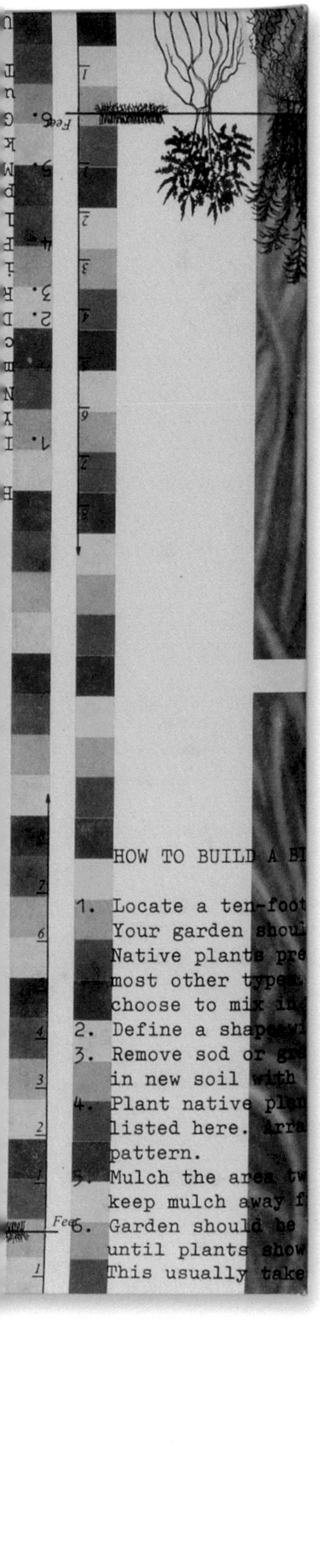

INSPIRATION. est. 2005
LIVING WITH
NATURE
INSPIRATION
est. 2005
a natural
neighborhood

INSPIRAT

INSPIRATION est. 2005
a natural neighbourhood

Page 158
–
–
–
Contemporary
Brochures
Catalogues
Documents
–
–
–
–
–
–
–
–
–
Description:
'Inspiration' is the name of a neighbourhood development committed to restoring 245 acres of land to its native prairie condition and to building homes that are sensitive to the environment. What the property developer is selling is more than land: it is a lifestyle for people nostalgic for a small town in a 'green' setting.
All of the elements that make up this document are designed to be warm and welcoming, and show home and nature juxtaposed in harmony. Ephemera are collected and displayed like bric-à-brac in a home. The brochure is designed to feel like recycled books and to show the high level of attention to detail that can be expected from the builders and developers of the site. The jacket unfolds to reveal both a decorative poster and a large, easy-to-use map that also makes an effective sales tool.
–
The document is mailed to potential buyers or handed out at the development site.
–
–
–
–
–
–

INSPIRATION
a natural neighborhood

1215 Inspiration Parkway
Bayport, Minnesota 55003
(651) 556-4572
www.inspirationbayport.com

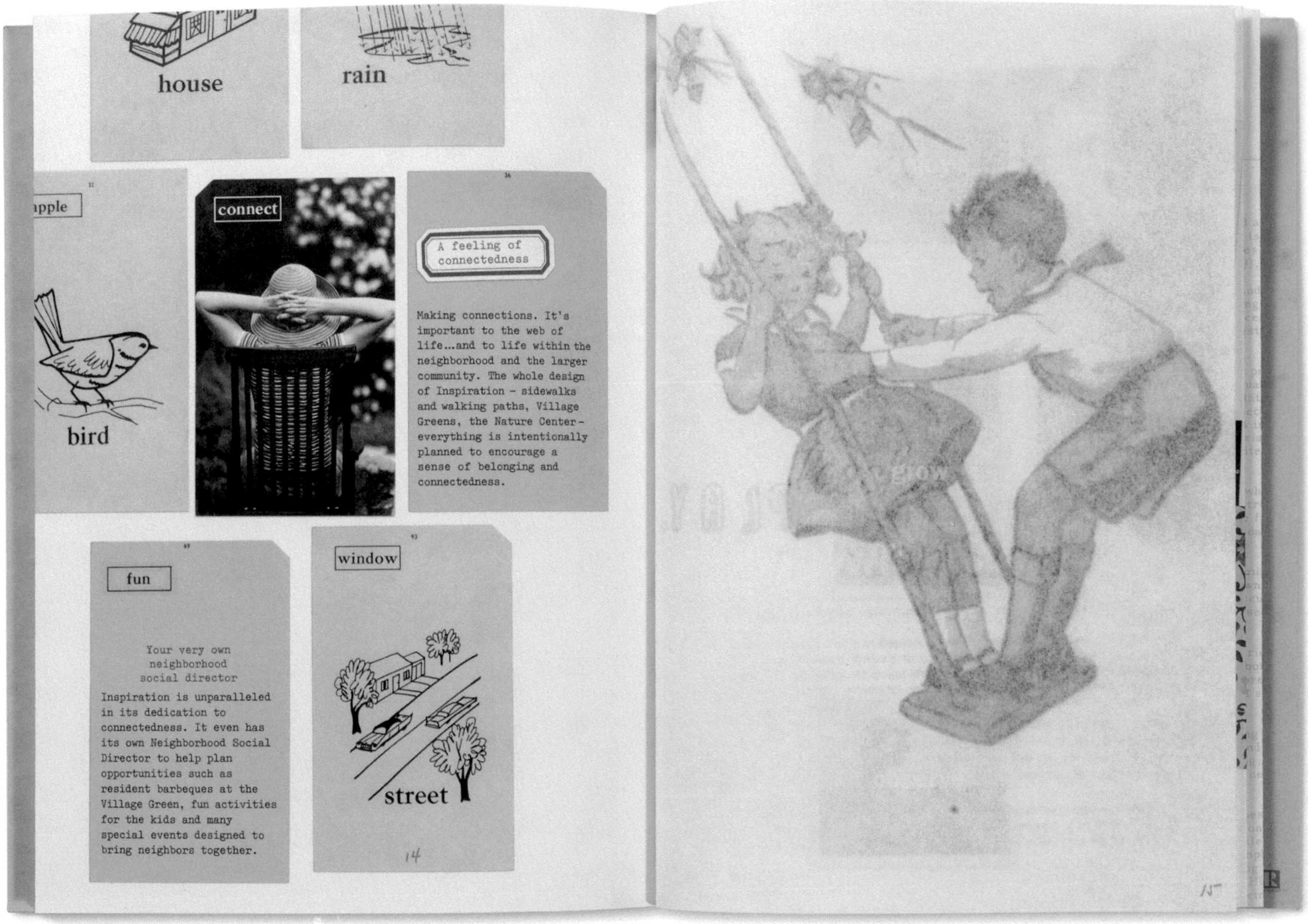
house
rain
apple
bird
connect
A feeling of connectedness
Making connections. It's important to the web of life…and to life within the neighborhood and the larger community. The whole design of Inspiration – sidewalks and walking paths, Village Greens, the Nature Center – everything is intentionally planned to encourage a sense of belonging and connectedness.
fun
Your very own neighborhood social director
Inspiration is unparalleled in its dedication to connectedness. It even has its own Neighborhood Social Director to help plan opportunities such as resident barbeques at the Village Green, fun activities for the kids and many special events designed to bring neighbors together.
window
street
14
15

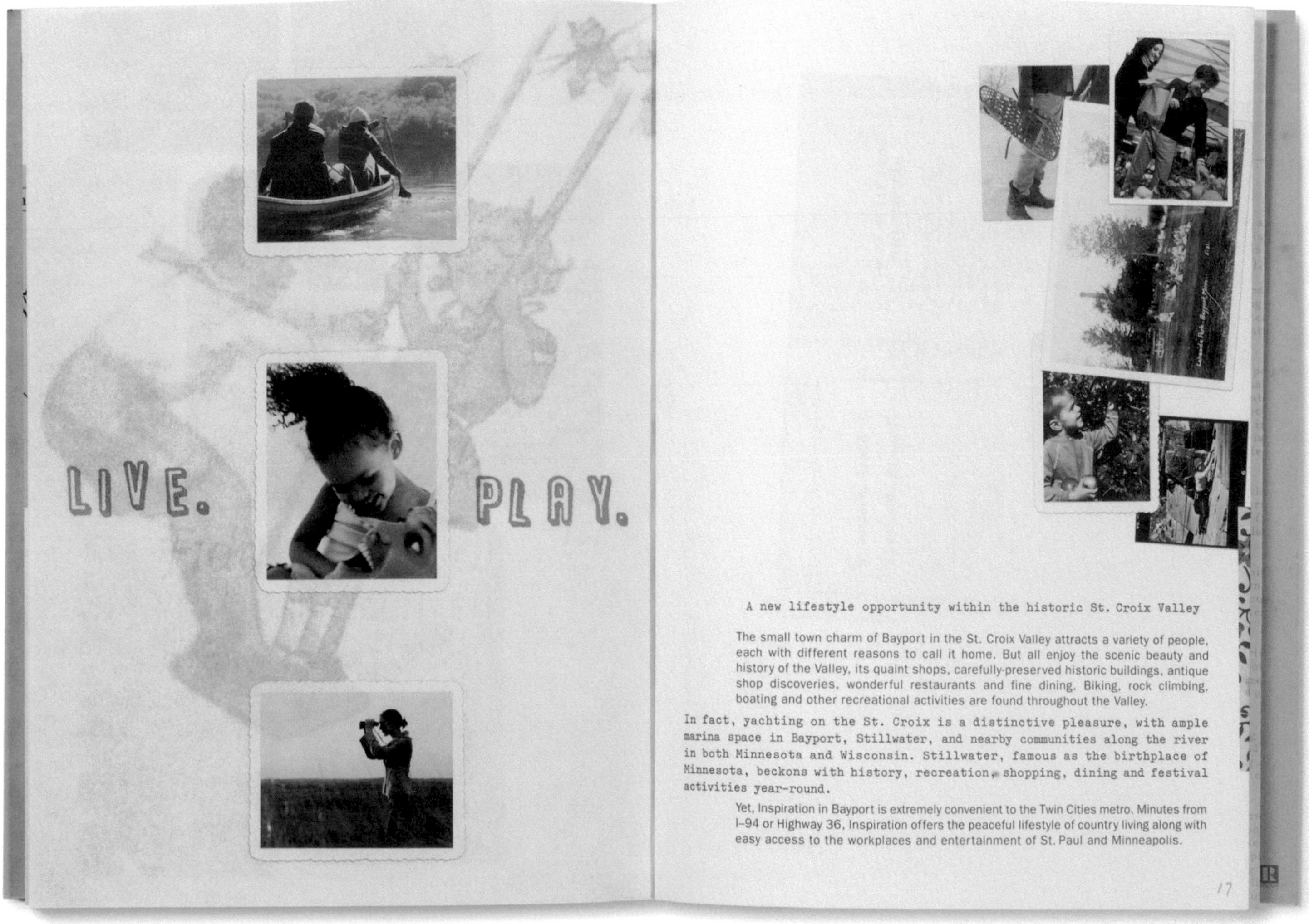
LIVE.
PLAY.
A new lifestyle opportunity within the historic St. Croix Valley
The small town charm of Bayport in the St. Croix Valley attracts a variety of people, each with different reasons to call it home. But all enjoy the scenic beauty and history of the Valley, its quaint shops, carefully-preserved historic buildings, antique shop discoveries, wonderful restaurants and fine dining. Biking, rock climbing, boating and other recreational activities are found throughout the Valley.
In fact, yachting on the St. Croix is a distinctive pleasure, with ample marina space in Bayport, Stillwater, and nearby communities along the river in both Minnesota and Wisconsin. Stillwater, famous as the birthplace of Minnesota, beckons with history, recreation, shopping, dining and festival activities year-round.
Yet, Inspiration in Bayport is extremely convenient to the Twin Cities metro. Minutes from I-94 or Highway 36, Inspiration offers the peaceful lifestyle of country living along with easy access to the workplaces and entertainment of St. Paul and Minneapolis.
17

Contem
Broc
Cat
Doc

Title:
The Curious Collection

Origin:
UK

Client:
Arjo Wiggins

Studio:
Design Project

Dimensions:
165mm x 199mm
6.5" x 7.8"

Description:
This 64-page 'specimen booklet' uses 16 unusual printing surfaces taken from the Curious Collection, 'a unique laboratory-developed range of papers, boards and plastics – all with enhanced aesthetic and surface properties' by the leading paper manufacturer Arjo Wiggins.

The booklet, which comes in a wallet with text in vibrant metallic silver ink, is designed to provide an introduction to the range, and to encourage experimentation. The collection comprises five stocks, named Translucents, Particles, Metallics, Touch and Plastics.

The designers have used an array of graphic effects (no text or photographic imagery) and printing techniques (scoring and metallic finishes) to demonstrate the robust reproduction qualities of these remarkable, technologically advanced paper stocks.

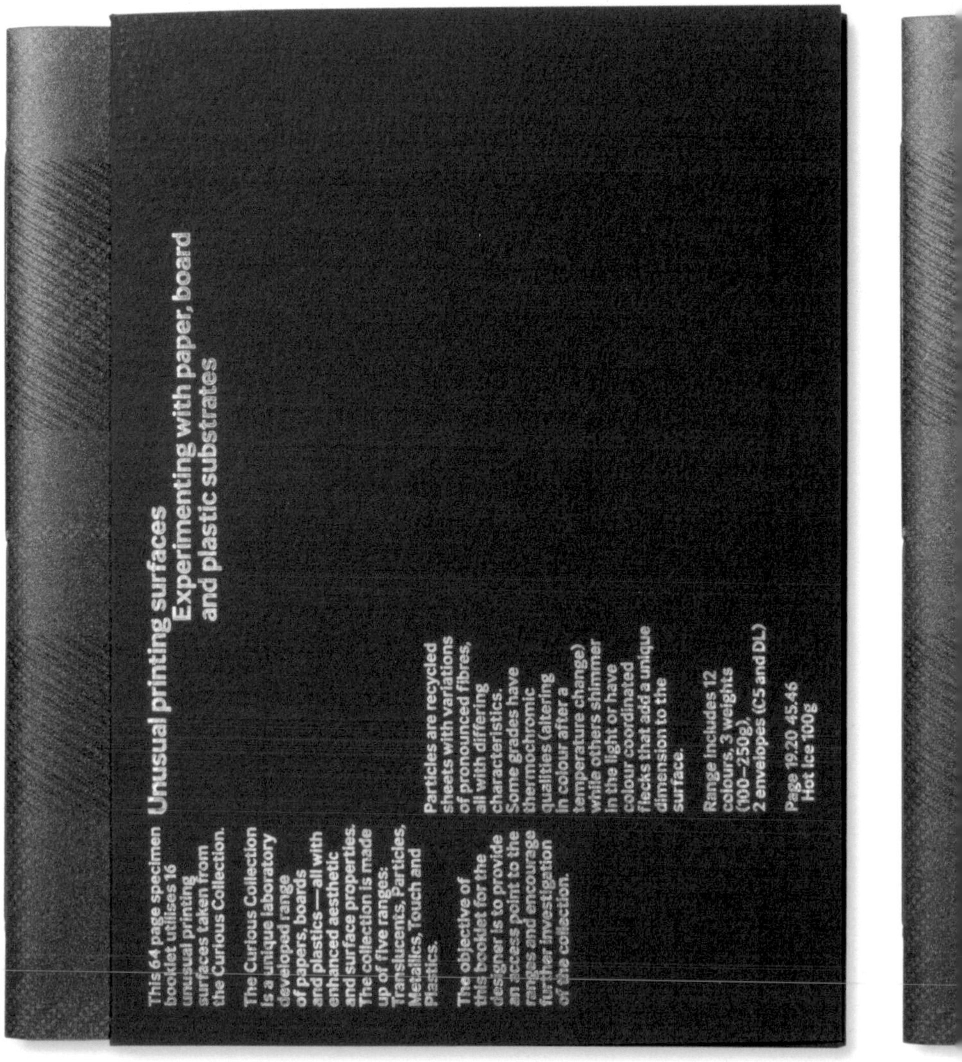
Unusual printing surfaces
Experimenting with paper, board and plastic substrates
This 64 page specimen booklet utilises 16 unusual printing surfaces taken from the Curious Collection.
The Curious Collection is a unique laboratory developed range of papers, boards and plastics—all with enhanced aesthetic and surface properties. The collection is made up of five ranges: Translucents, Particles, Metallics, Touch and Plastics.
The objective of this booklet for the designer is to provide an access point to the ranges and encourage further investigation of the collection.
Particles are recycled sheets with variations of pronounced fibres, all with differing characteristics. Some grades have thermochromic qualities (altering in colour after a temperature change) while others shimmer in the light or have colour coordinated flecks that add a unique dimension to the surface.
Range includes 12 colours, 3 weights (100–250g), 2 envelopes (C5 and DL)
Page 19.20 45.46 Hot Ice 100g

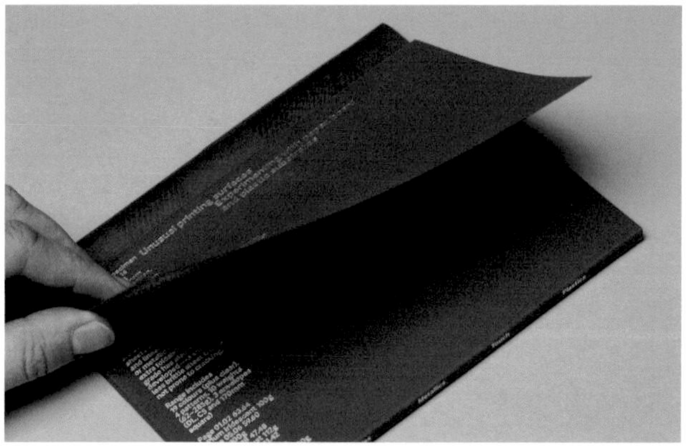

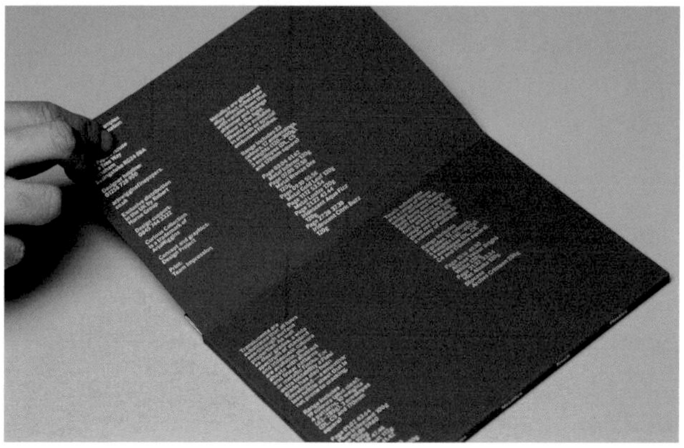

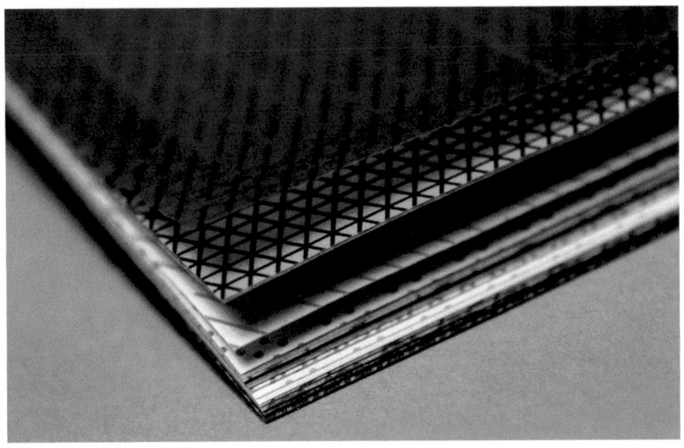

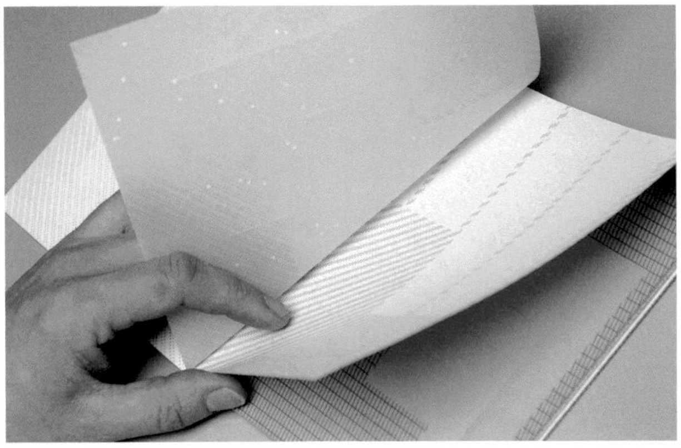

–
–
–
Contem
Broc
Cat
Doc
–
–
–
–
–
–
–
–
–
Title:
Maison Troisgros
–
Origin:
France
–
Client:
Maison Troisgros
–
Studio:
Ich&Kar
–
Dimensions:
180mm x 120mm
7" x 4.7"
–
–
–
–
–
–

MAISON TROISGROS
PLACE JEAN-TROISGROS 42300 ROANNE
T

–
–
–

Contemporary
Brochures
Catalogues
Documents

–
–
–
–
–
–
–
–
–

Description:
The brief from Michel Troisgros, owner of the restaurant and hotel Maison Troisgros in Roanne, France, was simply to 'design a brochure, no more'. Designer Helena Ichbiah, one half of the Ich&Kar partnership, explains how she approached the task: 'We set out to create an object which had a soul – an object that gives one the urge to keep it. We wanted to make something that was truthful, small, precious, fragile and cultivated – qualities that reflect the Troisgros ambience in a subtle way.' This delicate brochure – small enough to slip into a pocket or a handbag – hardly conforms to the usual image of the vapid 'leisure industry' document. It is quiet, delicate and understated. Its simple construction, thread-stitched binding and dreamy landscape photography create a lyrical statement.
'We wanted poetic images, put into perspective by texts of traditional literature, magnified by an unexpected graphic treatment. The idea was to create a "return ticket" between daydream and practical detail. The photographs (by Derek Hudson) are an invitation to discover the favourite walks of Michel Troisgros. We wanted show the beauty of the Roanne countryside, rather than endless photos of dishes and dining-tables.'

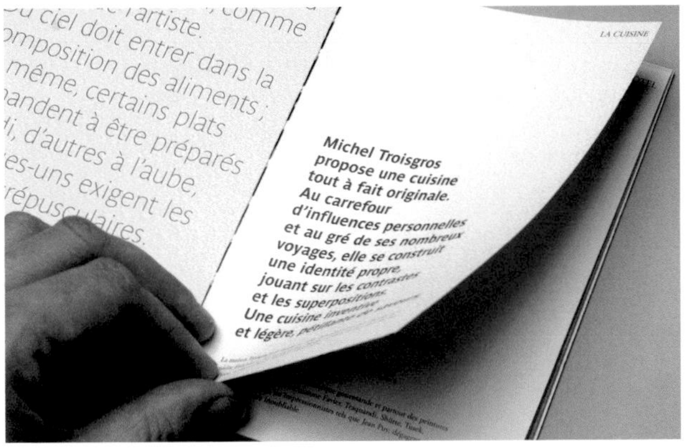
LA CUISINE
Michel Troisgros
propose une cuisine
tout à fait originale.
Au carrefour
d'influences personnelles
et au gré de ses nombreux
voyages, elle se construit
une identité propre,
jouant sur les contrastes
et les superpositions.

–
–
–
–
–
–

–
–
–
Contem
Broc
Cat
Doc
–
–
–
–
–
–
–
–
–
Title:
Not Just CMYK
–
Origin:
UK
–
Client:
G&B Printers
–
Studio:
North
–
Dimensions:
240mm x 173mm
9.4" x 6.8"
–
–
–
–
–
–

G&B Printers
North
Not Just CMYK

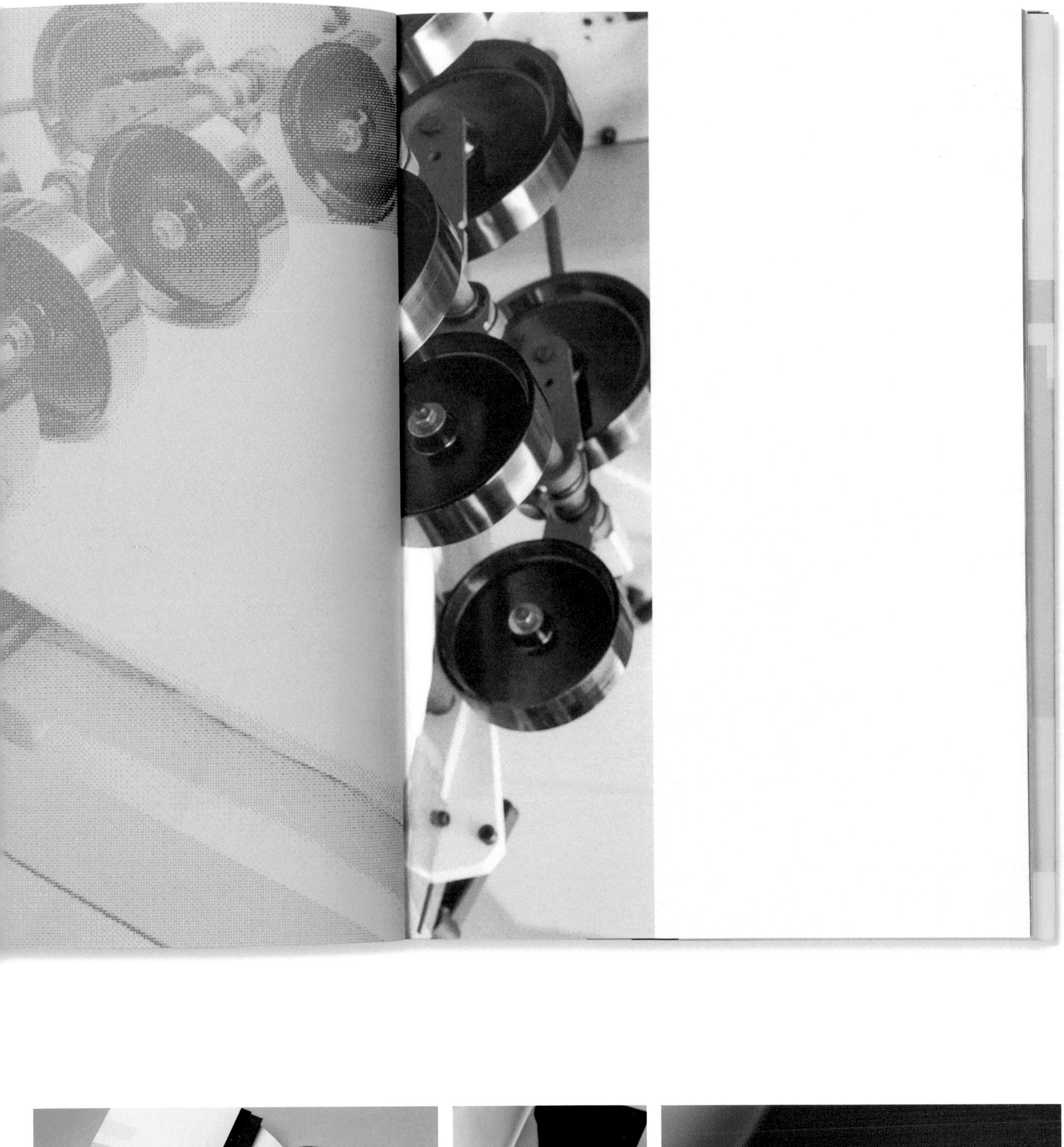

CMYK

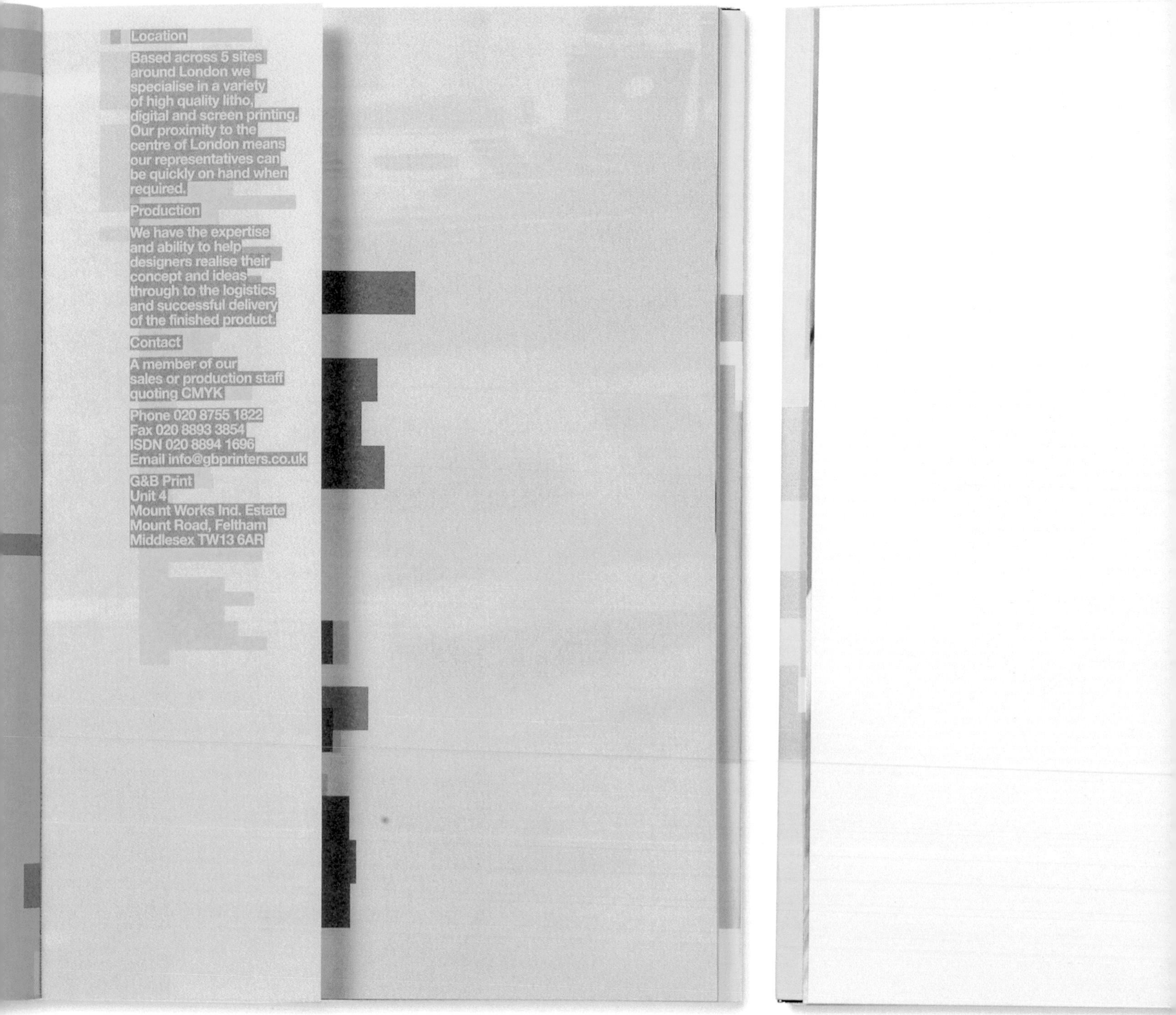
Location
Based across 5 sites around London we specialise in a variety of high quality litho, digital and screen printing. Our proximity to the centre of London means our representatives can be quickly on hand when required.
Production
We have the expertise and ability to help designers realise their concept and ideas through to the logistics and successful delivery of the finished product.
Contact
A member of our sales or production staff quoting CMYK
Phone 020 8755 1822
Fax 020 8893 3854
ISDN 020 8894 1696
Email info@gbprinters.co.uk
G&B Print
Unit 4
Mount Works Ind. Estate
Mount Road, Feltham
Middlesex TW13 6AR

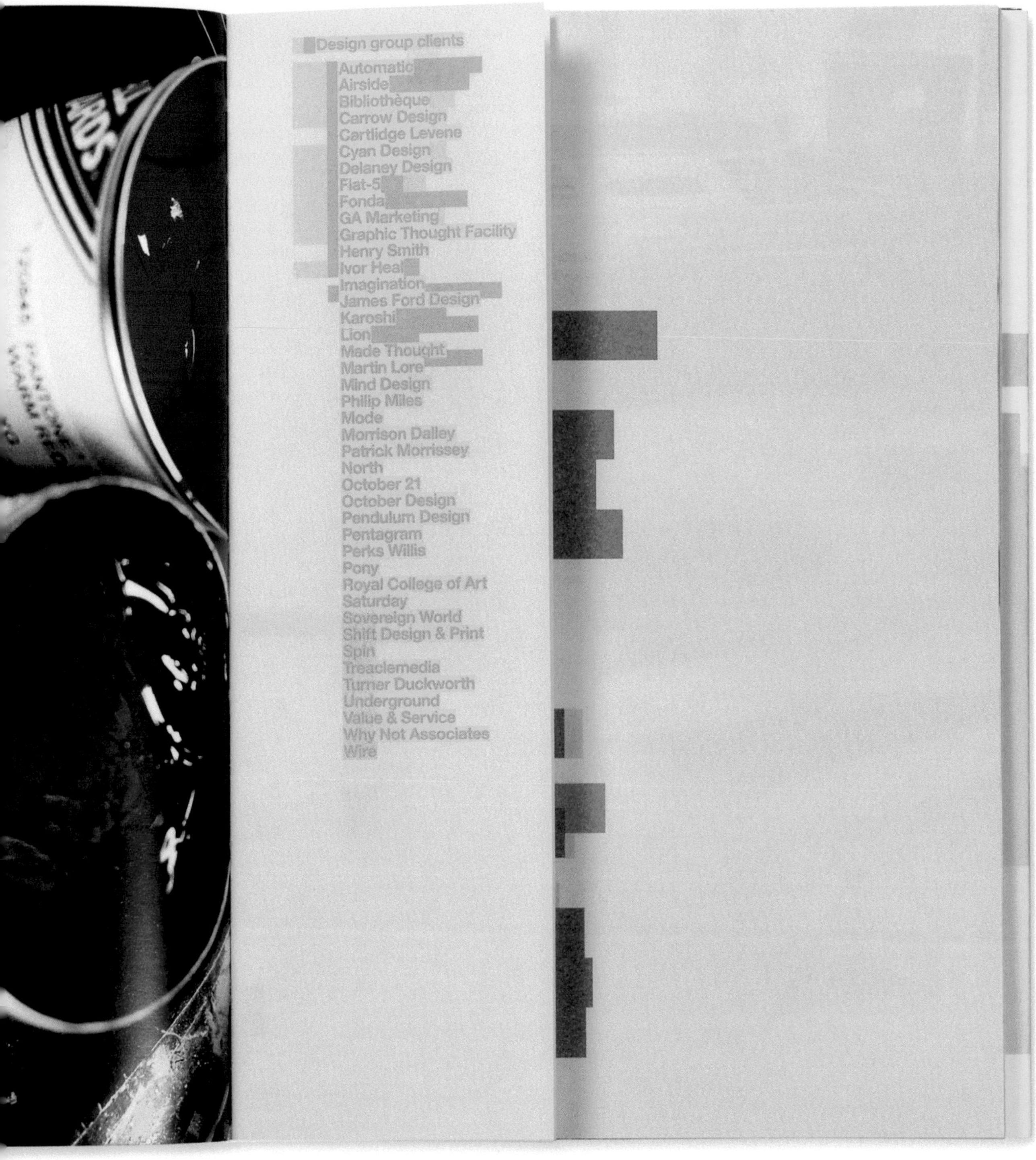
Design group clients
Automatic
Airside
Bibliothèque
Carrow Design
Cartlidge Levene
Cyan Design
Delaney Design
Flat-5
Fonda
GA Marketing
Graphic Thought Facility
Henry Smith
Ivor Heal
Imagination
James Ford Design
Karoshi
Lion
Made Thought
Martin Lore
Mind Design
Philip Miles
Mode
Morrison Dalley
Patrick Morrissey
North
October 21
October Design
Pendulum Design
Pentagram
Perks Willis
Pony
Royal College of Art
Saturday
Sovereign World
Shift Design & Print
Spin
Treaclemedia
Turner Duckworth
Underground
Value & Service
Why Not Associates
Wire

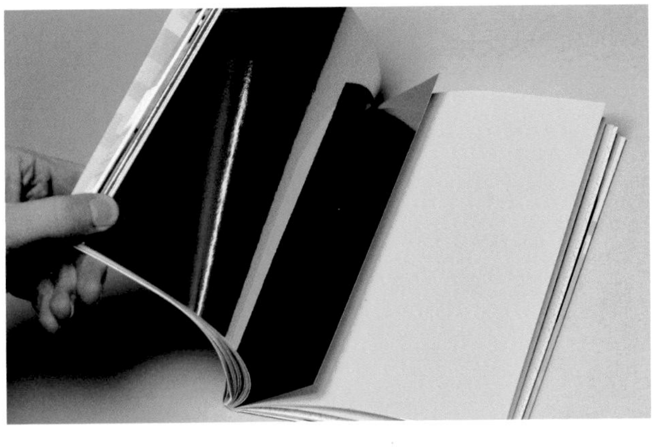

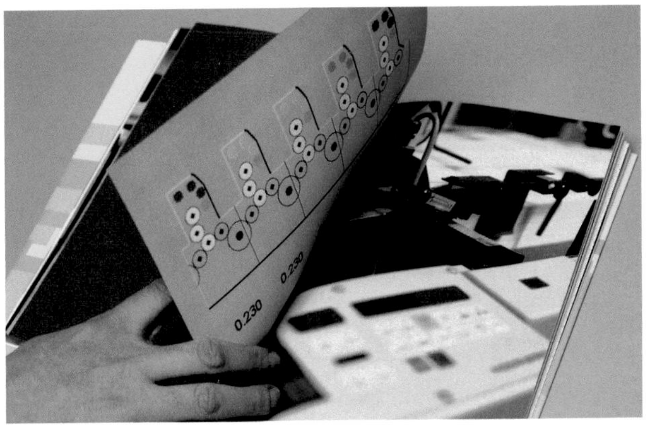
0.230
0.230

Contemporary
Brochures
Catalogues
Documents

Description:
Printers' catalogues have been around ever since printers first started touting their wares. After all, what better way is there for a smart print firm to present itself to potential customers than to display within a single document all its skills, specialities and attributes? G&B Printers are a leading UK firm, widely known for high-quality litho, screen and digital printing and used by many of the best UK design studios.

–

London designers North were commissioned by G&B, who had already been responsible for creating the company's corporate identity, to design and art-direct a brochure to serve as the print firm's promotional calling card when approaching design studios. The document avoids the normal 'plant' photography so often used by printers in their marketing literature. Instead, it uses atmospheric photography by Leon Chew, showing the minutiae of printing machinery and print-shop paraphernalia.

–

A lively mix of paper stocks and finishing techniques is used throughout, and the document is almost text-free, relying on pure graphic design and print production techniques for its impact. But one fragment of text includes the following statement: 'This book is a collaboration between G&B Printers and North Design. It has been produced as an inspirational reference guide to various papers, printing and finishing techniques by G&B.'

Conte
Broc
Cat
Doc

Title:
Moss Green, Brown, Lilac, Shocking Pink, Scarlet and Other Great Colours on Munken Print Extra 18 150 g/m²

Origin:
Sweden

Client:
Munken

Studio:
Happy F&B

Dimensions:
285mm x 210mm
11.2" x 8.3"

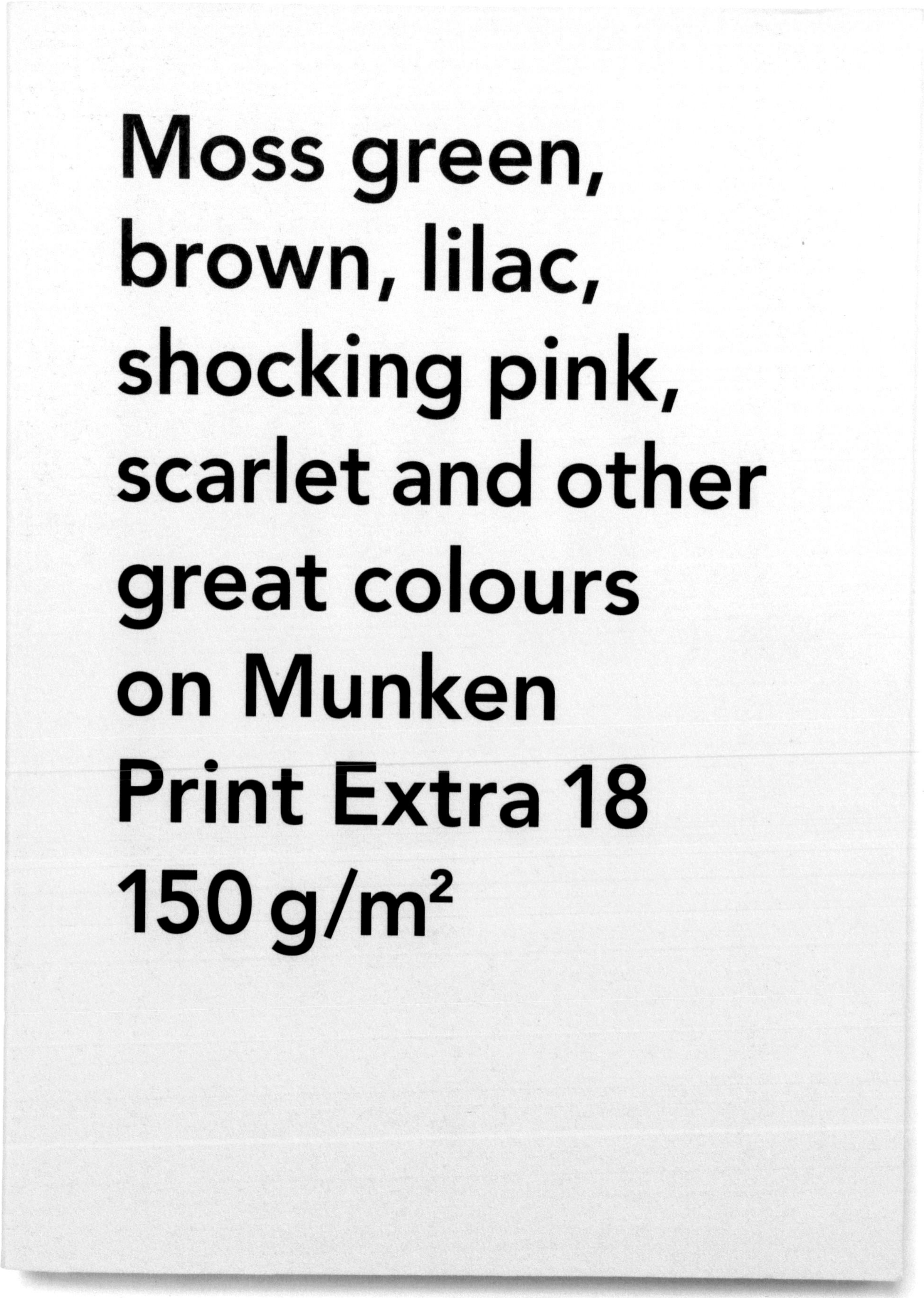
Moss green, brown, lilac, shocking pink, scarlet and other great colours on Munken Print Extra 18 150 g/m²

Description:
This chunky and tactile document, promoting the Munken range of uncoated paper stocks, is a paradigm of restrained graphic expression. A total of 45 Pantone colours were used – the most the brochure's printer had ever printed in a single document – creating dazzling spreads of pure colour.

–

But as designer Lisa Careborg explains, this was no act of designer indulgence; there was a hard-nosed purpose behind the textless and image-free pages: 'We wanted to inspire art directors and designers to print colour, and not just black type, on uncoated paper.'

–

Careborg and the designers at Happy F&B have cleverly demonstrated that colour on uncoated stock can have its own distinctive, unshowy and organic-looking vibrancy. 'We wanted to tell a story with colour', states Careborg. 'The decision not to use type was also a way to play with the fact that, when it comes down to it, not many art directors and designers really care about text – it's all about the visuals.'

–
–
–
–
–
–

Conte
Broc
Cat
Doc

Title:
George Womenswear
Autumn/Winter 2000

Origin:
UK

Client:
George at Asda

Studio:
Multistorey

Dimensions:
295mm x 244mm
11.6" x 9.6"

GEORGE
WOMENSWEAR
AUTUMN/WINTER
2000
GEORGE AT ASDA
www.georgeonline.co.uk
THANK YOU FOR SHOPPING
AT GEORGE. WHY PAY MORE?
THIS IS NOT A VAT RECEIPT

WOMENSWEAR

–
–
–
–
–
–
–
–
–

Description:
George at Asda is a successful fashion label that sells clothes through the Asda supermarket chain. Multistorey is a highly regarded British graphic design team, based in London. The design brief was to come up with a brochure that targeted both national and regional press, and which demonstrated the mix of glamour and affordability that is the label's most salient feature.

–

'We used a till receipt device', explains Multistorey partner Rhonda Drakeford, 'to clearly show the good-value price point, but we combined this with gold-foiled text and good-quality print on cotton-based card to express the unexpected glamour and quality of the brand. We printed part of each fashion shot onto the till receipt to create unity and texture.' Photography is by Lionel Guyou.

–
–
–
–
–
–

Contem
Broc
Cat
Doc

Title:
Artimo A-Z

Origin:
The Netherlands

Client:
Artimo

Studio:
Experimental Jetset

Dimensions:
296mm x 210mm
11.6" x 8.3"

Artimo A-Z

Contemporary
Brochures
Catalogues
Documents

Artimo

Artimo A-Z

Description:
Dutch design group Experimental Jetset designed a poster-catalogue for Amsterdam-based art publisher and bookshop Artimo A–Z. The document is a two-sided A2-size sheet, printed in black and white. Half the run was folded into A4 booklets; the other half was kept unfolded and used as A2 posters.

On one side (the reverse) all Artimo's publications are reproduced in black-and-white halftone.
On the other side (the front) silhouettes of the books are shown as empty white rectangles on a black background. And here we find a typical, idiosyncratic and playful Experimental Jetset gesture: when held up to the light, owing to the lightweight, semi-transparent stock used, it is possible to see the reproductions of the books inside the seemingly empty rectangles.

Based on their design for this elegant poster-catalogue, Experimental Jetset were invited to design Artimo A–Z's graphic identity, including stationery, a bookmark and signage.

Contem
Broc
Cat
Doc

Title:
Assignment Photography

Origin:
USA

Client:
Corbis

Studio:
Segura Inc.

Dimensions:
510mm x 348mm
20" x 13.7"

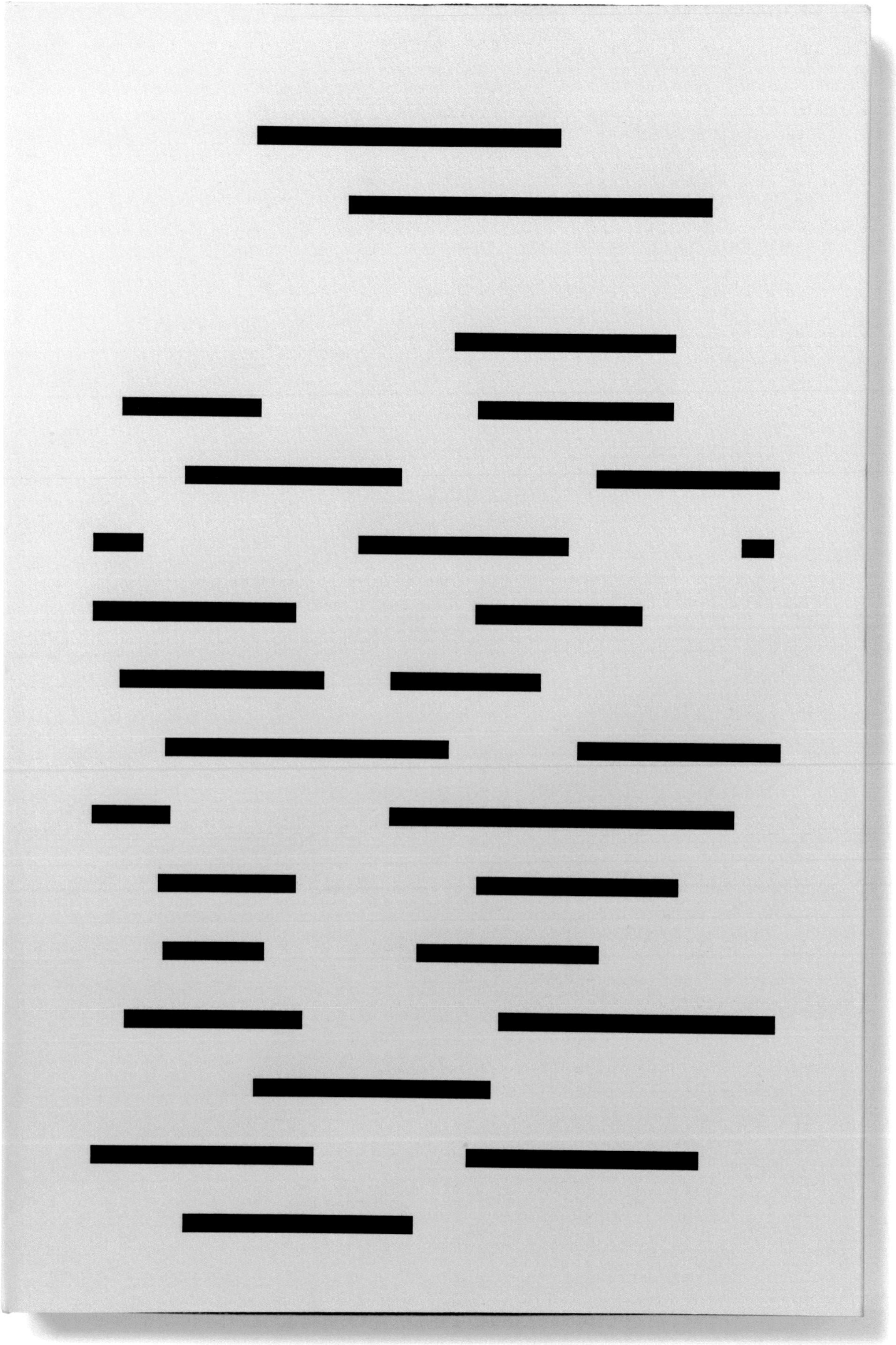

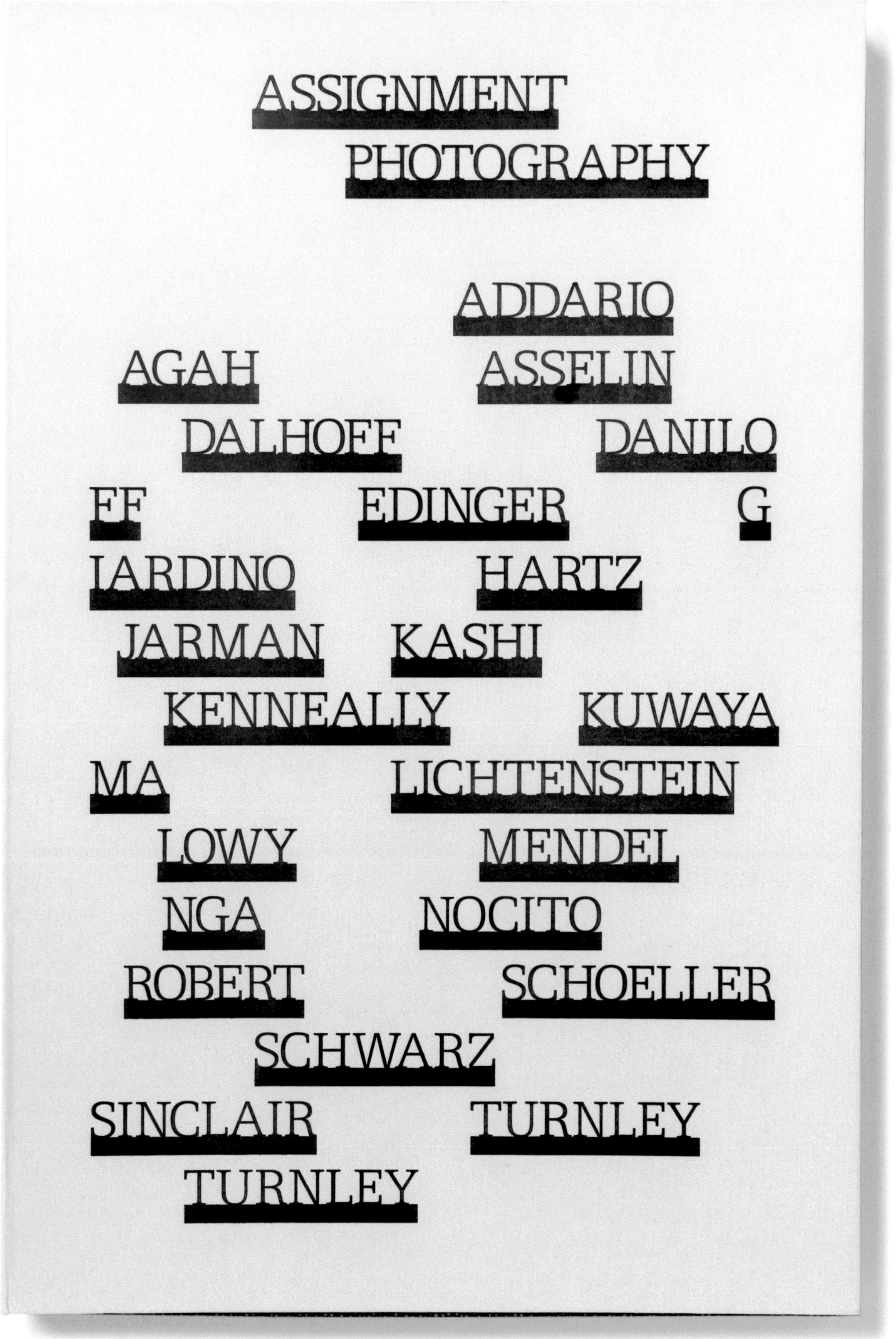
ASSIGNMENT
PHOTOGRAPHY
ADDARIO
AGAH
ASSELIN
DALHOFF
DANILO
EF
EDINGER
G
IARDINO
HARTZ
JARMAN
KASHI
KENNEALLY
KUWAYA
MA
LICHTENSTEIN
LOWY
MENDEL
NGA
NOCITO
ROBERT
SCHOELLER
SCHWARZ
SINCLAIR
TURNLEY
TURNLEY

2004

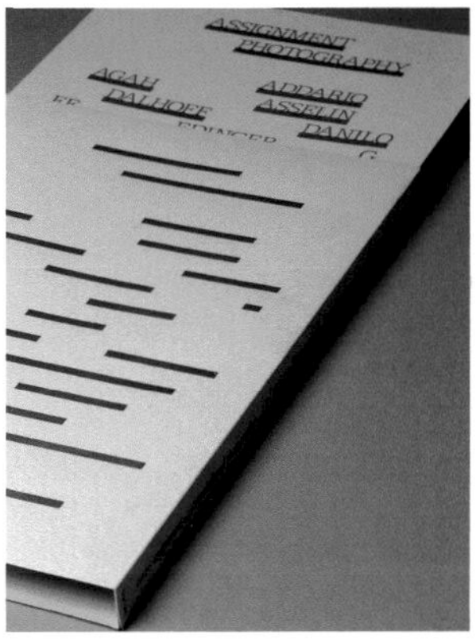

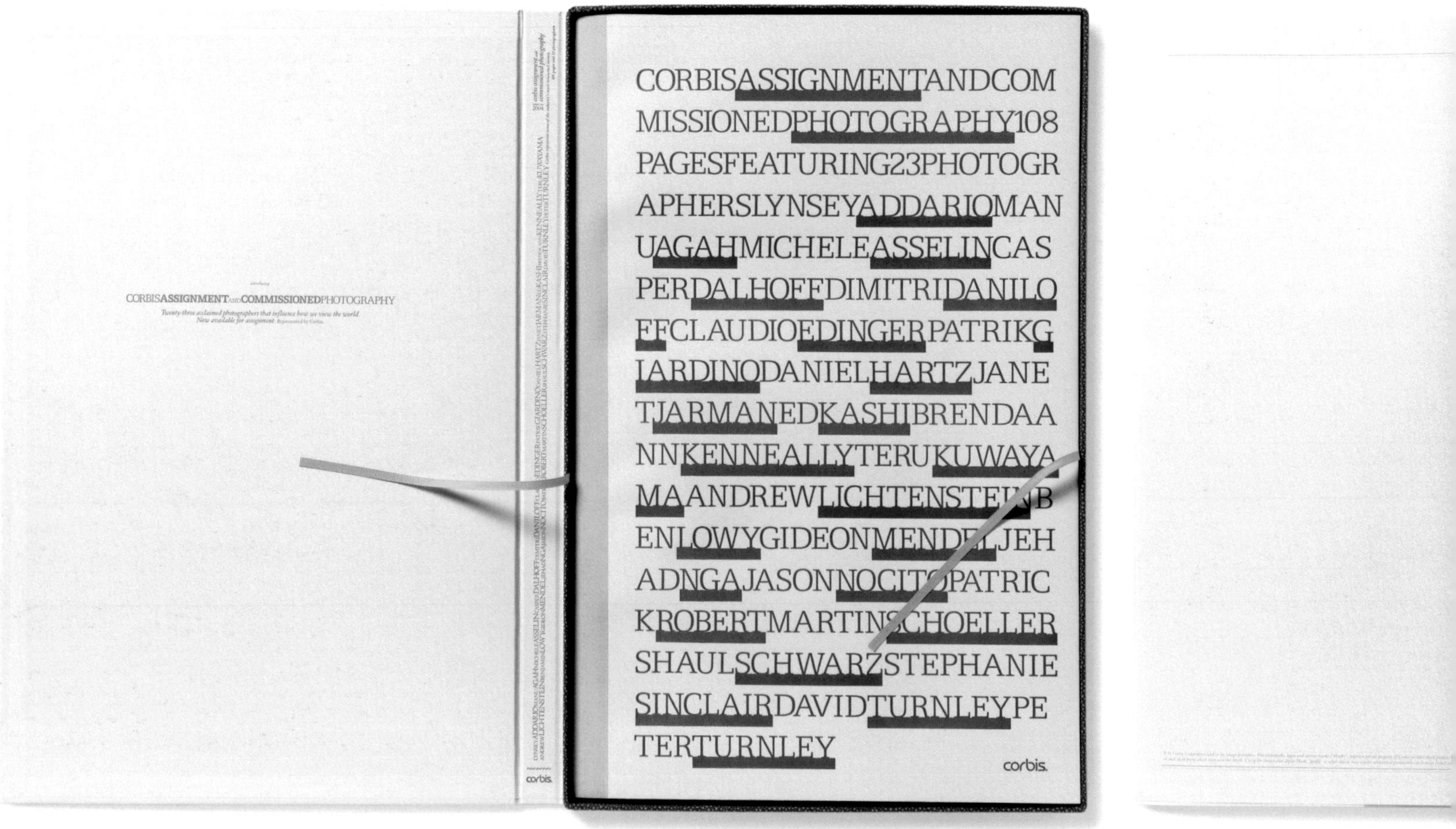
introducing
CORBISASSIGNMENTANDCOMMISSIONEDPHOTOGRAPHY
Twenty-three acclaimed photographers that influence how we view the world.
Now available for assignment. Represented by Corbis.
corbis.
CORBISASSIGNMENTANDCOM
MISSIONEDPHOTOGRAPHY108
PAGESFEATURING23PHOTOGR
APHERSLYNSEYADDARIOMAN
UAGAHMICHELEASSELINCAS
PERDALHOFFDIMITRIDANILO
FFCLAUDIOEDINGERPATRIKG
IARDINODANIELHARTZJANE
TJARMANEDKASHIBRENDAA
NNKENNEALLYTERUKUWAYA
MAANDREWLICHTENSTEINB
ENLOWYGIDEONMENDELJEH
ADNGAJASONNOCITOPATRIC
KROBERTMARTINSCHOELLER
SHAULSCHWARZSTEPHANIE
SINCLAIRDAVIDTURNLEYPE
TERTURNLEY
corbis.

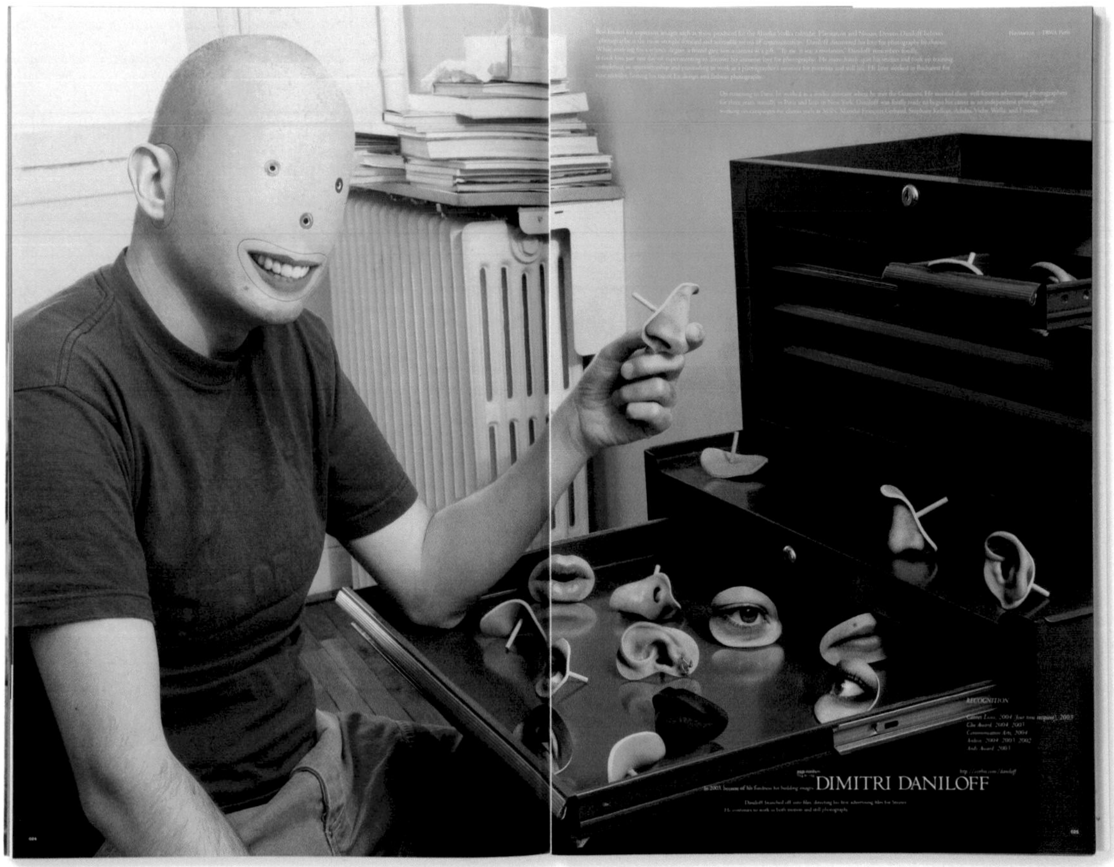
RECOGNITION
DIMITRI DANILOFF

corbis assignment and
commissioned photography
TABLE of CONTENTS
corbis

–
–
–

Contemporary
Brochures
Catalogues
Documents

–
–
–
–
–
–
–
–
–

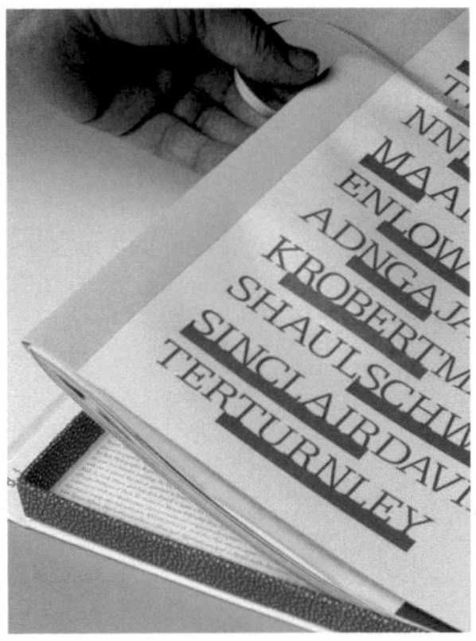

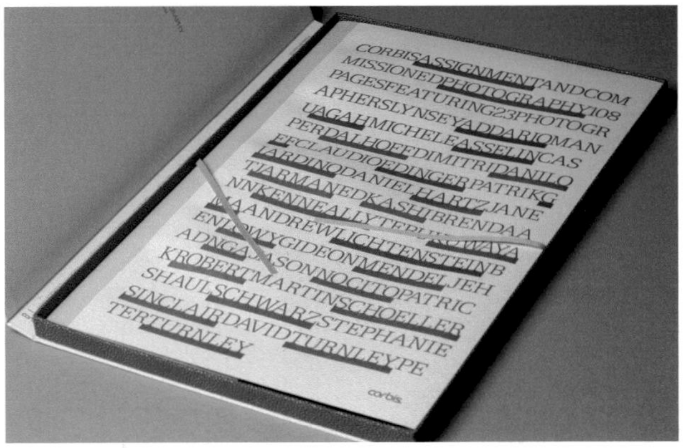

Description:
Segura Inc. was briefed by long-standing client Corbis to design a catalogue to announce the launch of the company's Assignment and Representation services. Known for its vast library of stock images, Corbis was now moving into the area of specific assignments. A powerful statement was needed to launch the new range of services to an image-hungry market.

–

With characteristic élan Segura Inc. created a striking document. It comes in a large, well-proportioned box and contains a handsome book with oddball graphics and off-kilter imagery. As with nearly all Segura Inc.'s work for Corbis, it is more an event than a document: receiving something from Corbis, when it's been designed by Segura, is like receiving a piece of theatre.

–

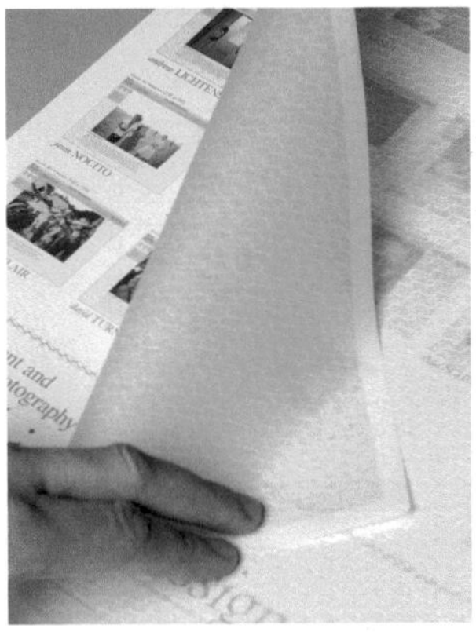

The substantial body of impressive print work that Segura Inc. has built up for Corbis in recent years appears almost to be an anomaly. Surely at a time when image libraries are moving to a near total reliance on the Internet, print is now redundant? Carlos Segura has no doubts about the importance of print: 'Humans require the interaction of feeling a document', he states. 'Print will never die.'

–
–
–
–
–
–

http://corbis.com/assignment

–
–
–
Contem
Broc
Cat
Doc
–
–
–
–
–
–
–
–
–
Title:
aiaiaiaiaiaizzzzzzzzz bummm
–
Origin:
Spain
–
Client:
Self-initiated
–
Designer:
David Torrents
–
Dimensions:
195mm x 125mm
7.7" x 4.9"
–
–
–
–
–
–

Narratives 013
Eumo Editorial
aiai
zzzzzzz
bummm
david torrents

–
–
–

Contemporary
Brochures
Catalogues
Documents

–
–
–
–
–
–
–
–
–

RING
RING
RING

BROOOOOOO
OOOOOOM..B
BROOM
MMMMMM BR
DOOM.BROM

Description:
A playground of typographic experimentation by Spanish graphic designer David Torrents, this document is subtitled 'Narratives 013' and is part of a series. The designer explains: 'I won a design competition, which is called Narratives 0, and which is also the name of a collection belonging to the publisher who organizes the awards. This is the 13th book of the series.'

–

Torrents's prize was to have his entry – a graphic depiction of a day in someone's life, explained only by the sounds the character makes and hears – published as a booklet. Torrents notes the influence of his teacher, the Dutch designer Melle Hammer, on the creation of this dazzling onomatopoeic typographic poem: 'I met him when I studied at the Gerrit Rietveld Academie in Amsterdam. He introduced me to the world of sound and typography. I made the book some years after graduating from there. It is a book for people who like poetry and typography.'

–
–
–
–
–
–

–
–
–
Contem
Broch
Cat
Doc
–
–
–
–
–
–
–
–
–

Title:
Abstract 03/04
–
Origin:
USA
–
Client:
Columbia University,
Graduate School of
Architecture, Planning and
Preservation
–
Studio:
Sagmeister Inc.
–
Dimensions:
272mm x 192mm
10.7" x 7.5"
–
–
–
–
–
–

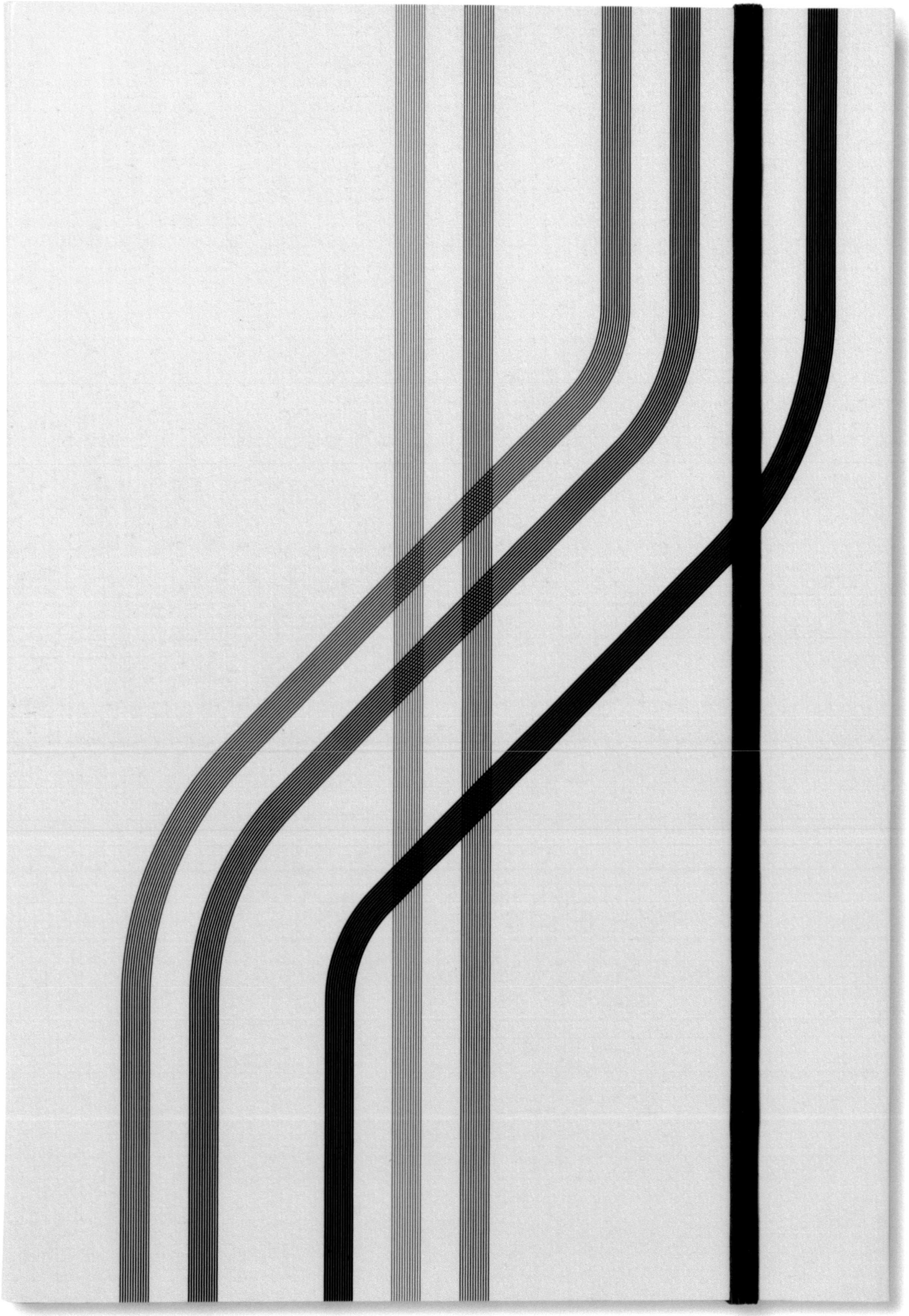

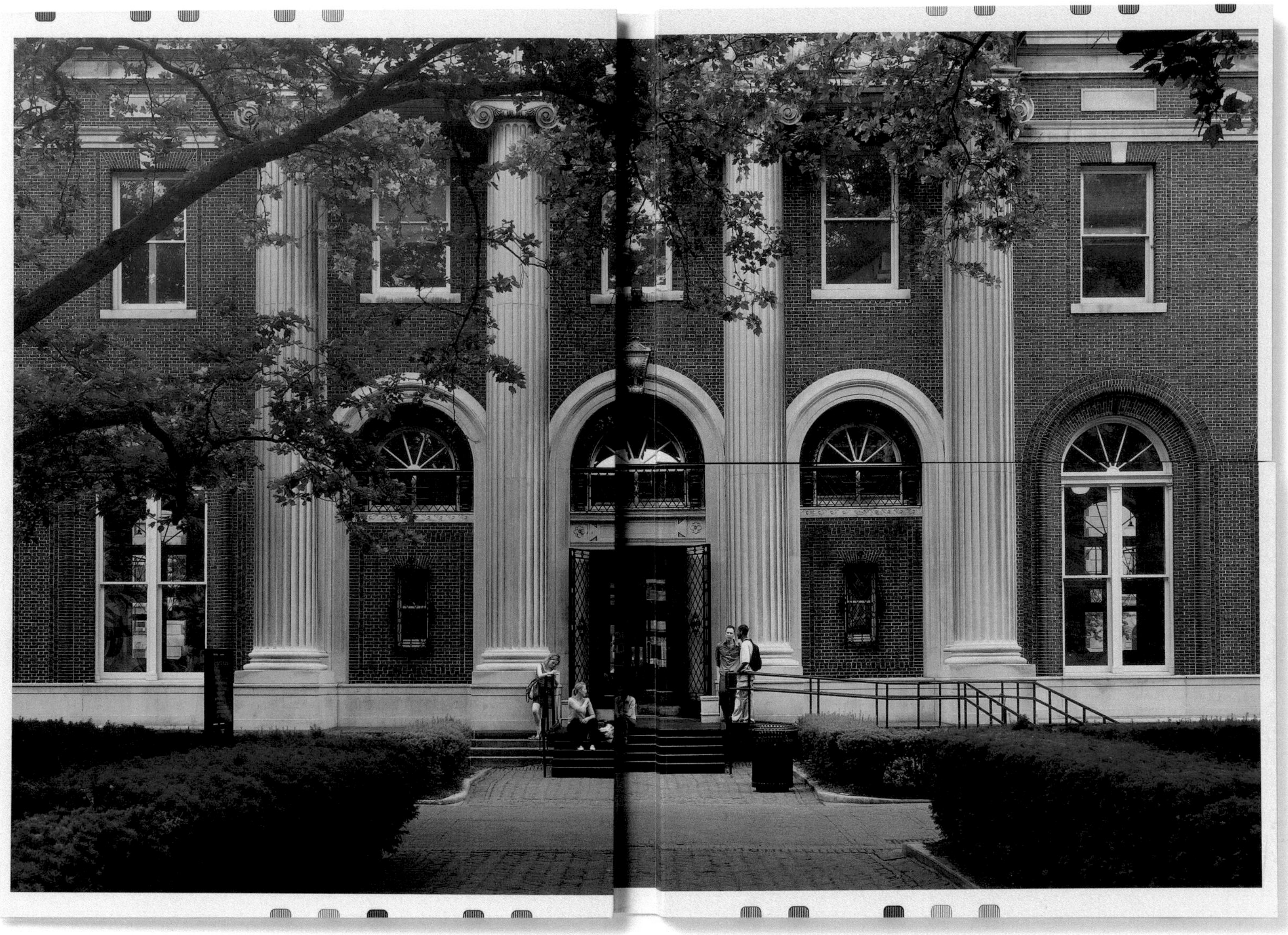

HISTORY/THEORY

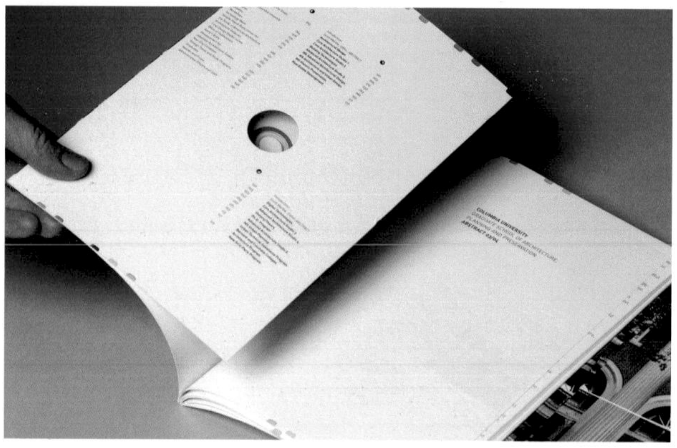

Description:
An untypically restrained and muted design by Stefan Sagmeister for this abstract of the academic year 2003–04 at the Graduate School of Architecture, Planning and Preservation at New York's famous Columbia University. Of necessity, and as befits a school of architecture and planning, the document is a serious piece of printed communication; it contains an essay from the Dean of the school and uses an 'archive of the student work, containing documentation of projects selected by the studio critics at the conclusion of each semester'.

However, despite the palpable restraint, a few idiosyncratic gestures of Sagmeisterian expressiveness have been injected. The cover (an unostentatious two colours) contains thick black lines that could represent the tracks of an underground railway in an urban planner's drawing. The document has a double spine and opens to reveal a gatefold picture of the university's façade and two internal brochures. On the right we find a typographically disciplined account of the school year; on the left is a second document (containing students' work), but this time split in two like a stable door. The effect is frankly architectural.

An elastic band holds the two documents together when closed. When removed, it reveals the document's title.

URBAN PLANNING
URBAN DESIGN
HISTORIC PRESERVATION

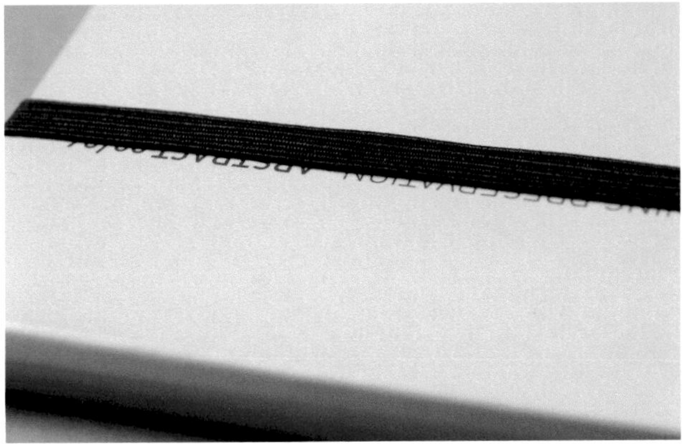

Conte
Broc
Cat
Doc

Title:
British Fashion Council Report of Activities 2002–2003

Origin:
UK

Client:
British Fashion Council

Studio:
Egelnick and Webb

Dimensions:
296mm x 210mm
11.6" x 8.3"

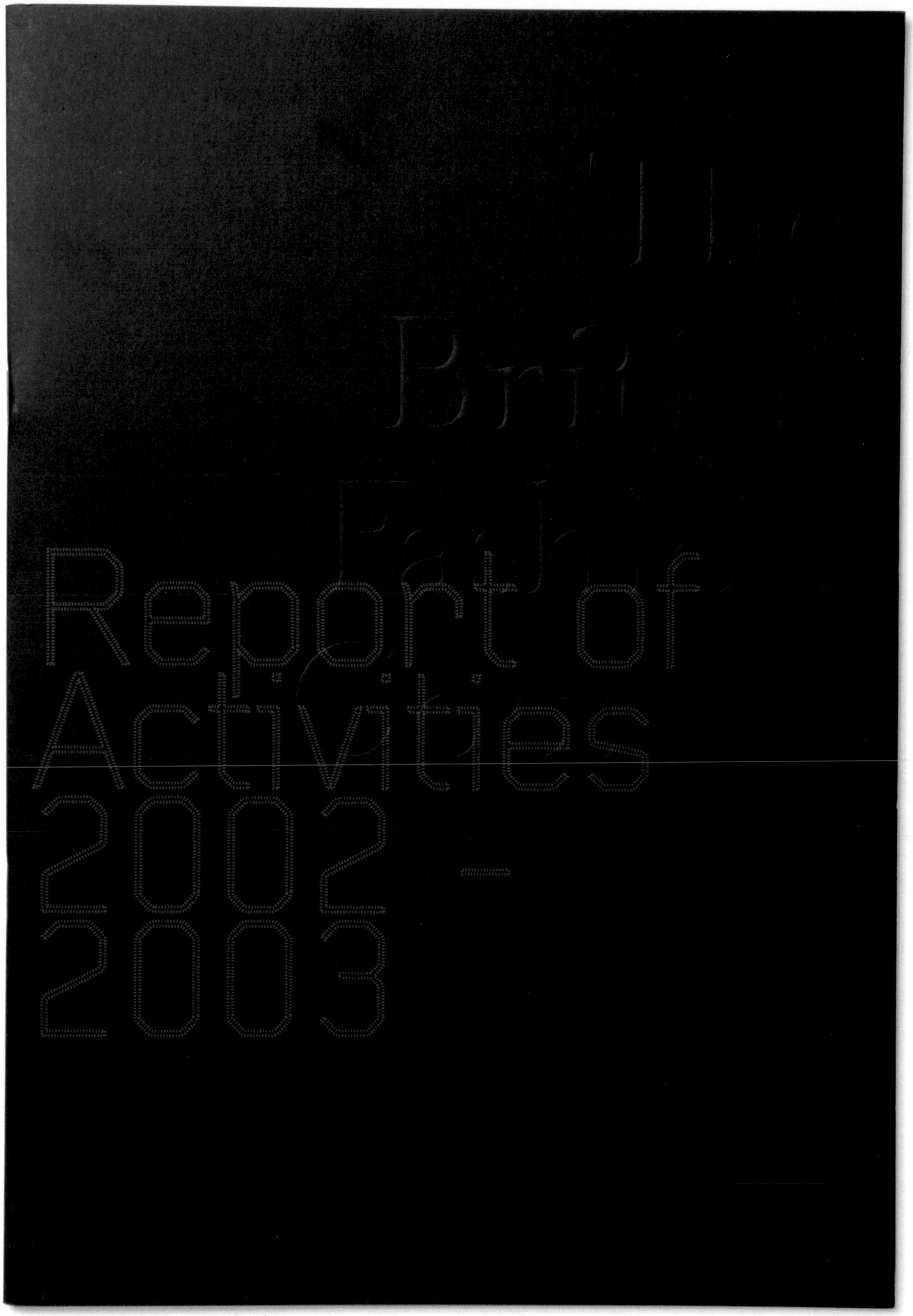
Report of
Activities
2002 –
2003

/4

British Style Awards
The re-focussed British Style Awards with a new sponsor, Lycra, and a range of celebrity awards in addition to the main fashion categories including British Designer of The Year, will be held in September 2003 as the finale event of the September London Fashion Week.

Prince's Trust Fashion Initiative
A number of initiatives have taken place under the auspices of the Prince's Trust fashion initiative, with was launched in 2001 and is supported by the BFC. A fashion stand at the 2002 Skill City event at Salford Quays was a major attraction for the 80,000 visitors from schools in the North West with an opportunity to see how a Manchester United team shirt is designed and made drawing large crowds. Free stand space for five Prince's Trust companies has been made available by the BFC at each London Fashion Week and work experience opportunities with major fashion retailers have proved a unique opportunity for a number of young people associated with the Prince's Trust. A major fund raising event for the Prince's Trust, 'Fashion Rocks', is planned for Autumn 2003.

British Style Awards

Prince's Trust Fashion Initiative

/5

Study of the UK Designer Fashion Sector
A Study of the UK Designer Fashion Sector was carried out during the year by the Malcolm Newbery Consulting Company. The Study sought to ascertain the impact of the designer sector on the wider clothing and textile industry, map existing support available to designers and identify the gaps in provision. Commissioned by the DTI and BFC, the Study sought views from a wide range of players in and supporting the designer sector and the findings were published at the February 2003 London Fashion Week. One major finding was that the designer sector has grown ten fold over the last decade with production in 2001 standing at £700 million.

The Study also focussed on the role of manufacturers and retailers in relation to the development of designer businesses and included recommendations for the development of closer links with schools and colleges. Discussions are being held with the DTI to identify how best the recommendations of the Study can be moved forward. Copies of the Conclusions and Recommendations are available from the BFC at 5 Portland Place.

Colleges Forum
The BFC Colleges Forum, chaired by Sally Smith OBE, provides an interface between the heads of the top British Fashion Colleges and the industry. The Forum's activities include an annual Open Day, held this year on 8th April at 5 Portland Place, when the industry had its first opportunity to see the portfolios of work from the students due to graduate in the summer.

Three competitions have been held during the year. The brief for the House of Fraser/FCUK/Glamour competition was to design a night through to morning outfit for a celebrity attending the BRIT Awards. The winner was Johanna Ericson of Ravensbourne. A competition with Tesco for a womenswear collection was won by Amy Baylis from Ravensbourne, whose winning outfit was produced and will be sold in store during Autumn/Winter 2003. The 3rd FAD (Fashion Awareness Direct) Graduate Fashion competition, the brief for which was to design an outfit on the theme of the opera Madame Butterfly and Venice, was won by Wendy Li of Salford University.

Study of the UK Designer Fashion Sector

Description:
After designing the previous year's document for the British Fashion Council's annual report, designers Egelnick and Webb decided to 'do something different and push the layout further than we did last time'.

–

It was decided that the photography ('generally snaps by one of the council members, or poor-quality grabs from the website') was of insufficient quality, so the images were converted to bitmaps and printed single-colour on the reverse of the French-folded pages – 'to produce a subtle effect of glowing out from under the text'. Initially it was planned to use Bible paper, but this proved difficult to find at the size required. In the end, paper company Antalis donated a lightweight stock that fitted the purpose.

–

The headline font was Gridnik, 'but done with a rough dashed outline in Freehand, to get a fashion/"fastenings" feel to it'. For the text Mrs Eaves, complete with ligatures, was used, to reflect the British Fashion Council's 'balance of heritage and history with the bleeding-edge nature of the fashion industry'.

–
–
–
–
–
–

–
–
–
Contem
Broc
Cat
Doc
–
–
–
–
–
–
–
–
Title:
Mark
–
Origin:
The Netherlands
–
Client:
Municipal Art
Acquisitions/Graphic
Design 2003–2004
–
Studio:
Hansje van Halem
–
Dimensions:
240mm x 161mm
9.4" x 6.3"
–
–
–
–
–
–

Mark
CATALOGUS/CATALOGUE
Gemeentelijke Kunstaankopen Grafische Vormgeving 2003-2004
Municipal Art Acquisitions Graphic Design 2003-2004

INZENDING 37
ENTRY 37 · DESIGN
ontwerp
164 Mark

Mark

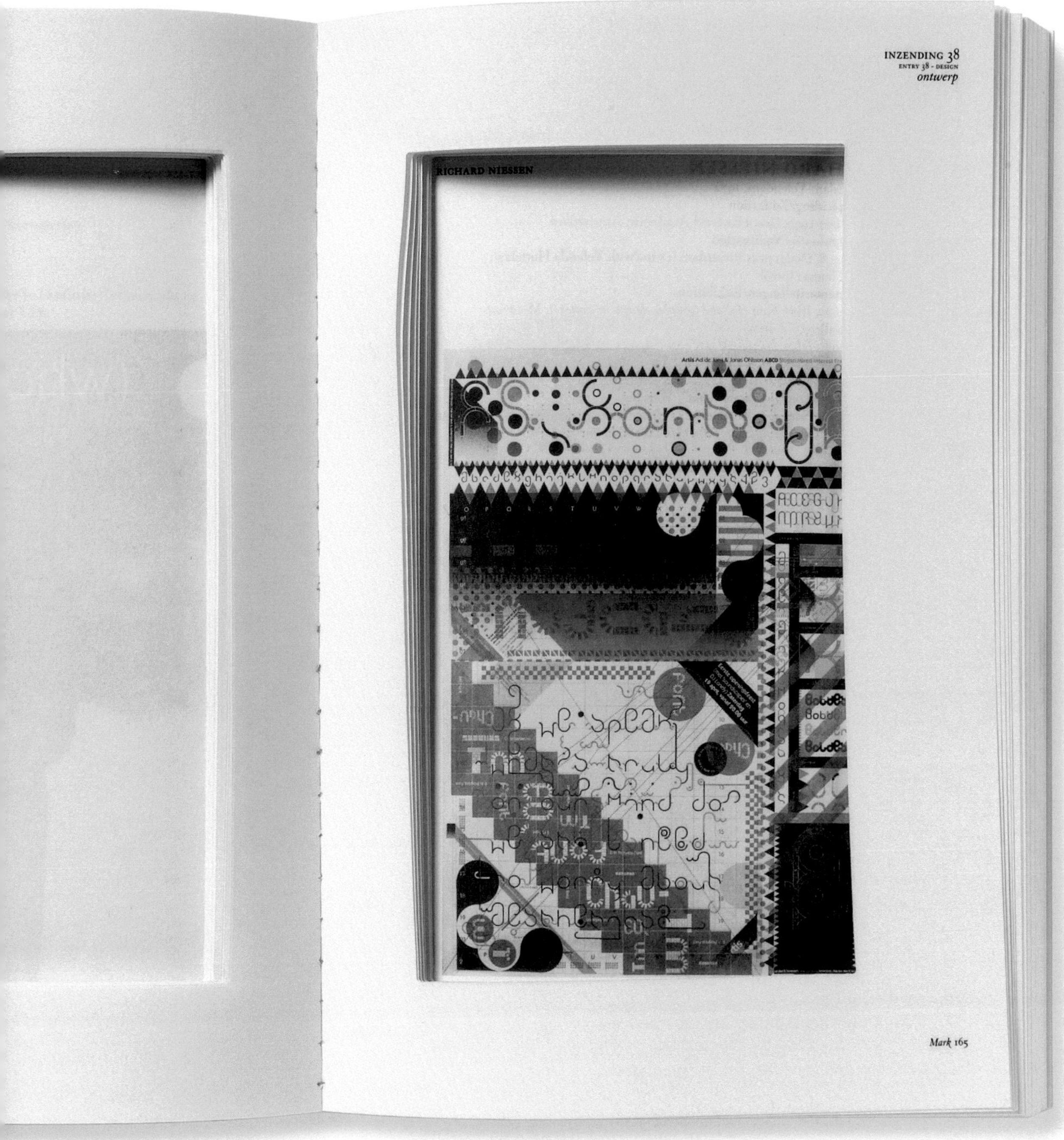
INZENDING 38
ENTRY 38 - DESIGN
ontwerp
RICHARD NIESSEN
Mark 165

–
–
–

Contemporary
Brochures
Catalogues
Documents

–
–
–
–
–
–
–
–
–

Description:
The world-famous Stedelijk Museum in Amsterdam invited graphic designers working in the city to submit their work to a jury sitting on behalf of a body called Amsterdam Municipal Art Acquisitions/Graphic Design. Successful participants had the opportunity to have their work acquired by the gallery for its permanent collection of graphic design and selected for a special exhibition.

–

Dutch designer Hansje van Halem was asked to design a catalogue showing the work of the successful candidates. Her remarkable design is a triumph of graphic design activism: graphic designers tend to be passive recipients of a client's brief, but van Halem challenged hers: 'There were 84 entries,' she recalls, 'but only 20 were selected by the jury, and I felt that all the entries should be included in the catalogue. So I put them all in. I wanted to make the point that the selection is part of a bigger whole, and I felt that the "bigger whole" was a better representation of the state of current graphic design in Amsterdam.'

–

Inside the book the selected artworks are catalogued by an intriguing system: each of the 84 entries has its own individual 'cut-out' window, which works as a framing device for each design. The effect is reminiscent of the hidden compartments in the books often found in murder or spy stories. But instead of concealing a key to a treasure chest or a priceless jewel, we find the work of the cream of contemporary Dutch graphic designers.

–
–
–
–

–
–
–
Conte
Broc
Cat
Doc
–
–
–
–
–
–
–
–
–
Title:
Late Shift 1/5
–
Origin:
Switzerland
–
Client:
Intershop Holdings
–
Studio:
Lehni-Trüb
(Urs Lehni and Alex Trüb)
–
Dimensions:
85mm x 85mm
3.3" x 3.3"
–
–
–
–
–
–

● LATE SHI 1/5
Peter Reg
im Puls 5.

● LATE SHIFT 2/5
16 Juni:
Roman Signer
im Puls 5.
22:00

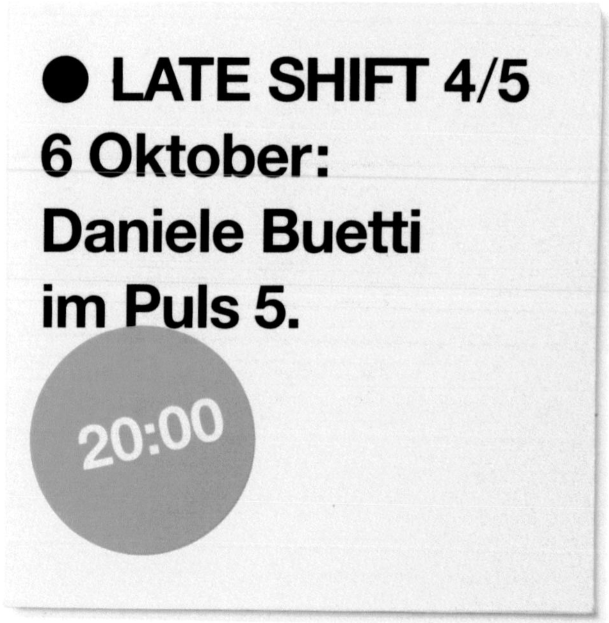
● LATE SHIFT 4/5
6 Oktober:
Daniele Buetti
im Puls 5.
20:00

LATE SHIFT 3/5
15 September:
Steiner/Lenzlinger
20:00
im Puls 5.

LATE SHIFT 5/5
20:00
Research
im Puls 5.

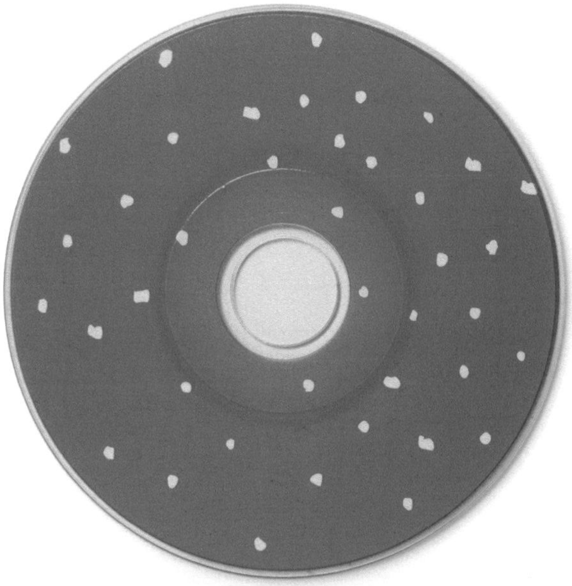

LATE SHIFT 4/5
6 Oktober:
Daniele Buetti
im Puls 5.
20:00

–
–
–
–
–
–
–
–
–

Description:
Late Shift is a series of 'artist's interventions' at Puls 5, a former Zurich foundry that was recently converted into a shopping mall and office complex. During construction work an old blast furnace, which was under a protection order, was accidentally destroyed. As compensation, the parties involved decided to launch an art project.

–

Rather than create static or monumental works of art, the project curators, Gianni Jetzer and Claudia Spinelli, evolved the concept of creating five 'ephemeral interventions' by five different artists: Peter Regli, Roman Signer, Steiner/Lenzlinger, Daniele Buetti and Knowbotic Research. A variety of works were created, including examples of performance art and installations using sound and light.

–

As an alternative to a printed catalogue, five 'audio catalogues' were produced. Graphic designer Alex Trüb explains: 'The aim was to communicate the history behind this project and to accurately portray the artists involved. So it was decided that allowing the artists to talk about their projects would be closer to the ephemeral character of their artworks. It also gave us the opportunity to pack in more information than we might have had in a small printed document. The CDs were handed out to customers frequenting the mall and given away in shops, foyers and bookstores to people interested in art.'

–
–
–
–
–
–

Contributors

Philippe Apeloig
41 Rue La Fayette
75009 Paris
France
www.apeloig.com
pages:
116–117
136–137

–

Chris Ashworth
Getty Images
Headquarters
601 North 34th Street
Seattle WA 98103
USA
http://creative.gettyimages.com
pages:
050–053

–

Marian Bantjes
Box X-15
1478 Tunstall Blvd.
Bowen Island BC, V0N 1G0
Canada
www.bantjes.com
pages:
074–075

–

BB/Saunders
Unit 2.08
The Tea Building
56 Shoreditch High Street
London E1 6JJ
United Kingdom
www.bbsaunders.com
pages:
058–063

–

Sander Boom
Weesperzijde 80-f
1091 EJ Amsterdam
The Netherlands
pages:
104–105

–

Stephen Coates
Studio 6
2nd floor
2-4 Hoxton Square
London N1 6NU
United Kingdom
pages:
092–093

–

Design Project
Round Foundry
Media Centre
Unit G15
Foundry Street
Leeds LS11 5QP
United Kingdom
www.designproject.co.uk
pages:
160–161

–

Egelnick and Webb
23 Charlotte Road
London EC2A 3PB
United Kingdom
www.egelnickandwebb.com
pages:
108–109
184–185

–

Elektrosmog
Pfingstweidstrasse 6
CH-8005 Zurich
Switzerland
www.esmog.org
pages:
134–135

–

Experimental Jetset
Jan Hanzenstraat 37/1
1053 SK Amsterdam
The Netherlands
www.experimentaljetset.nl
pages:
026–027
124–125
138–139
172–173

–

Ed Fella
c/o CalArts
24700 McBean Parkway
Valencia CA 91355-2397
www.edfella.com
pages:
148–149

–

Götz Gramlich
Treitschkestrasse 03
D-69117 Heidelberg
Germany
www.ggrafik.de
pages:
044–045

–

Hansje van Halem
Berberisstraat 16
1032 EL Amsterdam
The Netherlands
www.hansje.net
pages:
186–187

–

Happy F&B
Kungsgatan 51
Gothenburg SE-411 15
Sweden
www.happy.fb.se
pages:
024–025
038–039
076–077
168–169

–

IAMAS
Institute of Advanced
Media Arts and Sciences
3-95, Ryoke-cho
Ogaki City
Gifu, Japan 503-0014
www.iamas.ac.jp
pages:
114–115
126–127

–

Ich&Kar
51, rue du Sergent
Godefroy
93100 Montreuil
France
www.ichetkar.com
pages:
162–163

–

Karlssonwilker
536 6th Avenue
2nd and 3rd Floor
New York NY 10011
USA
www.karlssonwilker.com
pages:
144–147

–

Keller Maurer Design
Theresienstrasse 56 Hof 1
80333 Munich
Germany
www.km-d.com
pages:
090–091

–

Zak Kyes
Zak Group
Unit 12
Sunbury Workshops
Swanfield Street
London E2 7LF

United Kingdom
www.zak.to
pages:
120–121
–
–
–
Labomatic
25 Rue des Cascades
75020 Paris
France
www.labomatic.org
pages:
106–107
140–141
–
–
–
Multistorey
Studio 9
51 Derbyshire Street
London E2 6QJ
United Kingdom
www.multistorey.net
pages:
048–049
132–133
170–171
–
–
–
Nakajima Design
Kaiho Bldg-4F 4-11
Uguisudani-cho
Shibuya-ku
Tokyo, Japan 150-0032
www.nkjm-d.com
pages:
054–055
–
–
–
Non-Format
Lower Ground Floor
133 Curtain Road
London EC2A 3BX
United Kingdom
www.non-format.com
pages:
028–031
094–095
–
–
–
North
Unit 2, The Glasshouse
Royal Oak Yard
Bermondsey Street
London SE1 3GD
United Kingdom
www.northdesign.co.uk
pages:
040–043
130–131
164–167
–
–
–
Lippa Pearce
358a Richmond Road
Twickenham TW1 2DU
United Kingdom
www.lippapearce.com
pages:
096–097
–
–
–
Pentagram
11 Needham Road
London W11 2RP
United Kingdom
www.pentagram.co.uk
pages:
118–119
–
–
–
Tania Prill,
Alberto Vieceli
11 Lessingstrasse
CH-8002 Zurich
Switzerland
www.prill-vieceli.cc
pages:
016–017
056–057
128–129
–
–
–
Ranch Associates
23–24 Great James Street
London WC1N 3ES
United Kingdom
pages:
098–099
–
–
–
Sagmeister Inc.
222 West 14 Street
Suite 15A
New York NY 10011
USA
www.sagmeister.com
pages:
018–021
032–033
084–089
180–183
–
–
–
Segura Inc.
1110 North Milwaukee
Avenue
Chicago, IL 60622-4017
USA
www.segura-inc.com
pages:
122–123
174–177
–
–
–
Spin
12 Canterbury Court
Kennington Park
1–3 Brixton Road
London SW9 6DE
United Kingdom
www.spin.co.uk
pages:
070–071
078–081
142–143
150–151
–
–
–
surface
4 Petersstrasse
60313 Frankfurt am Main
159 Linienstrasse
10115 Berlin
Germany
www.surface.de
pages:
072–073
102–103
–
–
–
Thirst (the collaborative
studio of Rick Valicenti)
Postal: 117 South Cook
Street PMB 333
Studio: 132 West
Station Street
Barrington IL 60010
USA
www.3st.com
pages:
064–067
110–113
–
–
–
Toffe
6 Rue Thomas Francine
75014 Paris
France
www.toffe.net
pages:
068–069
–
–
–
David Torrents
Milà i Fontanals 14, 2–2
Barcelona 08012
Spain
www.torrents.info
pages:
034–037
100–101
178–179
–
–
–
Alex Trüb
Pfingstweidstrasse 31 A
CH-8005 Zurich
Switzerland
www.lehni-trueb.ch
pages:
188–189
–
–
–
Lonne Wennekendonk
Lloydstraat 17-d
Rotterdam
The Netherlands
www.lonnewennekendonk.nl
pages:
082–083
–
–
–
Werner Design Werks, Inc.
411 First Avenue North
Room 206
Minneapolis, MN 55401
USA
www.wdw.com
pages:
156–159
–
–
–
Cornel Windlin
Pfingstweidstrasse 6
CH-8005 Zurich
Switzerland
pages:
152–155
–
–
–
Winterhouse
PO Box 159
Falls Village
CT 06031
USA
www.belowthefold.org
pages:
046–047
–
–
–
–
–
–

LOOK AT THIS

Contemporary Brochures, Catalogues & Documents

Edited and written by
Adrian Shaughnessy

Art directed and designed
by Non-Format

Photography by Ian Jackson

Special thanks to all the designers who contributed work to this project. This book is fondly dedicated to you all.

Thanks also to:
Jon and Kjell, Jacko, Ed and Alice Shaughnessy, Hal Uden, Etienne Hervy, everyone at This is Real Art and the team at Laurence King Publishing for their support and patience.